A Guide to Teaching
Developmental Psychology

Teaching Psychological Science
Series editors: William Buskist and Douglas A. Bernstein

Each book in the *Teaching Psychological Science* series focuses on critical aspects of teaching core courses in psychology. The books share ideas, tips, and strategies for effective teaching and offer all the pedagogical tools an instructor needs to plan the course in one handy and concise volume. Written by outstanding teachers and edited by Bill Buskist and Doug Bernstein, well-respected authors and teachers, the volumes provide a wealth of concrete suggestions not found in other volumes and a clear roadmap for teaching. Each book focuses on practical, concrete, hands-on tips for novice teachers and experienced instructors alike.

The books include

- Ideas for beginning the course
- Sample lecture outlines for the entire course
- Examples and applications that link the course content to everyday student experience
- Classroom demonstrations and activities with an emphasis on promoting active learning and critical thinking
- Discussion of sensitive and difficult-to-teach topics and ethical issues likely to be encountered throughout the semester
- Course-specific options for evaluating student performance
- A chapter on available resources for teaching the course

1 *A Guide to Teaching Research Methods in Psychology*
   Bryan K. Saville

2 *A Guide to Teaching Introductory Psychology*
   Sandra Goss Lucas

3 *A Guide to Teaching Statistics*
   Michael R. Hulsizer and Linda M. Woolf

4 *A Guide to Teaching Developmental Psychology*
   Elizabeth Brestan Knight and Ember Lee

A Guide to Teaching Developmental Psychology

Elizabeth Brestan Knight and
Ember L. Lee

A John Wiley & Sons, Ltd., Publication

This edition first published 2008
© 2008 Elizabeth Brestan Knight and Ember L. Lee

Blackwell Publishing was acquired by John Wiley & Sons in February 2007. Blackwell's publishing program has been merged with Wiley's global Scientific, Technical, and Medical business to form Wiley-Blackwell.

Registered Office
John Wiley & Sons Ltd, The Atrium, Southern Gate, Chichester, West Sussex, PO19 8SQ, United Kingdom

Editorial Offices
350 Main Street, Malden, MA 02148-5020, USA
9600 Garsington Road, Oxford, OX4 2DQ, UK
The Atrium, Southern Gate, Chichester, West Sussex, PO19 8SQ, UK

For details of our global editorial offices, for customer services, and for information about how to apply for permission to reuse the copyright material in this book please see our website at www.wiley.com/wiley-blackwell.

The right of Elizabeth Brestan Knight and Ember L. Lee to be identified as the author of this work has been asserted in accordance with the Copyright, Designs and Patents Act 1988.

All rights reserved. No part of this publication may be reproduced, stored in a retrieval system, or transmitted, in any form or by any means, electronic, mechanical, photocopying, recording or otherwise, except as permitted by the UK Copyright, Designs and Patents Act 1988, without the prior permission of the publisher.

Wiley also publishes its books in a variety of electronic formats. Some content that appears in print may not be available in electronic books.

Designations used by companies to distinguish their products are often claimed as trademarks. All brand names and product names used in this book are trade names, service marks, trademarks or registered trademarks of their respective owners. The publisher is not associated with any product or vendor mentioned in this book. This publication is designed to provide accurate and authoritative information in regard to the subject matter covered. It is sold on the understanding that the publisher is not engaged in rendering professional services. If professional advice or other expert assistance is required, the services of a competent professional should be sought.

Library of Congress Cataloging-in-Publication Data

Knight, Elizabeth Brestan.
  A guide to teaching developmental psychology / Elizabeth Brestan Knight and Ember L. Lee.
    p. cm. – (Teaching psychological science; 4)
  Includes bibliographical references and index.
  ISBN 978-1-4051-5780-3 (hardcover : alk. paper) – ISBN 978-1-4051-5781-0 (pbk. : alk. paper) 1. Developmental psychology–Study and teaching.
I. Lee, Ember L. II. Title.
  BF713.K57 2008
  155.071′1–dc22
                                                                    2008009667

A catalogue record for this book is available from the British Library.

Set in 10.5/12.5pt Sabon by Graphicraft Limited, Hong Kong
Printed in Singapore by Markono Print Media Pte Ltd

1 2008

Contents

Series Editors' Preface vii
Preface xi
Acknowledgements xiii

1. Developing the Course 1
2. Contexts of Development: Research Methods 37
3. Prenatal Development; Labor and Delivery 65
4. Infant Development 87
5. Early Childhood Development 117
6. Middle Childhood Development 139
7. Adolescent Development 155
8. Young Adult Development 167
9. Middle Adult and Older Adult Development 181
10. Death and Dying 205

References 223
Author Index 251
Subject Index 261

Series Editors' Preface

As the best teachers among us can surely attest, teaching at college and university level is no easy task. Even psychology, as inherently interesting as it may be, is a difficult subject to teach well. Indeed, being an effective teacher of any discipline requires a steadfast commitment to self-improvement as a scholar, thinker, and communicator over the long haul. No one becomes a master teacher overnight.

Compared to other disciplines, though, psychology has been way ahead of the curve when it comes to taking its teaching seriously. The Society for the Teaching of Psychology (www.teachpsych.org/) was founded in 1946 and continues to be a powerful force in supporting the teaching of psychology in high schools, community colleges, and four-year schools. The annual National Institute on the Teaching of Psychology, or as it is more informally known, NITOP (www.nitop.org), has been featuring an impressive venue of pedagogical presentations for the past 30 years. In addition, several annual regional teaching of psychology conferences offer a variety of talks, workshops, and poster sessions on improving one's teaching.

Psychologists have also led the way in writing books on effective teaching. Perhaps the most well-known among these texts is McKeachie's (2006) *Teaching Tips*, now it's in twelfth edition (the first edition was published in 1951!). Although McKeachie wrote *Teaching Tips* for all teachers, regardless of discipline, other books focused specifically on teaching psychology have appeared in the past several years. (e.g., Buskist & Davis, 2006; Davis & Buskist, 2002; Forsyth, 2003; Goss Lucas & Bernstein, 2005). The common theme across these books is that they offer general advice for teaching any psychology course, and in McKeachie's case, for teaching any college course.

Blackwell's *Teaching Psychological Science* series differs from existing books. In one handy and concise source, each book provides all an instructor needs to help her in her course. Each volume in this series targets a specific course: introductory psychology, developmental psychology, research methods, statistics, behavioral neuroscience, memory and cognition, learning, abnormal behavior, and personality and social psychology. Each book is authored by accomplished, well-respected teachers who share their best strategies for teaching these courses effectively.

Each book in the series also features advice on how to teach particularly difficult topics; how to link course content to everyday student experiences; how to develop and use class presentations, lectures, and active learning ideas; and how to increase student interest in course topics. Each volume ends with a chapter that describes resources for teaching the particular course focused on in that book, as well as an appendix on widely available resources for the teaching of psychology in general.

The *Teaching Psychological Science* series is geared to assist all teachers at all levels to master the teaching of particular courses. Each volume focuses on how to teach specific content as opposed to processes involved in teaching more generally. Thus, veteran teachers as well as graduate students and new faculty will likely find these books a useful source of new ideas for teaching their courses.

As editors of this series, we are excited about the prospects these books offer for enhancing the teaching of specific courses within our field. We are delighted that Wiley-Blackwell shares our excitement for the series and we wish to thank our Editor Christine Cardone and our Development Project Manager Sarah Coleman for their devoted work behind the scenes to help us bring the series to fruition. We hope that you find this book, and all the books in the series, a helpful and welcome addition to your collection of teaching resources.

Douglas J. Bernstein
William Buskist
April 2007

References

Buskist, W., & Davis, S. F. (Eds.). (2006). *Handbook of the teaching of psychology*. Boston: Blackwell.

Davis, S. F., & Buskist, W. (Eds.). (2002). *The teaching of psychology: Essays in honor of Wilbert J. McKeachie and Charles L. Brewer*. Mahwah, NJ: Erlbaum.

Forsyth, D. R. (2003). *The professor's guide to teaching: Psychological principles and practices*. Washington, DC: American Psychological Association.

Goss Lucas, S., & Bernstein, D. A. (2005). *Teaching psychology: A step by step guide*. Mahwah, NJ: Erlbaum.

McKeachie, W. J. (2006). *McKeachie's teaching tips: Strategies, research, and theory for college and university teachers* (12th ed.). Boston: Houghton Mifflin.

Perlman, B., McCann, L. I., & Buskist, W. (Eds.). (2005). *Voices of NITOP: Memorable talks from the National Institute on the Teaching of Psychology*. Washington, DC: American Psychological Society.

Perlman, B., McCann, L. I., & McFadden, S. H. (2004). *Lessons learned: Practical advice for the teaching of psychology* (Volume 2). Washington, DC: American Psychological Society.

Preface

When I first began my academic career, I was asked to teach lifespan development as a favor to a more seasoned professor who had tired of the course. I was eager to help him and the department so I happily dove into the task of teaching a survey-level developmental psychology course. Having no previous teaching experience and a robust fear of public speaking, I felt sick to my stomach everyday for the first two weeks of class. I have now taught the course over two dozen times at Auburn University and, fortunately, my pre-class nausea has mostly dissipated. My goal in writing this book was to distil my experiences and the approaches that work best for me into the very handbook that would have been a valuable resource when I first taught developmental psychology. Hopefully, some of the techniques and approaches in this book will be helpful for you, too.

In preparing and refining the 20-odd lectures that comprise my lifespan development course, I learned more about the twists and turns of life and developed a greater appreciation for the human experience. Over the years I have also learned a good bit from my graduate teaching assistants and my undergraduates. Not surprisingly, I learned a huge amount about developmental psychology and my teaching objectives from writing this book. It is clearer for me now, for example, that my focus in class is not only on teaching the constructs and theories related to developmental psychology, but also on preparing my students for the unfolding development of their own lives.

Acknowledgements

Writing a book is a large undertaking and there are a number of people that deserve acknowledgement. First, I very much appreciate William Buskist and his faith in my abilities as an author. He has been an extremely helpful and patient editor throughout all of the twists and turns that life sent our way during the development of the book. I am especially grateful that my co-author, Ember Lee, was able to contribute to the project despite being in the midst of, quite possibly, the most hectic year of her graduate school training. My career has been nurtured by an absolute dream team of psychologists including Sheila Eyberg, Catherine Grus, Mark Chaffin, Barbara Bonner, Beverly Funderburk, and Roger Blashfield—hopefully, I will grow to be more like them some day. Finally, my dear friends and family (all the Brestans, Vigils, Tejedas, and Knights) deserve thanks as well. Anecdotes from their lives have helped me to illustrate developmental psychology for countless undergraduates. I am extremely grateful for their part in the development of my own life.

Elizabeth Brestan Knight, Ph.D
August 2, 2007
Auburn, Alabama

Chapter 1

Developing the Course

Because you are reading this book, you have probably agreed to teach a course on one of the most fascinating fields in psychology —lifespan developmental psychology. The job of teaching lifespan development to undergraduates can be daunting: A large number of non-psychology disciplines (e.g., biology, education, sociology, and medicine) and psychology subfields (e.g., experimental psychology, clinical psychology, health psychology, gerontology) relate to human development. However, it is our hope that this book will help you to organize your course and plan a semester that will be rewarding for both you and your undergraduates. We have written the book with the novice developmental psychology instructor in mind, but we hope that seasoned developmental psychology instructors will also find it helpful.

The overall purpose of this book is to focus on the critical aspects of teaching developmental psychology. We share ideas, tips, and strategies for effectively teaching lifespan development for undergraduate psychology majors and non-majors. Additionally, this book offers you advice on how to develop class presentations, lectures, and quizzes; how to teach potentially challenging topics; and how to link developmental psychology concepts to everyday student experiences. Because we focus solely on teaching lifespan development, you may be interested in learning more about the process of teaching by consulting such resources as *The Handbook of the Teaching of Psychology* (Buskist & Davis, 2006), *McKeachie's Teaching Tips* (McKeachie & Svinicki, 2006) or *Voices of Experience: Memorable Talks from the National Institute on the Teaching of Psychology* (Perlman, McCann, & Buskist, 2005). These books provide insight into topics that are beyond the immediate scope of this book, such as the basic mechanics of classroom management, how to present your subject matter passionately, how to build rapport with students, and how to deal with academic dishonesty.

In this chapter we highlight the relevant aspects to consider when planning a developmental psychology course. We begin by presenting a brief history of developmental psychology as a discipline. Next, we address typical course organization for a developmental psychology course with a lifespan perspective, offer some viable alternatives to the traditional course structure, and provide a blueprint for beginning the course. Finally, we focus on the characteristics of students who typically enroll in lifespan development courses.

History of Developmental Psychology

Developmental psychology has changed over the years but the discipline has been present since the early 1700s, as evidenced by the early work of Tetens (Dixon & Lerner, 1992). Early interest in developmental psychology was rooted in, and heavily influenced by, the evolutionary perspective. Various researchers, including Charles Darwin, made comparisons between humans and animals with the view that evolution was a developmental process and that distinct animal species were at different developmental stages of evolution (White, 2003). From human to animal comparisons emerged an interest in the comparison of adult and child forms of various species, including humans. Researchers were interested in describing which aspects change and which aspects remain the same during the transition from child to adult form (Dixon & Lerner, 1992). Thus, the evolutionary perspective was instrumental in the advancement of developmental psychology and remains an important influence (Dixon & Lerner, 1992; White, 2003). The evolutionary perspective currently describes development as a continuous process in which the present form of organisms developed from earlier forms. Additionally, modern evolutionary theory predicts that organisms will continue to develop into future forms (Dixon & Lerner, 1992).

However, developmental psychology did not become a psychology mainstay until the late 19th and early 20th centuries. In fact, the developmental psychology with which we are now familiar has been described as occurring in three waves (White, 2003). The first wave, from 1894–1904, has been called the Child Study Movement and is recognized for its emphasis on naturalistic observation and description of infant and child development (Hogan & Sussner, 2000; White, 2003). The second wave, from 1917–1950, has been coined the Child Development Movement and is distinguished by its normative and psychometric studies and the creation of catalogs of norms and standards for child development (Hogan & Sussner, 2000; White, 2003). The third wave, from 1960 to the present, has been called Developmental Psychology. This most current wave has involved research that is aligned with theory and is explanatory, rather than descriptive, in nature (Dixon & Lerner, 1992; White, 2003). The third wave encompasses all contemporary developmental psychology and entails myriad theories and perspectives.

The lifespan perspective is the most recent advancement in developmental psychology. This perspective gained prominence in the late 1960s; however, Tetens' work in 1777 was a precursor to our modern emphasis on lifespan development (Dixon & Lerner, 1992). The lifespan perspective views the changes that people display from conception through to death as developmental in nature (Dixon & Lerner, 1992). This perspective also takes into account that human life and all of its variables exist at multiple levels—and that those variables multi-directionally influence one another (Dixon & Lerner, 1992). It also emphasizes the need for interdisciplinary research on human development (Dixon & Lerner, 1992). This dual emphasis on lifespan development and interdisciplinary research has influenced the training curricula of many professional disciplines outside psychology to include a developmental psychology course.

Part of the appeal of learning how to teach courses in developmental psychology well is that it has become a requirement for a broad range of undergraduate majors in most four-year colleges, universities, and two-year colleges in the United States. In addition to psychology, these students represent a variety of disciplines such as nursing, communication disorders, elementary education, social work, criminology, and health sciences. This assortment of majors results in a diverse group of enrolled students in developmental psychology courses. Their past experiences and future career aspirations vary widely but you can draw upon these differences in class to illustrate developmental concepts. Often students have experiences that relate directly to the developmental psychology coursework and by asking them a few well-selected open-ended questions, they are generally very willing to discuss these experiences with the class. For example, nursing students may share their experiences of working in an infant labor and delivery hospital unit; early education majors may discuss their internship at a daycare or local elementary school; communication disorders majors may have additional insights about language acquisition to share. Although some students may view this information as tangential (you will never please everyone!) most students enjoy thinking about how these "real life" examples relate to the theory covered in lecture or the text.

Typical Course Organization

There are several approaches and many goals for teaching developmental psychology. Thus, new course instructors must consider "What sort of course am I teaching?" Are you preparing students for graduate study or for a university-specific graduation exam? Is your charge to teach a small course module for psychology majors or a larger, university-wide service course? Are you teaching a basic course or a capstone course at the end of the psychology curriculum (American Psychological Association (APA) Task Force on Strengthening the Teaching and Learning of Undergraduate Psychological Sciences, 2006)?

Your answer to these questions will help to determine the type of developmental psychology course that you will teach. In fact, the developmental psychology tradition in your department may also dictate the parameters of your course. The way that you choose to structure your course may be defined by something as simple as the course title. Courses usually have a short description in the undergraduate catalog and these descriptions may be in place because they fill a gap in the curriculum of your psychology department—as well as major areas of study across campus. For example, one of us (EBK) "inherited" a course called Lifespan Development when she was a brand new assistant professor. In her case, the title of the course dictated the perspective used for each subsequent semester. This course is considered a service course that our department provides for the university and, as such, has attracted a wide range of majors and students. If Lifespan Development is a "new prep" for you, we recommend that you talk to your department chair about the specific needs that your department may have for your course.

Developmental psychology is usually taught from one of three different perspectives: the lifespan development approach, particular age ranges, or thematic/topical areas. The lifespan development perspective follows a chronological time line, usually from conception through to death. There are discrete age ranges that fall within this time frame that most texts divide into stages corresponding to the prenatal period, infancy, the preschool period, the school-aged child period, adolescence, young adulthood, middle adulthood, late adulthood, death and dying. A developmental psychology course that specializes on a particular age range may focus solely on one stage (e.g., infant and child development, adolescent development, or gerontology). Thematic/topical courses in developmental psychology focus on one aspect of development such as cognitive development, physical development, personality development, or social development.

Regardless of the perspective that you choose for your developmental psychology course, it is important to examine the influence that your training and personal biases may have on your instruction. In light of our training as clinical child psychologists in the cognitive-behavioral tradition, we are always clear with students at the beginning of the semester that our perspective is the "lens" that we use to address lifespan development in our courses. We mention that there are five major theoretical perspectives (psychodynamic, behavioral, cognitive, humanistic, and evolutionary) and that in our courses we primarily emphasize the behavioral and cognitive perspectives. We point out to the class when alternative perspectives are available in the text but acknowledge that our bias as clinical child psychologists underscores the cognitive-behavioral perspective.

Although there are advantages and disadvantages to each perspective, the focus that we have chosen for our course is the lifespan development perspective. The advantage of using a linear approach to teaching developmental psychology is that students are exposed to a sampling of the individual changes that can occur over an entire lifetime. As a result, students leave the course with an appreciation for the perspective that development does not end after adolescence. In fact, this idea is one of the core themes that we believe students should learn in a lifespan development course. An additional advantage of teaching development in a linear format is the sense of closure that comes from studying the trajectory of an entire life! This focus can be rewarding for instructor and students alike. Many students

6 Developing the Course

have noted in their end-of-semester course evaluations that the linear, lifespan approach helped them to understand the concepts presented and the developmental stages of their own family members that they have observed.

One disadvantage of teaching a linear course such as lifespan development is the difficulty linking together topics corresponding to seven distinct life stages. Without careful planning, the course may seem disjointed because concepts related to several areas of functioning (physical, cognitive, social, personality) vary greatly with each life stage. For example, it may be difficult for students to appreciate the progression between the cognitive development of infancy and adolescence when a great deal of physical, social, and personality information must be consolidated along the way as well. As such, it is important to explain how development is linked from one stage to another during the course.

Related to the difficulty of integrating information about all of the life stages is the tremendous amount of information available for discussion and lecture in a lifespan development course. Because there is not enough time in any psychology course for every important topic, you need to be selective (Suddreth & Galloway, 2006). Throughout this text we have attempted to highlight key concepts for each life stage. At some point, however, you need to decide when to include breadth and when to include depth in your course. Similar to any psychology course that you might teach, it is best to teach to your strengths and interests. If you have research, clinical, or personal experience relating to some of the topics in the chapter but not others, choosing the area with which you are most familiar will serve you and the students well. In short, students will mirror your interest in these topics. If you are unsure of the material that you are presenting, students may be less interested it. However, if you are extremely enthusiastic about a topic and can pepper your lecture with related anecdotes or provide a context for how this material fits into the "big picture" of psychological theory, research, and application, students will respond to your enthusiasm and their learning is likely to be influenced positively.

Although covering relevant material in one semester is challenging when teaching development from a linear approach, it is not an impossible task. For example, a 50-minute, Monday-Wednesday-Friday course across a typical 15-week semester can typically cover selections from 19 chapters of material if two lectures are set aside for each chapter. We have found that lecture time can be redistributed easily in order to include the same amount of material in a Tuesday-Thursday schedule. One drawback to the Tuesday-Thursday schedule, however, is that it is harder for us to learn the students' names! At the end of this chapter we have provided a sample syllabus for a 75-minute Tuesday-Thursday course that may be used as a guide when planning a lifespan development course.

The challenge of covering material related to lifespan development becomes even greater when the course is taught as an abbreviated summer course. During a 5-week mini-semester in which the class meets daily for 90 minutes, we typically drop two chapters from the syllabus for brevity's sake. In our experience, providing less detail on the physical and cognitive development of young and middle adulthood (or bypassing this material entirely) does not detract demonstrably from the course. In this situation, we attempt to highlight the physical and cognitive aspects of the later adulthood period and how it is different from younger life stages. Additionally, although we typically assign a research paper during the fall and spring semesters, this requirement is dropped during the summer semester. Our rationale for this choice is that the pace of an abbreviated summer course is too fast for students to choose a topic and have adequate time to run a study or conduct an interview. The other, admittedly more selfish, rationale for dropping the paper requirement in the summer is that it would be difficult to grade papers for the entire class in a 5-week semester. Part of being a successful instructor is insuring that you are not an overly stressed instructor!

Choosing a Textbook

A vast array of textbooks and supplementary materials are available for lifespan development courses. The most common-sense method for narrowing the field of potential textbooks is to select a text that mirrors the perspective of the course that you plan to teach. Lifespan development texts often follow a chronological time line from conception through to death. We have organized the chapters of this book to be consistent with the order of these stages of life: prenatal and infant development, early childhood development, middle childhood development, adolescent development, young adult development, older adult development, and death and dying. Lifespan development texts typically cover the aspects of physical development, cognitive development, social development, and personality development corresponding to each stage of life.

A good place to start your search for a textbook is the syllabus from a previous lifespan development instructor in your department. Senior colleagues often have a sense for the level of difficulty that is appropriate for your institution, so the text that they selected will likely be appropriate for your own course (Christopher, 2006). If you do not like the text that was used previously, you should contact your local publishing representatives. They are often very eager to send materials related to your course once you indicate that you are looking for a text. Two texts that we have used successfully are Laura E. Berk's *Development Through the Lifespan* (2006) and Robert S. Feldman's *Development Across the Life Span* (2006). Both texts are currently in their fourth edition and are popular choices for undergraduate lifespan development courses. Berk's text has a higher level of difficulty than Feldman's book. While both texts are appropriate for middle-level undergraduate courses, there are a number of excellent texts available for lifespan development courses. You can acquire instructor's copies of the textbooks by contacting your local publisher's representative; both have a variety of pedagogical tools available such as supplementary instructor's manuals, test-item banks, and companion CD-ROMs.

Elements of the Syllabus

Most lifespan developmental courses include, at a minimum, lectures on core developmental concepts and theories, reading assignments, and, of course, quizzes and exams. Other lifespan developmental courses include papers, group projects, class discussion, videos, or in-class experiential activities. We have used all these pedagogical techniques in our lifespan development courses and most are listed in the sample syllabus at the end of this chapter.

Lecture schedule

Including a class schedule for the lectures in the syllabus is good policy when teaching any undergraduate course (Suddreth & Galloway, 2006). We have found that undergraduates respond well to structure and having a well-developed plan for lectures is an important ingredient of this structure. We rarely alter the lecture schedule;

however, occasionally we switch lecture topics to accommodate guest speakers' schedules. In the following chapters we provide guidelines for choosing class lecture material for each developmental stage as well as sample lecture outlines.

Reading quizzes

Lifespan development courses are busy courses simply because there is so much information to cover. For this reason, students find it helpful to have regularly scheduled reading quizzes throughout the semester. These quizzes help students to stay current with their class reading. It also motivates many students to attend class regularly. Our quizzes are generated from the review sections of each chapter to ensure that the questions reflect important concepts from the text. Our quizzes have five multiple-choice questions. We also typically add one bonus question based on something notable from a previous class (e.g., a student's comment that was relevant to the lecture material).

Exams

Because it is important to provide students with frequent feedback regarding their progress towards the learning goals of any course (APA Task Force on Strengthening the Teaching and Learning of Undergraduate Psychological Sciences, 2006; Suddreth & Galloway, 2006), we also frequently test our students (the sample syllabus in the Appendix lists four exams). We tend to use multiple-choice and short answer exams because we frequently teach large sections of the course (130 or more students). However, the material in the course lends itself well to essay exams and the instructor resources that accompany most lifespan developmental texts may assist you in writing excellent essay questions.

Short-project papers

Although students often dread having to write class papers, the short-project paper can be a valuable exercise in teaching students to think critically. This assignment works best during a full 15-week semester because the students have enough time to choose and research their topics for the paper. Most students have no problem deciding on a topic because there are so many interesting aspects of development in the course from which to choose. For the paper we assign, students have the option of conducting a "mini-experiment" that illustrates an aspect of developmental theory or conducting a developmentally-focused interview with an anonymous participant. We include guidelines for the short-project paper to help explain to students how to write papers in a psychology journal article format. In our experience, most non-majors are able to write a paper in APA-style if given a summary sheet and an explanation of how to cite material.

After hearing about research in class, most students relish the chance to conduct their own "experiment." Popular topics include Piaget's tasks of conservation, Kohlberg's theory of moral development, or short surveys related to mate selection. Because these projects are conducted within the context of class, and to avoid the IRB process, we urge students to include only two or three participants in their experiment (surprisingly, this advice did not stop one industrious undergraduate from developing her own anorexia questionnaire and surveying 40 sorority sisters about their eating habits). Our students report that they enjoy conducting their own research projects—and that these projects enhance their understanding of the course content.

Instead of conducting an experiment, some students choose to conduct an interview with someone who has experienced a life-changing event. The key to these interviews is for students to relate their subject's experience to lifespan development in some way. Each semester we receive a number of papers containing interviews with individuals who have experienced divorce, being fired from a job, or the death of a loved one. Rather than simply reporting on these difficult life events, students must inquire how the individual coped with the stressful life event and then relate the individual's coping to one of the coping styles described in the text. Typically, we do not accept clinical interviews that students conduct on themselves because it is awkward to give a student a letter grade on their own experience and because we would like them to have the experience of interviewing another person. However, one of our favorite papers was a self-study on stress and coping that a student wrote regarding his reaction to developing a topic and writing the short project paper itself!

Class attendance

Due to the size of our lifespan developmental courses, in the fall and spring semesters we do not provide grades for class discussion and class attendance. However, we substitute the short-project paper with a class attendance grade during the summer mini-semester because the class is usually much smaller (50 students) and there is not enough time for students to develop a short-project paper in a five-week summer mini-semester.

In-class activities

Although they are not listed on the syllabus in the appendix, we incorporate several in-class activities and videos throughout the semester. These activities are used to increase student learning and critical thinking about the topics we discuss in the course. Throughout the following chapters we provide ideas for in-class activities and appropriate videos. These in-class activities vary depending on the lecture material. For example, one successful in-class activity that we have used for infant development is to have students use a simple behavioral observation coding system to code a videotape of a 4-month-old infant. This activity gives students a flavor of what it is like to collect observational data for infant behavior. Another in-class activity that we use each semester involves bringing child visitors to class. Bringing children to class helps to demonstrate Piaget's theory of cognitive development and the motor abilities associated with the preschool age range. These child guests can be a very powerful demonstration tool. We do not grade students on the activities themselves but we consider material associated with in-class activities and videos as "fair game" for exam questions (e.g., what aspect of Piaget's tasks of conservation did our child guest have difficulty understanding?). When using a video in class, we have found it helpful to provide the class with "Swiss cheese notes" (i.e., part of the video transcript with key concepts/key words missing) to help guide their viewing of the video. The students enjoy having these notes to help them study for exams.

Extra credit

Our psychology department has three graduate programs, which translates into dozens of graduate students scouring undergraduate classes for thesis and dissertation research participants every semester. In the name of science, we typically allow our students the opportunity to participate in this research for extra credit. The extra credit arrangement serves mutually beneficial functions in that the graduate students are able to complete their research and our undergraduate students experience research participation first-hand and receive a few points to offset whatever difficulties they might have encountered on the last exam.

Some students are unable to attend extra credit sessions due to work or athletic schedules. For this reason, we allow students the opportunity to turn in reaction papers for extra credit. These papers require students to summarize a recent developmental psychology journal article. A typical grading rubric for the extra credit reaction papers is 1 point for using an appropriate journal article, 1 point for a description of the participants, 1 point for describing the data collection method, 1 point for a well-described reaction to the article, and 1 point for including a copy of the journal article and submitting a paper that is at least two to three pages in length.

Alternative Formats for the Course

In addition to the standard teaching practices that we have already outlined, a number of innovative teaching techniques can also be used to promote student learning in an undergraduate lifespan development course. These teaching practices have gained prominence over the last several years and include Problem Based Learning, Focused Interactive Learning, Interteaching, and Service Learning.

Problem-based learning

Problem-based learning (PBL) is a student-directed learning exercise that has been found to be an effective teaching technique (Connor-Greene, 2006). PBL is a form of laboratory-based instruction that provides students with first-hand experience of solving applied problems (Coppola, 2002). Instructors often precede the PBL activity by lecturing on concepts that will be important to PBL activities. After the lecture, the instructor then presents students with a case example to solve either individually or by working in small groups. Because the exercise is self directed, instructors may facilitate working groups but students must decide what information they need to solve the problem and when they have completed the exercise. An example of a PBL exercise that would lend itself well to a Lifespan Development course could include some of the following activities: design your own daycare using a lifespan development perspective, describe how parenting may be different depending on a family's income level or racial/ethnic background, or design a bedroom for an adolescent and explain the pros and cons of including a computer in this bedroom.

Focused interactive learning

Focused interactive learning (FIL) is an active learning technique that uses the principles of dynamic social impact theory to facilitate student participation in class discussion (Harton, Green, Jackson, & Latané, 1998). FIL centers on teaching fundamental concepts via focused discussions with other students (Harton, Richardson, Barreras, Rockloff, & Latané, 2002). FIL has demonstrated increases in student test performance, rapport with other students in class, and students report participation and interest in the material (Harton et al., 2002). Instructors generally give students approximately six multiple-choice questions to answer on their own at the beginning of the class period. Once the students have answered the questions, they discuss each item in small groups (usually the students sitting next to them) for one or two minutes per question. Instructors expect students to discuss each answer's alternative and provide arguments for why that is or is not the correct answer. Following the discussion, the students answer the questions again. The instructor then leads a short discussion of the items. FIL can be conducted in as little as 10 minutes and has been argued to enhance learning by involving students and allowing them to process information (Johnson & Johnson, 1994). FIL also allows students access to immediate feedback on their level of understanding of the material (Harton et al., 2002). Questions that are viable options for FIL include multiple-choice items that are complex and thought provoking, multiple-choice opinion questions with no single correct answer (e.g., choosing a research method to study a developmental concept or stage); or having students give their opinion on a Likert type scale (Harton et al., 2002).

Interteaching

Interteaching (Boyce & Hineline, 2002) is an instructional method based on behavior-analytic principles and includes elements of other behaviorally based methods such as Personalized System of Instruction (Keller, 1968), reciprocal peer tutoring, and cooperative learning (Saville & Zinn, 2005; Saville, Zinn, Neef, Van Norman, & Ferreri,

2006). Interteaching engages students in discussions with each other that are both probing and informative. Typically, instructors assemble "preparation guides" that provide structure for what material will be discussed in the next class period and contain questions that assess factual knowledge as well as a student's ability to apply and synthesize the material.

During the following class period, students work in pairs or small groups to discuss the questions in the preparation guide. The discussion generally uses approximately three-quarters of the class time (Saville & Zinn, 2005). The instructor (and teaching assistants, if available) monitor and facilitate the discussions, clarify concepts and assess students' understanding of the material. Following the discussion, students complete a record that gives the instructor feedback about which questions they found difficult, which concepts they would like reviewed during lecture, and any other information that the instructor believes would be useful in evaluating student performance (e.g., quality of discussion with partner, partner's preparedness). The instructor uses the students' feedback to design the lecture for the next class. The class begins with a lecture that clarifies the concepts from the preceding interteaching session and then may progress to another interteaching session. For a more complete discussion of interteaching, readers are directed to Boyce and Hineline (2002).

Service learning

Service learning is another viable alternative to traditional lecture-based courses in psychology (Osborne & Renick, 2006). Students enroll in a psychology class for course credit and learn course content as directed by an instructor. In addition, they concurrently engage in an applied outreach activity designed to provide them with opportunities for experiential learning that is related to the course content. Students then reflect on their experiences through graded assignments such as a mock grant proposal that would describe the perceived needs of the agency or an essay in which students are asked to relate in-class material to outreach experiences.

The ultimate goal for a service learning course is to establish a mutually beneficial venture in which students gain intellectually from opportunities to apply course content to the community placement while the community simultaneously benefits from services provided by the students. It is important to include graded "reflection activities" in the course structure so that students have a chance to describe what they have learned from the application of course content to the "real world" problem they are engaged in during the semester. (For a detailed summary of best practices for service-learning courses and best practices for service-learning programs, see Osborne & Renick (2006)).

The lifespan development course lends itself well to the service-learning paradigm. For example, students who enroll in a service-learning oriented lifespan development course could volunteer at a local Child Advocacy Center (CAC). CACs can be found in most communities throughout the United States (as well as many other countries) and their focus is to prevent and respond to child abuse and neglect (www.nationalcac.org). Most CACs are non-profit organizations that rely on donations and volunteer assistance to maintain operations. Service-learning students could provide a valuable service to the community by helping in the day-to-day operations of such an agency. As students learn about child, adolescent, and adult development in the classroom, they can apply their knowledge to various CAC activities (e.g., the link between cognitive development and understanding the procedures of a forensic interview, the link between social development and the benefits of a support group for the children and non-offending parents, physical development across the lifespan and how caregivers physically respond to abuse).

Because child maltreatment involves several disciplines (law enforcement, the legal system, medical personnel, school officials, social services, and psychotherapists) and individuals from different stages of the lifespan, this type of service-learning course could be attractive to a variety of undergraduate majors. Additional examples of service learning activities could include working in a Head Start center, tutoring school children with reading or math or other school-based problems, volunteering at a domestic violence shelter, or spending time in an assisted-living facility or nursing home. Should you decide to use a service-learning component for your course, Baird (2005) provides a comprehensive guide for undergraduates who are engaged in field placements.

Infusing Diversity into Lifespan Development

The United States is becoming an increasingly more culturally diverse context within which to live. It is predicted that by the year 2050, half of the US population will consist of "people of color" (Hall,

1997). Given this prediction, it is no longer practical to ignore the influence of cultural factors on lifespan development. We suggest that undergraduate instructors continue to increase their multicultural competency by attending conference workshops on teaching courses with a diversity perspective and reading material related to this topic (e.g., Constantine & Sue, 2005).

Discussion regarding how to incorporate multiculturalism into an undergraduate psychology curriculum has received increased attention in the past decade (Balls Organista, Chun, & Marin, 2000; Hackney, 2005; Hill, 2000; Ocampo et al., 2003; Warren, 2006). Fortunately, there are several chapters (Freeman, 2006; Goldstein, 2005; Lloyd, 2006), books (Balls Organista, Chun, & Marin, 1998; Whittlesey, 2001), and internet resources (Society for the Teaching of Psychology's (STP) Office of Teaching Resources [www.lemoyne.edu/OTRP/index.html]) available on the topic should you choose to include a diversity focus in your class. We would argue, in fact, that it is difficult to teach a class on developmental psychology without including some coverage of a diversity-related topic. In our view, teaching lifespan development is a chance to infuse diversity into a specific content course that is not typically perceived as a multicultural course. For this reason, we have identified key lifespan development topics that can be discussed from a diversity perspective throughout the following chapters in this book. We have also included a list of multicultural resources at the end of this chapter.

Although college professors recognize the importance of including diversity in the undergraduate psychology curriculum, such recognition does not always translate into practice. A survey conducted by STP Task Force on Diversity found that STP members reported the importance of including cultural diversity education in their courses, but only 13% reported including discussion about diversity throughout "most of their course" and 20% reported spending a "couple of weeks" of class time on diversity issues (Simoni, Sexton-Radek, Yescavage, Richard & Lundquist, 1999). Survey participants cited their lack of comfort with diversity issues as a primary barrier to including diversity-related topics in psychology courses (Simoni et al., 1999). This lack of comfort with diversity probably includes the instructor's self-perception that he or she is not "expert" enough to include these issues in class or fears about the emergence of their own personal assumptions and biases (Gloria, Rieckmann, & Rush, 2000).

Another challenge to teaching topics that touch on diversity is that students are at different levels of ethnic/cultural identity development and have differing levels of tolerance for diversity-related topics (Gloria et al., 2000). In fact, if you assume that the entire class has an equally developed understanding of diversity, you are in danger of losing your connection with students who are not tolerant of diversity differences (Gloria et al., 2000). A lack of student appreciation for diversity-related influences on development, or "tunnel vision" for their own perspective, can be especially challenging for even seasoned course instructors. This lack of appreciation for diversity may be a by-product of the type of students that enroll in your class. For example, your students' understanding of socio-cultural influences on development may be limited if your institution does not have many students of color, students from varying economic backgrounds, or returning adult students.

One recommendation for infusing diversity into your lifespan development course is to start small. For example, a presentation or lecture on language development in infancy is a good place to engage students in a discussion of how and why regional accents occur. This topic is a non-threatening way to introduce individual differences among your students, which can easily lead to discussions about how an important behavioral process like language can be shaped by region of the country, education, social class, and historical influences. We have found that if we start our lifespan developmental course by acknowledging that we are all different or diverse in some way and provide non-judgmental encouragement about sharing "differences" for smaller issues, students are willing to share examples throughout the semester when we discuss more controversial topics such as mate selection, gender and the workplace, or death and dying.

Despite possible pitfalls to including a diversity focus, there are many benefits associated with integrating this perspective into lifespan development. For successful infusion of diversity into your courses we offer the following suggestions:

- Maintain perspective regarding your students' level of cultural identity (Gloria et al., 2000). Much like abstract reasoning, cultural identity is a developmental phenomenon that takes time to mature.
- Include guest speakers to expand student perspectives towards diversity beyond that which the instructor can provide (Santos de Barona & Reid, 1992). For example, you might invite a guest to

speak to your class about how having a physical disability affected his or her social or emotional development.
- During lectures, avoid taking the Caucasian, middle-class stance as "normative" for development. This point is especially important to remember when reviewing research findings (e.g., Kohlberg developed his moral development theory with exclusively Caucasian, male participants).
- Finally, remember that there is a wide diversity among your students even if you can't "see" it (e.g., religion and sexual orientation).

We encourage interested instructors to join a listserv that provides a forum for discussion relevant to the teaching of diversity. The APA Division 2 listserv for the Teaching of Diversity (DIVTEACH; diversity-teach-l@listserv.bsu.edu) has helped us to develop as instructors in that comments relevant to pertinent diversity issues (e.g., "how do I work with students who are resistant to the notion of racial privilege?") are frequently posted.

Effective Use of Teaching Assistants

You may have a graduate student or upper level undergraduate student assigned to work with you as a Teaching Assistant (TA). Working with a TA can be very helpful for you in terms of course management, providing assistance with lectures, and meeting with students. Students often benefit from having a TA assigned to their lifespan development course because this individual can double the available office hours for the course and provide another perspective about course content. Some students feel more comfortable approaching a TA with problems in the course because TAs are typically closer in age to the students and may be perceived as more of a "peer" than the course instructor. TAs are generally graduate students who can answer questions about how to gain admission into graduate school in psychology. Finally, TAs can enhance their professional development through their position by honing their public speaking skills, learning to edit papers, and mastering the art of course management with computerized systems such as WebCT or Blackboard. As an aside, most undergraduate and graduate students enjoy working as a TA for lifespan development for the same reasons that the course appeals to undergraduate students. Because this course will apply to their own lives in some way, we have found that TAs are rarely at a loss for examples to illustrate class material.

Your experience with TAs will vary depending on their strengths and weaknesses for the TA job skills set. However, you can maximize the potential for a positive collaboration with your TAs by meeting with them before the semester begins to discuss your expectations (Kipp & Wilson, 2006). We recommend providing your TAs with a class syllabus, a course schedule indicating whether the TAs or instructor is responsible for specific lectures, and a TA syllabus that outlines their duties for the semester.

Generally, graduate student TAs will be able to perform more duties than undergraduate TAs. Typical duties that you may ask of an undergraduate TA would be to facilitate discussion groups focusing on specific age ranges, tutor students who are having problems in the course, provide study sessions, manage grade information, monitor class attendance, photocopy exam papers and handouts, and conduct office hours. Most graduate TAs will be able to handle all the tasks that you would ask of undergraduate TAs and they can participate in more complex tasks such as providing class lectures, generating handouts, grading papers, and writing and grading exams (Kipp & Wilson, 2006).

If you would like your TAs to be in charge of downloading documents to your computerized course management system or walking scantron exams to the university testing center, be specific about these duties and explain how they are done. To maximize the learning experience for your TA, it is important to assess the comfort level and skills set that he or she has at the beginning of the academic term and use this information to determine their assigned duties throughout the remainder of the academic term. Experienced TAs will likely become frustrated if their only job is entering grades; inexperienced TAs would not be qualified to prepare a majority of the class lectures. In other words, use Vygotsky for your inspiration and check in regularly with your TAs during the semester to assess how they are performing and to provide "scaffolding" as needed.

Teaching Psychology Majors vs. Non-Majors

There are a few things to consider when teaching developmental psychology to psychology majors. In some departments developmental psychology is open to students soon after they have taken an introductory psychology course but in other departments, developmental psychology students may not have any experience with psychology. Even within a class full of psychology majors, it is important to assess whether everyone in the class has had exposure to topics before proceeding if for no other reason that different introductory psychology teachers in your department may cover different content in their courses. For example, some teachers of this course may omit developmental psychology from their coverage.

Some adaptations to your course are necessary to teach developmental psychology to non-psychology majors. We often ask questions of the class to see if anyone who has taken introductory psychology before might be able to explain the concept of developmental psychology to the rest of the class (an early example in our course is the "nature vs. nurture" debate). We find that this question fosters an atmosphere that encourages engaging class participation. It allows psychology majors a chance to show what they have learned, and it keeps the class fresh because we are not droning on in "lecture mode" for the entire class period. We tend to teach to the lowest common denominator of psychological knowledge—especially when we cover statistics and research design. Those students who have learned the material in class before often benefit from hearing the information again.

Teaching Today's Developmental Psychology Students

Psychology courses are more popular that ever (Brewer, 2006) and developmental psychology probably appeals to many students because it involves an examination of their own lives. Although not all students are in the business of learning how to "analyze" their friends and families, most students do choose courses based on whether (a) they fill a graduation requirement and (b) they are interesting. Certainly reputation of the instructor, perceived workload, the time of day that the course is offered, and the day scheduled for the final exam *(sigh)* have some bearing on their decision to enroll in any particular developmental psychology course. Some students are interested in the prenatal and infancy periods because they either hope to be parents in the future or they will be parents in the very near future (in our courses, we average one pregnant student a semester).

Some students prefer to study the young adult period because it applies to their everyday efforts to establish an identity separate from their family of origin, establish intimate relationships, and determine which career path to follow. Many students will enroll in your course simply because they have an interest in working with children in their future careers.

Teaching today's developmental psychology students can be both rewarding and challenging. In some respects, teaching lifespan development is rewarding for the instructor simply because the topic area is intrinsically interesting for most students, which makes it an extremely enjoyable course to teach. Lifespan development courses are often offered early in the psychology major curriculum sequence. For this reason, many motivated first and second year students enroll in the course. Many students are fresh from completing an introductory psychology course and they are eager to learn more about psychology. It is our experience that our lifespan developmental course has helped some students determine whether they prefer to work with children or adults following graduation. (Of course, those of us in the helping professions know that working with children means that you will necessarily also work with adults and vice versa!)

Nonetheless, teaching lifespan developmental psychology has its challenges. One challenge to teaching this course is the increased demand for coursework that stimulates the class through multimedia effects and demonstration. For this reason alone, the pace of your lectures is an important consideration when preparing your lectures. For example, video clips can be especially helpful when covering the early sections of the course such as prenatal development, infant reflexes, early language development, and stranger anxiety. All of these topics are easy to understand when observed rather than just writing lecture notes about them. We find it helpful to lecture on material, show examples of the material through video clips, and then discuss the video clips with the class. This sequence provides some natural breaks for the class so that they are not spending the entire class taking copious notes or absently watching a video.

Many of your students will be technologically savvy and will expect to be "entertained" by technological aspects of the course. Fortunately, developmental psychology lends itself quite well to the use of technology as there are numerous videos that can be used to illustrate the concepts of the course. We have included references for a selection of video resources throughout this text.

Another challenge to teaching lifespan development is that you will have students with varied learning styles in your course. As a product of our training as clinical child psychologists, we tend to think about children with learning disabilities when deciding how to present information to undergraduate students. Many younger children with auditory processing problems can understand material better when they *read* information. Others with reading difficulties understand material better when they *hear* about it. Much like school-aged children, there is a continuum of learning styles in the typical undergraduate class. To help make the material accessible to for all students, we recommend presenting important topics through a few modalities (straight lecture, class examples, video clips, and textbook reading). Of course, this point is true for all undergraduate courses.

Culturally inclusive teaching has become an important goal for most undergraduate psychology instructors (Hill, 2000). One way to promote culturally inclusive teaching is to include a variety of examples to illustrate lecture material. Some of these examples can include topics that would be familiar to majority culture students, but you should also include examples that are relevant to the experience of minority culture students as well. Carefully selecting video clips that include diverse participants is another way to promote cultural inclusion in your classroom. We find it helpful to allow students to share personal experiences with pre-established ground rules regarding classroom acceptance for all perspectives. A final common-sense guideline is to avoid calling on any one student to speak for an entire group simply because they are—or appear to be—representative of the group being discussed.

Beginning the Course

Any effective public speaker will tell you that to capture the attention of your audience you must understand them and what they are hoping to learn from your presentation. The same is true for teaching a course on lifespan development. To understand development and its myriad nuances and complications, teachers must consider the context of their courses; in particular, the experiences and perspectives that your students bring with them to the classroom.

On the first day of class we discuss the syllabus and then tell the students some basic biographical information about ourselves (e.g., our hometown, where we went to school and a few of our hobbies). We then distribute index cards to the class and ask them to "write your name and something about you." Most students include their major area of study, their year in school, and some information about their hobbies and/or future career choices. We have found this "ice breaker" activity to be a valuable tool for learning more about our "audience" for the upcoming semester. The comments we receive each semester generally include a wide range of interests and experiences and we read them with curiosity. As you will note from the selection of comments below, our students have unique life experiences and expectations about lifespan development! We try to integrate these interests and future career goals into our lecture whenever possible. For example, if someone in the class had experience working in a labor and delivery unit, we would ask them for any insights they might have during our lecture on labor and delivery. We have found that including students in the teaching process can be a very engaging technique for undergraduates.

- "I am an early childhood special education major. I love it and hope to use some of the information that I learn here with my kids."
- "I want to work with kids but I am not really sure what ages yet."
- "I really enjoyed my Intro to Psychology course last summer and I am looking forward to this course."
- "I am from South Carolina and have traveled and lived all around the world. I am ready to learn what you have to teach me."
- "One day I would like to be a missionary and go to Africa."
- "I enjoy reality shows, 'Red Stripe' beer, and classic rock."
- "I don't have a life. I work, sleep, and go to school."

An additional activity to conduct at the beginning of the course is to set the context for the course. For example, giving students a brief history of the field of developmental psychology helps connect the subject matter to our society. Because students have an intrinsic interest in human development, it is relatively simple to combine a brief history of the field with relevant sociopolitical events to set the stage for drawing similar links throughout the semester.

For example, your lecture on the history of developmental psychology can provide a time line that follows the progression and overlap of the various theoretical perspectives related to developmental psychology. This time line will allow you to highlight the perspective from which you will teach the remainder of the course. In addition, a fun activity to use to engage the students in this material would be either for you to provide (or have the students generate) a list of social policies or programs with which they are familiar (or of which they have at least heard). Select one or two of these suggestions and briefly discuss how developmental psychology has influenced them. Let the students know that most, if not all, of the remaining programs have been influenced in some way by developmental psychology. Some examples with which students are likely familiar are Head Start, Medicaid, Women Infants and Children (WIC). Throughout the remaining chapters we offer tips and ideas on how to infuse information about prominent historical players in developmental psychology and their contributions to current social policies within the course content.

Appendix A

Sample Syllabus for Lifespan Development (PSY 2120)

2:00 pm–3:15 pm Tuesdays and Thursdays, Thach 112

Elizabeth Brestan Knight, Ph.D., Course Instructor
Office Hours: Tuesdays at 3:30pm or by appointment
Phone: 844–6486; office: 208C Thach; E-mail: brestev@auburn.edu
"Bright Student," Graduate Teaching Assistant
Office Hours: Tuesdays at 1:00pm or by appointment
Office: Thach 210; E-mail: bright@auburn.edu

Course objectives:

This course is intended to familiarize students with the psychologically important physical, cognitive, personality, and social changes that individuals experience from conception through to old age. In examining these changes, students will be introduced to the methods through which psychological development is studied and to the major theoretical perspectives used to make sense of developmental change. The impact of social and cultural variables on psychological development will also be considered.

Textbook

Feldman, R. S. (2006). *Development Across the Lifespan*. Upper Saddle River, NJ: Pearson/Prentice Hall.

Lecture, assignment, and examination schedule

Date	Lecture topic	Quiz/examination
Thursday, Aug 18	Chapter 1	
Tuesday, Aug 23	Chapters 1 and 2	Quiz 1 [Chapters 1 and 2]
Thursday, Aug 25	Chapters 2 and 3	
Tuesday, Aug 30	Chapter 3	
Thursday, Sep 1	Chapter 4	Quiz 2 [Chapters 3 and 4]
Tuesday, Sep 6	Chapters 4 and 5	
Thursday, Sep 8	Chapters 5 and 6	Quiz 3 [Chapters 5 and 6]
Tuesday, Sep 13	Chapter 6 and review	
Thursday, Sep 15		*Examination 1* [*Chapters 1, 2, 3, 4, 5, 6]*

26   Developing the Course

Date	Lecture topic	Quiz/examination
Tuesday, Sep 20	Chapter 7	
Thursday, Sep 22	Chapters 7 and 8	Quiz 4 [Chapters 7 and 8]
Tuesday, Sep 27	Chapters 8 and 9	
Thursday, Sep 29	Chapter 9	Quiz 5 [Chapters 9 and 10]
Tuesday, Oct 4	Chapter 10 and review	
Thursday, Oct 6		*Examination 2 [Chapters 7, 8, 9, 10]*
Tuesday, Oct 11	Chapter 11	
Thursday, Oct 13	Chapters 11 and 12	Quiz 6 [Chapters 11 and 12]
Tuesday, Oct 18	Chapter 12	
Thursday, Oct 20	Chapter 13	
Tuesday, Oct 25	Chapters 13 and 14	Quiz 7 [Chapters 13 and 14]
Thursday, Oct 27	Chapter 14 and review	
Tuesday, Nov 1		*Examination 3 [Chapters 11, 12, 13, 14]*
Thursday, Nov 3	Chapter 15	Quiz 8 [Chapters 15 and 16]
Tuesday, Nov 8	NO CLASS	
Thursday, Nov 10	Chapter 16	Short project due [See below – may be turned in early]
Tuesday, Nov 15	Chapter 17	
Thursday, Nov 17	Chapters 17 and 18	Quiz 9 [Chapters 17 and 18]
Tuesday, Nov 22	NO CLASS	*THANKSGIVING*
Thursday, Nov 24	NO CLASS	*THANKSGIVING*
Tuesday, Nov 29	Chapter 18	
Thursday, Dec 1	Chapter 19	
Tuesday, Dec 6	Chapter 19 and evaluations	Quiz 10 [Chapter 19]
Monday, Dec 12	5:00pm – 7:30pm	*Examination 4 [Chapters 15, 16, 17, 18, 19]*

Reading quizzes: [Required]

There will be 10 reading quizzes, each consisting of 5 questions earning 1 point each (5 points per quiz). The quizzes will cover the "Looking Back" summary at the end of the assigned chapters and also any "From Research to Practice," "Review and Rethink," and "Developmental Diversity" sections contained in the assigned chapters. A sixth "bonus question" may be added to the reading quizzes.

Short project: [Required – due Thursday, Nov 10]

You may earn a maximum of 50 points by writing a report of a "project" satisfying the following criteria:

1. Summarize the material in the course/text that relates to your topic [background].
2. Indicate what you did [method].
3. Indicate what you found [results].
4. Indicate what *you* conclude from the results [conclusions].
5. *Include proper references for the material you cite from the text or other materials.*
6. *Include headings for each section (background, method, etc.).*

Please type your report and limit the length to between three and four pages, double-spaced. Note that *plagiarism of any sort will not be tolerated.*

Report options

1. Ask a child from two different age groups "What are you like as a person?" Record their answers and provide an analysis of their responses.
2. Administer Piaget's conservation tasks to a 3- or 4-year-old and a 7- or 9-year-old. Compare your findings to those of Piaget.
3. Interview an adolescent about the moral choices they face in their life. Next ask him/her how they go about deciding what to do. Relate their responses to Kohlberg's theory of moral decision-making.
4. Interview an adult who has experienced a major life change (divorce, death, job change, empty nest, etc.) Ask him/her to tell you how they have tried to cope and relate their responses to the text material on coping and stress.
5. Visit a hospice (there is one at 665 Opelika Road in Auburn) and interview a staff member about the hospice philosophy. Briefly indicate that philosophy and your personal reactions to your visit.
6. Propose a relevant project to the instructor or GTA and follow their guidance.

We will provide more detailed guidelines for the short project later in class.

Extra credit: [Optional]

Ten points can be earned by either or both of the following:

1. *Research subject participation*: Participate as a research subject in projects conducted by faculty or students in the Department of Psychology.

Each hour of participation will earn 5 points up to a maximum of 2 hours (10 points). Many of these opportunities are posted on a bulletin board in the Psychology Department; others will be announced in class. *No extra credit slips will be accepted after 5pm on Tuesday, December 6th (our last day of class).*

2. *Reaction papers to articles about human development*: Write a reaction paper to an article about some aspect of human development published in 2003, 2004, or 2005. Provide a complete reference, a brief summary of the article, and your critical reaction to the article. *Include a copy of the article with your paper.* Please type and double-space each paper; 2–3 pages each. *No reaction papers will be accepted after 5pm on Tuesday, December 6th (our last day of class).*

Each reaction paper can earn a maximum of 5 extra credit points, and no more than 10 extra credit points can be earned in total. Reviews of magazine articles are *not* permitted. The reaction paper must present a full description of who the subjects were and how the data were collected. You must use an article from one of the journals presented below:

Child Development
Journal of Gerontology
Journal of Applied Developmental Psychology
Monographs of the Society for Research in Child Development
Developmental Psychology
Infant Behavior and Development
Merrill-Palmer Quarterly
Journal of Marriage and the Family
Developmental Psychobiology
Human Development
Development

Special needs

Students needing accommodations must be formally registered with the Program for Students with Disabilities located in 1244 Haley Center (phone 844-2096).

You must see the instructor or GTA at the beginning of the semester to make necessary arrangements.

Attendance policy

The instructor does not take attendance. However, students should be aware that the instructor and GTA do lecture on topics not covered in the textbook. Examination questions will reflect this additional material. Lectures are intended to elaborate material that is likely to be on exams and is intended to provide a deeper understanding of *some* of the topics that are covered in the textbook. However, students should understand that they are responsible for *all* textbook material, even when that material is not elaborated in class. Although the instructor does not take attendance, you *must be seated in class in order to take the in-class reading quizzes*. No quiz will be given to anyone who arrives after the quiz has already been administered to the class.

Exam/Quiz make up policy

Exams and quizzes can be made up when the student documents a University sanctioned absence (see the "Rules" section of the Tiger Cub under "Class Attendance"; can also be found at the following web address: www.auburn.edu/academic/provost/handbook instruction.html#class). Note: All missed exams and quizzes must be made up within two weeks (10 class days) of the day of the exam or quiz was scheduled, unless the sanctioned absence covered a period of more than 5 class days, in which case the students will have 10 class days from the end of the extended absence to make up the exam or quiz. Any student who does not show for a scheduled make up exam will be given a zero mark for that exam unless he or she can document a University sanctioned absence for the make up exam. *If you miss class due to an illness, you need to present a note from the doctor excusing you from class for that day in particular.* Exams and quizzes may be made up without a University sanctioned excuse, but a deduction of 15% will be taken.

Grading

A total of 500 points can be earned in the course (extra credit points will be added to your total for a maximum of 510). Course grades will be assigned based on the following point totals:

A: 450–500   B: 400–449   C: 350–399   D: 300–349   F: <299

Points

Examinations 1, 2, 3, and 4 [100 points each]	(400)
Reading Quizzes [5 points each]	(50)
Short Project [50 points maximum]	(50)
	Total Possible = (500)
Extra Credit [5pts/research hour; 10pts/reaction paper]	+10

30 Developing the Course

Please note that Exam 4 is not a cumulative exam. This final exam will cover material from Chapters 15, 16, 17, 18, & 19.

All final grades are based on total points. NO grade will be rounded up (even if you are one point away from an A), so it is in your best interest to participate in the extra credit activities and attend class regularly.

The authors would like to acknowledge Phil Lewis, Ph.D for sharing portions of his syllabus with us.

Appendix B

Sample Short Project Guidelines

The short project is required of all PSYC 2120 students and is due *on Thursday, Nov 10th.*

You may earn a maximum of 50 points by writing a report of a "project" satisfying the following criteria.

Report organization

The report should be organized into the following five distinct, ordered, *and labeled* sections:

1. *Background:* This section will include information from the textbook (and other sources as applicable) that describes, explains, and justifies/makes obvious the significance of the project topic you have chosen.
    a. Introduce the topic on which you conducted your project and indicate how what you did relates to material in the course. (e.g., "This relates to the material in Chapter X (Feldman, 2003)....)
    b. Summarize the theories and/or research relevant to your project.
    c. Elaborate. Not just one or two sentences.
    d. Include proper references where appropriate.
2. *Method:* This section will be a straight-forward account of *precisely* what you did. Your method should be so explicit that a reader could exactly replicate your project by reading the method section alone.
    a. Indicate what you did.
        i. (e.g., "I administered Piaget's conservation of liquid task to a 6-year-old female and a 12-year-old male...")
        ii. (e.g., "I conducted an interview with a 46-year-old female...")
    b. Include the actual questions you asked, detailed descriptions of the tests/tasks you administered, etc.
    c. If you develop a long questionnaire, you might include it as an Appendix at the end of your paper rather than in the body of the paper, but you should refer to the appendix in the text.
3. *Results:* This section will be a straight-forward account of precisely what you found, that is, what happened, how your participant(s) responded.
    a. Indicate what you found.
        i. (e.g., "The female participants were able to solve the conservation task...")

ii. (e.g., "Ms. X reported that the death of her husband has been a very difficult event . . .")
   b. Report what your participants' answers to your questions were, the scores they received on any tasks you administered, etc.
   c. *Keep opinions and conclusions out of the results section*; simply report what you found/what happened. Your conclusions and opinions are for the next section . . .
4. *Conclusions:* This section should pull the project together. It will include a brief summary of the main results and what conclusions *you* draw from your findings in relation to what you know about the topic from the text and any other sources (if you choose to use other sources).
   a. Indicate what *you* conclude from the results. What do the results mean to you?
      i. (e.g., "I was able to replicate Piaget's conservation task and his view of child intellectual functioning was well supported by my project.")
      ii. (e.g., "The death of a spouse is a very traumatic event. It seems that family support is crucial for the grieving process.")
   b. How do your findings "fit" with the theory or previously reported research (which you discussed in your background section)? What doesn't fit?
   c. Include your opinions and conclusions in this section. What do *you* think about it? (e.g., does it change or how does it influence your perspective on the topic?)
   d. Do you have remaining questions or "hindsight" realizations of how you could have improved your project?
5. *References:* Include proper references for the material you cite. This includes any material you cite from the text or other outside materials. You are *required* to use the *textbook* as a source, but you may use any other additional resources you choose as well.
   a. You <u>must</u> include proper citations in the body of your paper whenever you are quoting, summarizing, or otherwise using information or ideas that are not your own. There essentially are two ways of doing in-text citations.
      i. If you are using a direct quotation (no matter how large or small the amount you're quoting), the in-text citation must include the author, year, and page number, *along with quotation marks*. For example:
      "Feldman (2003) writes, 'stress may also lead to psychosomatic disorders, medical problems caused by the interaction of psychological, emotional, and physical difficulties' (p. 452)."
      ii. If you are paraphrasing or summarizing information in your own words, the in-text citation must include the author and publication year. For example: "Stress also can be expressed

through physical complaints or psychosomatic disorders (Feldman, 2003)."
b. You also *must* include a reference page at the end of your project that includes the full reference citation for *each and every* source you have used and cited in the text of your project. A full citation includes: author (date of publication). *Italicize title*. City of publication: Publisher. Example of a reference page, using two sources:

References

Bornstein, M. H. & Lamb, M. E. (1992). *Developmental psychology: An advanced textbook* (3rd ed.). Hillsdale, NJ: Lawrence Erlbaum Associates.

Maccoby, E. E. (1998). *The two sexes: Growing up apart, coming together*. Cambridge, MA: Harvard University Press.

c. You will not receive full credit for a paper that includes plagiarism. Plagiarism can be loosely defined as passing off someone else's words or ideas as your own. This includes copying something from the book (or another source) word for word without providing a proper reference, including proper quotations. This also includes turning in a paper that you did not write: turning in someone else's work will result in a grade of zero for the paper.

The report should be typed, double-spaced, and 3–4 pages in length. The reports will be graded on their readability, clarity of content, and the overall quality of the project. *Please note that any paper originally written for another class and only loosely resembling a topic in lifespan development will receive no points.*

Report options

Please note that you can do your project on anything that relates to the readings—even if we have not yet covered the material.

1. Ask a child from two different age groups "What are you like as a person?" Record their answers and provide an analysis of their responses.
2. Administer Piaget's conservation tasks to a 3 or 4 year old and a 7 or 9 year old. Compare your findings to those of Piaget.
3. Interview an adolescent about the moral choices they face in their life. Next ask him/her how they go about deciding what to do. Relate their responses to Kohlberg's and/or Gilligan's theory of moral decision-making.
4. Interview an adult who has experienced a major life change (divorce, death, job change, empty nest, etc.) Ask him/her to tell you how they have tried to cope.

5. Visit a hospice (there is one at 665 Opelika Road in Auburn) and interview a staff member about the hospice philosophy. Briefly indicate that philosophy and your personal reactions to your visit.
6. Propose a relevant project to the instructor or GTA and follow their guidance.

The authors would like to acknowledge L. Kimberly Epting, Ph.D for providing Appendix B.

Appendix C

Sample lifespan development schedule for a summer semester

Date	Lecture topic	Topic	Quiz/examination
Monday, May 23	Chapter 1	Intro, Nature vs. Nurture	
Tuesday, May 24	Chapter 1	Research Methods	
Wednesday, May 25	Chapter 2	Genetics, Pediatric Psychology, Prenatal Growth	Quiz 1 [Chapters 1 and 2]
Thursday, May 26	Chapter 3	Stages of Labor	
Friday, May 27	Chapter 4	Infant Development, Reflexes, Senses	Quiz 2 [Chapters 3 and 4]
Monday, May 30	NO CLASS		
Tuesday, May 31	Chapter 5	Piaget, Language Development	
Wednesday, June 1	Chapter 6	Attachment, Temperament	Quiz 3 [Chapters 5 and 6]
Thursday, June 2			Examination 1 [Chapters 1, 2, 3, 4, 5, 6]
Friday, June 3	NO CLASS		
Monday, June 6	Chapter 7	Piaget, Vygotsky	Quiz 4 [Chapters 7 and 8]
Tuesday, June 7	Chapter 8	Child Maltreatment	
Wednesday, June 8	Chapter 9	ADHD	
Thursday, June 9	Chapter 10	Kohlberg, Gilligan, Self Esteem	Quiz 5 [Chapters 9 and 10]
Friday, June 10			Examination 2 [Chapters 7, 8, 9, 10]
Monday, June 13	Chapter 11	Adolescent Cognition Video Body Image	
Tuesday, June 14	Chapter 11/ Chapter 12	Anorexia Video	Quiz 6 [Chapters 11 and 12]
Wednesday, June 15	Chapter 12	Depression/Suicide	
Thursday, June 16	Chapter 14	Mate Selection	Quiz 7 [Chapter 14]
Friday, June 17	NO CLASS		
Monday, June 20			Examination 3 [Chapters 11, 12, 14]

Date	Lecture topic	Topic	Quiz/examination
Tuesday, June 21	Chapter 16	Personality Development in Middle Adulthood	Quiz 8 [Chapter 16]
Wednesday, June 22	Chapter 17	Alzheimer's Disease	
Thursday, June 23	Chapter 18	The Big Fire	Quiz 9 [Chapters 17 and 18]
Friday, June 24	Chapter 19	Death and Dying	Quiz 10 [Chapter 19]
Monday, June 27			Examination 4 [Chapters 16, 17, 18, 19]

Helpful resources for Teaching Lifespan Developmental Psychology

Brislin, R. (2000). *Understanding culture's influence on behavior.* South Melbourne, Australia: Wadsworth/Thompson Learning.

Eisler, R. M. & Hersen, M. (Eds.). (2000). *Handbook of gender, culture, and health.* Mahwah, N.J.: Lawrence Erlbaum.

Goldberger, N. R., & Veroff, J. B. (Eds.). (1995). *The culture and psychology reader.* New York: New York University Press.

Mio, J. S., Barker-Hackett, L., & Tumambing, J. (2006). *Multicultural psychology: Understanding our diverse communities.* Boston: McGraw Hill.

Paludi, M. (Ed.). (2002). *Human development in multicultural contexts: A book of readings.* Upper Saddle River, N.J.: Prentice Hall.

Shiraev, E., & Levy, D. (2007). *Cross-cultural psychology: Critical thinking and contemporary applications.* Boston: Pearson.

Smith, T. B. (Ed.). (2004). *Practicing multiculturalism.* Boston: Pearson.

Squire, C. (Ed.). (2000). *Culture in psychology.* London: Routledge.

The Office of Teaching Resources Web page has many resources devoted to diversity issues in psychology at the following website: www.lemoyne.edu/OTRP/teachingresources.html#diversity

Chapter 2

Contexts of Development: Research Methods

The content of this chapter is important because, together, research methods and the contexts of development provide the foundation for developmental psychology. To understand development, the context of the developing individual must be considered. Likewise, an understanding of how developmental knowledge is generated through scientific inquiry is important for all of our students to know.

The content discussed here also serves as an "ice breaker" as it is the first opportunity that we have to engage the students in class discussion. As you know, every class has its own personality. Some classes have outspoken students and discussion flows freely. Other semesters you may have a class that is so quiet that generating class discussion is a serious challenge to your teaching skills. Your first reaction to a quiet class may be that they do not respond to your teaching style; however, we recommend that you do not take their silence personally. There are probably several reasons for your quiet class, most of which do not have anything to do with you. First, time of day and semester variables are likely to play a part. In our experience, students in early morning courses and spring semester courses tend to be more reticent. Mid-term fatigued students can also be a challenge to engage in class discussion. Second, you may have a roomful of students who are simply shy. These classes do not have a critical mass of "talkers" and they would probably be quiet with most teachers. Third, some classes demonstrate social loafing by relying on a few talkative students to carry class discussion. Finally, some students simply prefer to sit and have you do all the talking. Several times we have received feedback from students that they prefer to hear what they need to know for the exam and nothing more. You may feel as though the semester is not going well if you have a quiet class but their exam grades and class evaluations will likely be comparable to more actively engaged classes (except for those students who only want to hear what will be on the exam—they are not yet lifelong learners).

There are a few things that you can do to increase the chances that students contribute to class discussion. They may worry that they might appear foolish if their answer or comment is incorrect. Guidance regarding the particulars of classroom management is beyond the scope of this chapter; however, there are some excellent resources available on dealing with classroom problems and establishing classroom etiquette (Damour, 2006; Wilson & Hackney, 2006). In our training as child therapists, we have learned the value of using praise with individuals in clinical settings. Fortunately, praise also works extremely well in the classroom, too. The use of praise is one of the most powerful behavioral family therapy techniques because it helps to increase appropriate, prosocial behavior. As such, you can use praise to increase most classroom behaviors. In the type of parent training that we use, Parent-Child Interaction Therapy (PCIT) (Brinkmeyer & Eyberg, 2003) we focus on using a particular type of praise called "labeled praise." Most praises that adults give to one another are unlabeled praises. "Good," "nice job," and "thanks" are all examples of unlabeled praises that instructors may give to students. Labeled praises, however, are more specific praises that tell the student exactly what you like about his or her behavior. Some examples of in-class labeled praises that you could use would include "Sharon, thank you for sharing that example." "I like how everyone in this class is thinking so creatively." "I really appreciate how everyone gave their undivided attention to the last guest speaker." "Thanks for bringing that point up, it is a great segue into my next slide..." We like using labeled praise because it shows appreciation for our students. They are more likely to perform appropriate student behaviors when you provide them with positive reinforcement following their demonstration of these behaviors. Also, it helps to create warmth within the classroom.

In this chapter we summarize the key concepts relating to the contexts of development and research methods that we believe are the most important to include in a course on lifespan development. We provide examples of class activities that would help to enhance your teaching of these key concepts. Finally, we provide suggestions for Web sites and resources that you can use to highlight the key concepts from this section.

Contexts of Development

In the lifespan development course that we teach, the first lecture covers issues relating to the contexts of development in developmental psychology. Teaching material related to the contexts of development is fairly straightforward and an excellent way to introduce the course. Additionally, students tend to understand this material well. The developmental science themes that we consider to be the most crucial for this section include coverage of the topical areas in lifespan development, the contexts of development (including Bronfenbrenner's (1979) Ecological Systems Theory), the importance of nature and nurture for the maturation process, the distinction between discontinuous and continuous development, and the distinction between sensitive periods and critical periods. In this chapter we present more topics than you will be able to cover in one lecture. We typically take two lecture periods to cover this information—although there is variation per semester depending on the amount of discussion generated by the class.

Topical areas in lifespan development

Because the text that we use in our class divides each stage of life into chapters that correspond to topical areas of development (i.e., physical, cognitive, social, and personality development), we begin the course by providing brief definitions and examples of these areas. Next, we present a slide show that lists the age ranges of the developmental stages that we cover in class. Due to our training as clinical psychologists, we also like to provide a few examples to show why children, adolescents, and adults may be referred for clinical treatment. Although developmental psychopathology may not be recognized as an essential component of lifespan development, we find that including these examples helps to illustrate the intra- and inter-personal challenges faced by individuals at different life stages. As clinical psychologists, it is also a chance for us to teach to our strength of clinical experience.

In short, our brief coverage of developmental psychopathology serves as an introduction to the topic of lifespan development and provides examples for the topical areas. The first lecture is your chance to help students understand why topics related to lifespan development are relevant. Additionally, the first class is our chance to set the tone for the rest of the semester. Our hope for every semester is to create an interesting and energetic atmosphere. As such, we include interesting photographs to capture the various age ranges.

Unique contexts of development

Evaluating the contexts of development places the individual within their cultural and historical context. This topic is an easy introduction to the course because most students appear to enjoy generating examples for the cultural and historical influences on development. We recommend reviewing a detailed graduate textbook for any aspects of human developmental science that you feel need clarification in your mind as you prepare your lectures. One resource that we have found helpful in developing our understanding of developmental psychology is a book edited by Bornstein and Lamb (2005) entitled *Developmental Science: An Advanced Textbook*. Notably, this book contains a chapter on the concepts and theories of human development that apply directly to this section (Lerner, Theokas, & Bobek, 2005).

Normative age-graded influences Normative age-graded influences are developmentally relevant influences determined through biology or the environment. The onset of a child's formal education is one example of an age-graded influence on development (Feldman, 2006). The beginning of school typically occurs once a child is potty trained. Thus, attending school is biologically influenced and this event typically occurs on the same time schedule, regardless of an individual's culture or nationality. Frequent student-generated examples of normative age-graded influences have included becoming potty trained, losing your first tooth, menarche, and menopause. Regardless of the example that a student contributes to class discussion, we try to help them determine how the point given may influence human development.

Normative sociocultural-graded influences Normative sociocultural-graded influences are developmental influences related to an individual's ecological niche. In particular, an understanding of an individual's ethnicity and social class is needed to describe the sociocultural influences on their development (Feldman, 2006). One of the first things that we do to elaborate on this concept is to define "socio-economic status" (SES) for our students. Many of them are not psychology majors and they do not know what SES means. We have gone so far as to describe how SES is measured in many developmental research studies (e.g., Hollingshead, 1975). Most undergraduate students have not considered how their cultural environment influences different aspects of their development so this topic can be an opportunity to broaden their perspective on their own lives.

Once the class understands what specific examples of sociocultural influences might include, students are quick to point out how poverty could impact a child's development. Dangerous neighborhoods, poor air quality, few books in the home, and low parental involvement in school-related activities are all examples of the insidious ways that poverty could negatively effect human development (Evans, 2004). However, we find it interesting to discuss how coming from a high SES background may negatively impact child and adolescent development as well (Luthar, 2003).

History-graded influences History-graded influences are biological and environmental developmental influences that are related to the unique historical period during which an individual develops (Feldman, 2006). Wartime is one example of a history-graded influence on development. Another frequent student-generated example includes individuals who lived through the US economic depression of the 1930s. For each historical event that students generate in class discussion, you will want to help them think about how the historical event influenced human development. For example, stories about older relatives re-using tin foil, having a lack of consumer debt (i.e., not carrying a credit card balance), using bars of soap until there is nothing but "mush" left, and keeping cash under the mattress, could all be related to the thriftiness and social development of these individuals.

Since we have been teaching lifespan development, events relating to the September 11, 2001 terrorist attacks on the US have been frequently cited by our students as an historical event that has influenced the development of their cohort. Of course, there are numerous examples of past and current terrorist attacks on other countries and wars around the globe that parents and educators must explain to younger children (Goldman, 2002). However, given the sociocultural and historical experience of our students, they typically generate current US centered examples.

Occasionally students have difficulty generating examples for the possible influence of historical events on development. In these cases, historical movies could serve as a handy reference point. We recommend mentioning well known blockbuster films. *Gone with the Wind* (Selznick & Fleming, 1939), *Little Women* (DiNovi & Armstrong, 1994), *Sixteen Candles* (Green & Hughes, 1984), and *American Graffiti* (Coppola & Lucas, 1973) are films that could be used as examples to illustrate the influences of different historical eras on young adult development.

Non-normative influences Non-normative influences are atypical developmentally relevant influences for the average person (Feldman, 2006). We tend to give the example of a child whose parent dies while he or she is in elementary school. When the class is asked to provide examples of ways in which this child's development could be impacted, they typically generate the following negative influences on development: the child may need to deal with grief issues, the child may not be able to focus on school work due to sadness or anxiety, the child's academic performance may suffer, social relationships may suffer if the remaining parent is also grieving and not able to provide adequate support, the home financial situation may change for the worse (see Adler (2005) for examples from the current Iraq war). These are all negative examples, and occasionally we point out to the class that there could be some positive outcomes relating to the death of a parent such as removal of unhealthy marital conflict (e.g., if the parent was physically abusive). Additionally, the death of a parent could be a motivating force for a child in that it may serve as a reminder that life is short and there is limited time to generate "good works" for the community. Counter-intuitively, the finances of the home could actually improve following the death of a parent.

A less morbid example for the non-normative influences on development would be when someone wins the lottery. It can be quite entertaining to think about how your department chair's life could change as a result of winning millions in the state lottery. Popular media examples could be used to describe some of the benefits—and challenges—related to winning a large amount of money in a lottery. The Nicholas Cage and Bridget Fonda movie, *It Could Happen to You* (Lobell & Bergman, 1994), about a cop and a waitress who win the lottery could help to promote some discussion on how winning the lottery could influence an individual's development.

The nature vs. nurture controversy A great deal of recent writing has focused on the history and current research relating to the nature vs. nurture debate (Ceci & Williams, 1999; Collins, Maccoby, Steinberg, Hetherington, & Bornstein, 2000; Pinker, 2002; Ridley, 2003). Indeed, many students in your class will have already heard about the nature vs. nurture debate from their general psychology course. We tend to cover this topic in moderate detail by providing a brief history and examples of both nature (genetics) and nurture (environment). One way to conceptualize the nature vs. nurture debate is to ask the class whether genetics or environment is most important for height, language development, the ability to speak French, or social skills.

To illustrate the standpoint of a staunch behaviorist (i.e., a proponent of the nurture side of the debate), occasionally we read the following quote from John B. Watson:

> Give me a dozen healthy infants, well-formed, and my own specified world to bring them up in and I'll guarantee to take any one at random and train him to become any type of specialist I might select – doctor, lawyer, artist, merchant-chief, and yes, even beggar-man and thief, regardless of his talents, penchants, tendencies, and abilities ...
> (Watson, 1925)

We like this quote because it provides an example of an individual with a strong opinion regarding the developmental importance of environmental process. Watson's view that he could mold an infant into any profession is particularly striking in its absolute emphasis on environment—and complete disregard of genetics! This quote could also provide a springboard for a class discussion on the ethics of using humans—especially children—in psychological research.

The "nature vs. nurture" philosophical debate is so well known that it occasionally appears in popular media. One way to highlight this point in your course is to provide students with extra credit if they bring to class examples of developmental psychology constructs as depicted by the media—this approach has been a productive activity for us. We have shown varied nature/nurture-related items such as a video clip from the science fiction television show *Andromeda* (Wolfe & Montesi, 2000) starring Kevin Sorbo and a magazine ad for Playskool toys. In the *Andromeda* episode, children were held captive in a penal colony for a crime committed by their parents before the children were born. The question raised by one of the characters in the episode was whether crime was an inevitable part of these children's natures or whether the children were held unfairly in the penal colony. The magazine advertisement used a play on the words "nature" and "nurture" (the caption read "We put the nurture in nature" and was accompanied by a child playing with a plastic toy squirrel). Looking for psychological examples in the media can be helpful for students because it may help them to become more aware of the impact that the discipline of psychology has in modern society.

Aside from the theoretical importance of the nature vs. nurture controversy, your coverage of this debate is an excellent time in the course to point out to students that psychology is a developing science and, as such, prevailing thought changes over time. Currently most developmental psychologists would agree that the nature vs. nurture controversy on the importance of these factors in human development is best considered as a dynamic fusion between nature *and* nurture (Lerner et al., 2005). It is misguided to think that either nature or nurture influences development independent of one another because all humans develop in a context that always includes both aspects (Lerner et al., 2005). There are few other such examples in developmental psychology in which developmental theories have evolved over time (e.g., critical periods vs. sensitive periods) and we try to acknowledge that psychology is dynamic and constantly evolving. For example, our understanding of developmental psychology has evolved related to the emergence of new scientific technologies (e.g., computer technology and Piaget's theory) and because society and the developmental challenges faced by individuals within different life stages has changed over time (Guest, 2007).

Our coverage of the nature vs. nurture controversy is also a good time to help our students move away from dualistic thinking (that something is completely right or completely wrong) and shift towards multiple thinking (understanding that there can be multiple truths about a particular issue; Perry, 1970). Of course, we cover William Perry's (1970) theory of multiple thinking during our lecture on young adult cognition—but we find it helpful to incorporate this notion into our teaching early in the semester as it is a common thread that we visit throughout the semester.

Continuous change vs. discontinuous change There are many times in teaching lifespan development when it is beneficial to show a picture to help students understand a lecture concept. The lecture on continuous vs. discontinuous development is one of those times. We have used a very simple drawing that we spontaneously once drew in class to demonstrate the difference between the two types of developmental theories. We have also used a picture provided from a textbook publisher. We have had success with both types of illustrations but because neither one of us is a very gifted artist; we have used the textbook picture most often.

We approach the concept of continuous and discontinuous stage theories by explaining that there is some debate among developmentalists as to whether development occurs in a step-like process or in a more continuous, gradual process (Feldman, 2006). Have your students ever been to a butterfly garden? (There is a fantastic butterfly garden in near us in Calloway Gardens, Georgia, where the life stages of different varieties of butterflies are on display.) The developmental trajectory of a butterfly could be used to illustrate discontinuous development in that initially a caterpillar forms a cocoon, that later develops into a butterfly. One could argue that the insect is qualitatively different during each of the distinct developmental stages of caterpillar, cocoon, and butterfly. The insect also relates to the world in a different way depending on its current developmental stage. We usually mention Jean Piaget as an example of a developmental scientist who proposed a discontinuous stage theory of development. Later in the semester, we remind students that Piaget's theory suggests that cognitive development occurs in qualitatively different stages.

Alternatively, other psychologists believe that development is a more continuous process. In the continuous view of development, the living organism is believed to change in a quantitative way, with new skills building on previous skills (Feldman, 2006). Although we do not cover the information processing approach to human cognition in great detail in our course, you could describe this model as a quantitative theory. The recent documentary film, *March of the Penguins* (Girard & Jacquet, 2005), could provide a visual example for continuous development. This film follows infant Emperor penguins during the first nine months of their life. The Emperor penguin chick initially develops in an egg but once hatched, it grows more feathers and grows in size. Gradually, the chick learns to eat, walk, and swim. The young penguin has similar features as time goes by; however, it develops gradually into an adult.

Of course, one could argue that the middle ground between continuous and discontinuous development is the best way to conceptualize development (Feldman, 2006). It is likely that some aspects of human development actually follow a hybrid trajectory in which there are certain stages of development, but there is gradual development within those stages. Finally, some types of development may be more discontinuous while other types of development may be more continuous in nature.

Sensitive periods vs. critical periods Originally, developmentalists believed that all humans had critical periods for development—a period of time during which an event has its greatest consequence or effect (Feldman, 2006). According to the critical period model, there are some events that must occur during the critical period for development to proceed in a normative fashion. For example, if infant kittens live in a completely dark environment during their first few weeks of life, the visual center of their brain will atrophy and they will have permanently impaired vision. In this case, the kittens need to have regular exposure to a visual array during the critical period for vision. It is also possible, however, for an event occurring during a critical period to have a teratogenic effect (Poole, Warren, & Nunez, 2007). To use a human example, prenatal exposure to large amounts of maternal alcohol consumption can lead to mental retardation in the developing fetus. In this case, the presence of a toxic environmental agent during an important fetal critical period can have a long-standing negative impact on the developing human.

There has been a shift in the way that developmentalists describe human development over the past few decades in that critical periods are currently described as less important (Belsky, 2006). Rather, developmentalists currently suggest that the term "sensitive period" should be used to describe the critical period because the human brain is more malleable—and better able to accommodate following an insult or deprivation—than originally thought.

Our favorite example of a non-human animal critical period is the description of ethologist (and Nobel Prize winner) Konrad Lorenz's work with newborn geese. Lorenz was interested in demonstrating how non-human animals' genetic makeup could influence behavior.

Because newly hatched goslings are genetically programmed to imprint, or attach to the first moving object that crosses their visual field, Lorenz was able to demonstrate that goslings are capable of attaching to other objects, including humans. He illustrated his point by allowing newborn goslings to imprint on him during their critical period for attachment (or imprinting). Consequently, Lorenz was permanently able to alter the goslings' social development. (Note: This part of lecture is more entertaining if you can include a picture of Lorenz from a textbook in which he is walking through a field followed by a small gaggle of goslings.)

To provide an example of a sensitive period, we usually ask students if anyone in the class is trying to learn a new language. Inevitably someone in the class is studying a foreign language for the first time. Once someone volunteers that they are talking a language (let's say German, for example) we ask them how the semester is going and how they like learning German. In a very non-confrontational way, we then ask them whether they would be able to speak like a native German if we were to drop them on a street corner in Berlin. Almost always, the student admits that there is no way that he or she could speak German as well as a native. This line of questioning becomes our hook to describe how developmentalists would say that the student's sensitive period for learning a new language has already passed. Although the student's sensitive period for learning to speak German without an accent has already passed, it does not mean that he is not able to learn the language. Rather, the human brain is able to assimilate new linguistic information. However, the student will probably always be identified as a "German as a second language" student due to his accent. We then ask the class at what age the individual would need to start learning a language to speak as well as a native. This question is partially a matter of speculation, but we do tell the students about existing research that supports the notion that infants have the ability to discriminate the sounds for every language on earth—a skill that infants lose over their second 'sixth months' of life.

Depending on the time available for discussion on critical periods, you could talk to the class about Genie, the classic case study in psychology of a young girl who was raised as a feral child in Los Angeles. When Genie was discovered by authorities in 1970 following extreme neglect and seclusion for 13 years, she had limited language ability and was severely delayed in her cognitive, physical, and social development (NOVA, 1994). Even with a very enriching environment following her discovery, Genie never learned age-appropriate social or language skills. Thus, it appears that she did not receive adequate social interactions during her sensitive period for optimal language and social skill development. This case study could also be a tie-in to an extended discussion on nature vs. nurture.

A final example that we have used to describe the sensitive period of human development involves athletic ability. We start by asking our students for examples of sports for which early exposure is important for development of athletic skill. Many sports are mentioned as candidates by our students (e.g., golf, gymnastics, basketball, tennis). In this course our teaching style allows for lecture-relevant self disclosure. In fact, we often share our own experiences with the class to help illustrate particular concepts. For example, one of us (EBK) once talked to a professional boxer at a party about the ideal age for a child to learn the basic mechanics of boxing. Imagine our surprise when the boxer stated his opinion that children should start boxing around 8 years of age to master the necessary reflexes and techniques for boxing!

Bronfenbrenner's ecological systems theory of development In order to understand child development, one must strive to understand the unique "belongingness" that each family member possesses. Bronfenbrenner's (1979) ecological theory of development is a helpful way to conceptualize lifespan development. It can also be used to understand the role of culture in development. We like to cover Bronfenbrenner's theory due to its inclusion of broad contextual factors in human development. However, a word of caution is needed in that most of our students have never considered their developmental context in a way that is consistent with Bronfenbrenner's theory. The names of the theory sub-systems sound very similar, so you may have to explain the different structures a few times to ensure that your students understand this theory.

According to Bronfenbrenner (1979), each individual lives within multiple circles of influence. These circles of influence can be conceptualized as nesting structures, with larger structures incorporating smaller ones. Children typically develop within the context of their environment (e.g., home, school, and neighborhood), so one must consider the broader context within these bi-directional "circles" to understand a child's current level of development.

Microsystems include the immediate settings within which the child operates. Typically the child has daily contact with individuals and entities within these microsystems. The family microsystem can include the child's siblings, caregivers, extended family living within the household, and the child. Subsystems important to development also exist within each microsystem, including the marital relationship, sibling relationships, and interactions between parents and the child. An infant or very young child may have a limited number of microsystems. However, older children can be members of several microsystems, including school, peers, after-school programs, daycare, and the neighborhood. We usually use examples that include school-aged children for Bronfenbrenner's theory. Thus, to illustrate the microsystem we discuss how the child's parents are part of the microsystem.

The next "circle" in the child's environment is the *mesosystem*, which includes interactions between different *microsystems*. For example, parents attending a parent-teacher conference, a family therapy session at a psychology clinic, the family's involvement in church activities, or an extended visit from out-of town grandparents are all examples of mesosystem interactions. For children living in isolated households, mesosystem interactions may be scarce. In these situations, the lack of a support network for isolated caregivers may have a negative influence on the child (Wahler & Afton, 1980). Alternatively, some children may have an extended group of individuals from the community (e.g., church family, non-relative kinship network in the neighborhood) who are considered family (Gushue, Greenan, & Brazaitis, 2005). The social support that can result from the community operating as family can serve as a buffer for children. Occasionally, we mention that social support has been reported to be a strength for some racial/ethnic minority families—and African American families in particular (Boyd-Franklin, 2003).

The next structure in Bronfenbrenner's ecological theory is the *exosystem*, which includes a member of the child's microsystem (e.g., a parent or a sibling) and an outside organization (e.g., parent's workplace, sibling's peer group), but not the child directly. When considering the exosystem, one should consider the indirect influence of larger entities such as the parent's workplace or the parent's social network on the child. For example, a parent may experience a great deal of stress from her workplace and as a result have less patience with her child during home discipline situations.

Finally, the *macrosystem* includes the influence of cultural values and attitudes of the family's social environment on the child. One way that we have described the macrosystem for our students has been to use the example of physically abusive parents and their children. In our clinical work with physically abusive families, we have found it useful to discuss the current mainstream US cultural views towards corporal punishment. Not surprisingly, we often find a discrepancy between the parent's view on corporal punishment and the stance of child protective services. Ultimately, it is important to discuss the potential end-result of this macrosystem-level disparity for the child (i.e., a substantiated report of physical abuse) in therapy.

Although we have used child examples to illustrate Bronfenbrenner's ecological theory, this theory can also be used to explain adolescent or adult development as well. To use an adolescent example, you could ask the class to think about an adolescent with anorexia and how the teen's family (microsystem), peers (microsystem), and images of attractive people displayed by the media (macrosystem) work in concert to influence the development and maintenance of the individual's eating disorder.

In summary, Bronfenbrenner's theory can serve as a helpful rubric for teachers to consider when conceptualizing the role of the family and community in child development. Indeed, it is important to consider the context within which an individual lives and how these "circles of influence" may serve to support or challenge the individual's functioning.

Tools of the trade: research methods

As we have mentioned previously, it is helpful to "teach to your strength" when you are preparing a psychology course. We incorporate our knowledge of treatment outcome research for children with behavior problems when we cover the section on research methods. You may decide to use a different technique for teaching research methods but the following approach has worked well for us in the past. Whenever applicable, we "teach to our strength" by including examples from our own research in an effort to help explain research constructs. If you are not able to use examples from your own research, you might describe the developmental research conducted by a colleague. Additionally, you could cite studies from the text as your examples. Should you decide that you need a refresher on the methods associated with developmental research, we recommend a very comprehensive chapter by Hartmann and Pelzel (2005).

One semester we had a guest speaker from the nursing school who asked for our permission to have students complete her health survey at the end of her guest lecture. Following the class participation in the study, we used the IRB form and the health-related questionnaire study as an example for our next lecture, which happened to be on research methods. It was a coincidence that we were able to allow the students the experience of being a participant in a research study prior to our lecture on the topic, but the students seemed to enjoy having this "real life" exposure to research. Most of the students who take your course have little direct experience with research. Thus, merely describing what it is like to collect developmentally relevant data, enter data into a database, analyze the data, and write up and present findings interest most students. The students who are deciding whether to major in psychology—or whether they would like to pursue a graduate degree in psychology—will probably appreciate hearing a first-person account of research. In this spirit, we often bring a copy of one of our publications so that we can briefly describe the process that led to the end result of a publication.

The developmental science themes that we consider to be the most crucial for this section include naturalistic observation, case study, correlational study, experimental design, independent variables and dependent variables, and three research designs for measuring developmental change (longitudinal, cross-sectional, and cross-sequential designs). We choose to cover all of these developmental research designs because we want students to understand the benefits and the drawbacks of different research methods. Throughout the course we present summaries of empirical literature and we hope that students have an appreciation for the research methods that were used to collect the data we present.

Research methods can be challenging to teach because of time constraints, variability in your students' previous exposure to research methods, and student hesitancy to ask questions early in the semester. However, it is important for students to understand the "tools of the trade" with regard to generating scientific knowledge (Belsky, 2007). Without a basic understanding of how research is generated, your students' ability to engage in critical thinking about developmental science is seriously hampered. Because there is not much time available to teach the concepts related to research methods, we recommend that you introduce basic concepts early in the semester and use future lectures as opportunities to reiterate and reinforce the applications of specific research methods.

There will be considerable variability in your students' previous exposure to research methods. Many of the undergraduates have never taken a research methods course. Some of these students have not taken a research methods course because they are not psychology majors. Other students who are psychology majors may avoid research methods because they have heard that it is a difficult course. We have found that only a small minority of the students in our courses have previously taken research methods and are familiar with the concepts from this section.

Finally, research methods can be challenging to teach because this material falls at the beginning of the semester. Even after the general class discussion on the contexts of development, students are often hesitant to ask questions that might make them "look stupid" in front of their peers. Our recommendation for a stress-free introduction to research methods includes the following:

1. *Explain the rationale for why you are asking students to learn the material.* Some students expect to start the course by watching videos of babies and are disappointed to learn that they are responsible for learning about research methods. At the beginning of this section we tell students that research methods are important to learn because they are crucial for the development and revision of the knowledge base for the discipline. We also inform them that we will refer to developmental research design throughout the course and that future lectures will elaborate and highlight the concepts generated by research. Finally, we tell our students that it is our hope that they will become critical consumers of science as a result of taking this course. You can't believe everything that you read in the paper or see on the Internet about psychological research!
2. *Tell the class that you know most of them have never taken research methods.* Non-majors are often very concerned that they are at a disadvantage because they have not taken psychology courses prior to lifespan development. We try to cover only the most basic material related to developmental science and we reassure students that they will only need to recognize the concepts—not generate or understand statistics!
3. *Give concrete examples.* To help students understand the various research methods, we try to use the most basic of examples to explain the constructs of interest. In addition to incorporating easy-to-understand examples, we rely on graphs and charts to help explain the research concepts for this section.

4. *Repeat yourself...repeat yourself...repeat yourself.* Again, because most of the students have not had previous exposure to research methods, you need to cover the material slowly so as not to overwhelm them. We recommend repeating key concepts several times.
5. *Monitor your audience.* You will need to monitor your audience to assess whether or not they understand the material. Look for confused faces or students desperately conferring with their neighbor to get information that they may have missed. Because this material is presented at the beginning of the course, some students are hesitant to speak up if they have a specific question or a request for you to repeat information. We work more diligently during this lecture to make sure that the students understand the material.

Examples of research methods concepts

Naturalistic observation Our main goal for students is to help them understand why one research method would be used over another method given a particular research question. Fortunately, naturalistic observation is an easy research method for students to understand. We typically start this section by defining naturalistic observation, explaining the benefits of using an observation, and providing an example of what an observation could entail. We often use the example of observing a child on the playground and we talk about our personal experiences conducting behavior observations in the school setting (e.g., having to wear sunglasses once so that the target child did not know that we were watching him).

Because naturalistic observations can be done for research purposes or clinical purposes, we try to explain why a researcher or clinician would choose to conduct an observation on a child. Ideally, you could lead the students in a discussion about the potential variables of interest that could be assessed using an observation of a child on the playground. Once a few variables of interest are suggested by our students (e.g., peer aggression, cooperative play), we help them to develop an operational definition of the variables (e.g., number of times that the target child hits another child on the playground). We usually end our discussion of naturalistic observation by repeating the benefits of using this method and briefly describing the negative aspects of using an observational method to answer a research question.

Case study We typically start this section by defining case study, explaining the benefits of using a case study, and providing an example for how a researcher may conduct a case study. One example that we like to use is a case study in which an intervention is provided to a child with autism. Because most students have heard of autism but are not sure what it is, we briefly describe the disorder and associated symptoms. Our graduate program in clinical psychology staffs a developmental disabilities clinic so we briefly explain the clinical activities conducted by the clinic and the behaviors that clinicians attempt to address through Applied Behavior Analysis (ABA) interventions.

Our goal for this case study discussion is to expose the class to a simple AB design (baseline (A) and intervention (B)). Several variables could be used as examples (e.g., training the child to use a particular word, training the child to sit in a chair, teaching the child to stay in the classroom). We usually use "time in seat" as the behavior to increase through our case study example. It helps to show the class a graph depicting mock data from an AB design intervention. First, we explain the difference between the two conditions (baseline and intervention) and then we explain what the data would look like if the intervention were successful. We usually end our case study discussion by repeating the benefits of using this method and briefly describing the negative aspects of using a case study.

Correlational study We typically start this section by defining the term correlation, describing a correlational study, explaining the benefits of using a correlational design, and providing a few examples for correlational studies. We use a few mock scatter plots to describe the "made up" correlation between shoe size and height, the correlation between shoe size and math ability, and the correlation between time spent studying and performance on a math test.

Our goal for the lecture on correlation is for the class to understand the well known maxim "correlation does not equal causation" and that a correlation simply reflects an association between two variables. We also want them to recognize that a correlation coefficient can range from −1.0 to 1.0 and that there are positive correlations and negative correlations.

To illustrate a negative correlation, we show a picture of a brand new car and mention that a car typically becomes less reliable as it gets older. The next slide has a mock plot of the negative correlation between the variables of (a) car age and (b) reliability.

To illustrate a positive correlation, one of us (EBK) tells the class about her dissertation research in which she asked 300 mothers of children between the ages of two and ten to answer questions about their tolerance for child misbehavior. After a brief anecdote about conducting a dissertation, the main finding of the research study (that mothers are less tolerant of misbehavior from older children than from younger children) is given as an example of a positive correlation.

Experimental design Our student learning goals for this topic include a basic understanding of random assignment, the difference between an independent variable and a dependent variable, and the benefits of using an experimental design. We attempt to meet these goals by presenting an experimental design within the context of a treatment outcome study.

Our university psychology clinic conducts a treatment group for children with social skills problems each spring. Using this real-life treatment group as an example, we describe the general procedure for the project (e.g., random assignment, measures used for the pre- and post-treatment assessment, use of an intervention group and a control group, and the nature of the intervention) as well as our hypothesized outcomes for the project. The time line and different components of a treatment outcome study can be difficult to understand for some students, so we always use a chart to illustrate the important aspects of this research design. Helping children gain social skills is a fairly common-sense reason for parents to seek services for their children so students seem to understand the rationale for this experimental research design.

Designs for measuring developmental change The research designs for measuring developmental change can be confusing for some students. Cross-sectional and cross-sequential designs sound very similar in name—and in method—so you will likely need to cover these concepts carefully. We typically start this section by defining and describing a longitudinal study before describing the other two types of development designs in detail. It is also helpful to refer to a chart that illustrates the difference between the three developmental designs during your lecture on this section.

First, we describe what a longitudinal study would look like to a participant and why a researcher would want to conduct a longitudinal design. The longitudinal study that we like to use as an example is Lewis Terman's long-standing study on 1,500 gifted children that he initiated 75 years ago (Terman & Oden, 1959). It is conceptually easy to understand why a researcher would want to use a longitudinal design and students are usually able to generate the major pros and cons of using a longitudinal research design once you describe it to them. However, the monumental task of following 1,500 individuals over 75 years may not be so apparent to your students since most of them have little research experience. Sometimes we point out how expensive questionnaires can be when you buy them from a publisher (upwards of $50 for a pack of 25) as well as how difficult and expensive it can be to keep track of research participants (the researcher might have to pay transportation costs such as airplane fare or hotel accommodations!).

Cross-sectional study Because cohort effects are the main concern to a researcher when using a cross-sectional design, we try to use an example that has the potential to exaggerate these effects. We start by giving the definition of a cohort effect and we ask if their parents or grandparents have trouble checking e-mail. Although there is almost always someone in the class with a 90-year-old grandmother who likes to surf the Internet, usually the class consensus is that college students are better with computers than their grandparents. Once facility with computers is defined as a potential cohort effect (you could tie-in this cohort effect to the historical context within which the students have been raised) we then talk about the possible confound of studying psychomotor speed with a computerized task for a group of 20-year-olds, 50-year-olds, and 70-year-olds (we always define psychomotor speed, too). Next, we describe why a researcher would want to conduct a cross-sectional design as well as the negative aspects of a cross-sectional study.

Cross-sequential study At this point in the lecture you are almost done with coverage of research methods in the field developmental psychology! We typically explain how cross-sequential designs are different from longitudinal and cross-sectional designs and list the benefits and challenges to using a cross-sequential design.

Final thoughts on research methods

If you teach a course for many semesters you may become bored with the examples that you use in class if you use them repeatedly. To avoid burn-out and boredom we do rotate our examples to make things more fun for ourselves. In fact, some of our best teaching moments are spontaneous. We find that the creativity required to explain a new example that we are improvising in class helps to keep our teaching fresh. For example, instead of always using a case study example of a child with autism we have been known to describe an AB case study involving Anna Nicole Smith (the now deceased US reality-TV actress and model). In this case study evaluating the effectiveness of Trim Spa, Anna Nicole's weight is the dependant variable and treatment with Trim Spa is the independent variable. Similarly, instead of repeatedly using an example of a social skills intervention for school-aged children we have used the example of a social skills intervention for dateless college students (our students do have fun coming up with the components of the intervention that could be most effective for these clients).

Critical Thinking Opportunities

Whether you are teaching in a traditional lecture format or incorporating alternative formats into your class, we suggest trying to add opportunities for your students to engage in critical thinking. Critical thinking activities increase students' ability to remember course material (Williams, Oliver, & Stockdale, 2004) and may help them to make connections from what is learned in the classroom to how it relates to the world outside the classroom. In addition, critical thinking is one of the most important outcomes of a college education (Halpern, 1988; Jones, 1995; Resnick & Peterson, 1991; Williams et al., 2004).

Critical thinking activities can take a variety of forms; they can be conducted in-class or out-of-class, and can be done individually or in groups. In this chapter as well as chapters to follow we provide potential topics and formats for presenting occasions for critical thinking to your students.

Contexts of development

Students tend to enjoy the discussion of contexts of development, which makes it another welcome opportunity for critical thinking activities. Some activities that we think may be useful in exploring the contexts of development include class discussions or assignments that examine:

- How do we know whether nature or nurture is more important?
  - For example, you and your students can explore twin studies that investigate both sides of the nature-nurture debate. There

are also short readings available that address either side of the debate, like those found in Guest's book (2007).
- ○ Students could be split into groups to present one side of the argument that nature or nurture is more important and have a debate in the classroom.
- How did nature influence the way that we as individuals were raised by our parents?
  - ○ Students could be asked to list different aspects of "nature" that may have affected the way in which individuals are raised.
- How do different contexts affect the way that we were raised by our parents?
  - ○ Students could be asked to list different aspects of the environment or "nurture" that may have affected the way in which individuals are raised.
- Which micro-, exo-, and macrosystem level factors influenced our lives?
  - ○ Have students identify the different levels of influence on their lives and have a class discussion about similarities and possible differences that occur in the class.
  - ○ Give a vignette of a family or individual and have students identify micro-, exo-, and macrosystems involved in the vignette and possible influences on the family/individual.
- How might Bronfenbrenner's theory differ in countries other than the US?
  - ○ Explore similarities and differences in the weighted influence of the micro-, exo-, and macrosystem levels in other countries.

In addition to having activities that are specific to research methods or contexts of development, you could try to have the students engage in activities that link the two concepts together. One activity that may allow the opportunity to link research methods to contexts of development and provide an occasion for critical thinking might be to give students a research question related to contexts of development- have students work in groups to design an experiment to answer the research question.

The activities that we suggest represent only a few of which we have used. Any activity that sparks meaningful discussion and thoughts that link the study of human development to the students' lives and the world around them are likely to engage them in critical thinking.

Research methods

Research methods can be a wonderful way to use critical thinking activities. An activity that can prove useful for linking critical thinking with research methods is the evaluation of research studies. Students can be asked to determine what is gained by the studies and how the studies may be flawed. Whether the activities are presented as a group activity or an individual activity or in-class vs. out-of-class, the opportunity exists to discuss the methods used in the studies as well as the contexts that may affect the results. We recommend using short research articles in which the methods are relatively straightforward so that students can be successful in their identification of the research method concepts that you would like them to master.

Some activities that we think may be useful in examining the intricacies of research methods include:

- Giving students a short research paper and having them identify particular concepts related to research methods that you would like them to understand. For example, you could ask them to identify the type of research design (case study, longitudinal, cross-sectional), have them summarize the methods, or state the research question in their own words.
- Give students a research question and have them work in groups to design a study to investigate the question.

These activities do not necessarily have to take place only when you are teaching research methods explicitly—you can use activities such as these throughout the semester to reiterate research methods concepts in addition to other developmental concepts. Critical thinking opportunities can build on one another throughout the semester and become more complex as the course moves along.

Controversial Topics

Many of the topics discussed in a class related to human development may create controversy in the classroom (Guest, 2007). Often instructors avoid such topics for fear of creating or experiencing an "awkward moment" in the classroom. The potential for awkward moments are high, especially with controversial topics, but Guest suggests that controversy can be meaningful and worthwhile in advancing the knowledge of your students (Uline, Tschannen-Moran, & Perez, 2003).

Topics that have the potential to be controversial are those that create "instinctual reactions and beliefs" from you or your students based on your life and learning experiences (Guest, 2007; Lusk & Weinberg, 1994). It is important as an instructor to be aware of what your reactions and beliefs are and to remember that your students may have similar or different reactions or beliefs. Guest suggests one way in which to approach controversial topics is to establish a ground rule that maintains that controversies should be evaluated predominantly in terms of available evidence. Ground rules limit students' contributions to classroom discussion to statements with supportive evidence rather than personal opinion. By limiting students' statements to those that have evidence to support them, you may be able to minimize the personalization to controversial topics that may arise otherwise. In this chapter as well as chapters to follow, we highlight topics that we foresee as potentially controversial topics.

One resource for controversial topics in psychology is Guest's book (2007). This book provides a compendium of readings that provide differing expert perspectives for 20 issues. The issues follow the stages of a lifespan development course (e.g., general issues in the study of lifespan development, prenatal development, infancy, etc) and an instructor's manual with test items is available from the publisher. We recommend assigning readings related the issue before having a discussion about how the students in your class view a particular issue. Although controversial topics can be intimidating, frustrating, and confusing for both instructors and students, they provide wonderful opportunities for class discussion as well as critical thinking. Guest (2007) suggested that the "educational value" of controversy "lies in the space between evidence and beliefs." It is your role as instructor to help students navigate that space in an environment that is safe as well as welcoming. Topics that we consider potentially controversial include:

- Nature vs. nurture
    - One discussion question that we typically ask the class is to think about how the government would spend taxpayers' money depending on a nature vs. nurture stance. What type of programs would the government fund if nature was

considered to be the most important aspect of development? What type of programs would the government fund if nurture was the most important aspect of development? This is an early class discussion question that typically works to enhance student critical thinking.
- Genetics research vs. Head Start
- Genetic engineering (e.g., designer babies, choosing genders, harvesting organs)
  - Stem cell research
  - Sexual orientation
- Research methods
  - Have students form small groups and answer the following thought questions (Suggett, 2006).
    - What is a theory?
    - What is a developmental theory?
    - What sets developmental research apart from other types of research?
  - Selecting subjects
    - Animals vs. humans
    - Race/ethnicity of subjects
    - Age of subjects
  - Selecting measures
    - IQ
  - Implications for government funding
    - Research findings lead to government funding and government funding leads to the types of research studies that are conducted

Developmental Diversity

As we discussed in the first chapter, diversity is difficult to ignore in a course on lifespan development. In addition, we argue that discussing diversity in your course is a wonderful way to create critical thinking opportunities as well as address the already present and ever increasing diverse context within which we live. Diversity as it relates to the contexts of human development can include such variables as race, ethnicity, physical handicaps, family structure, and cultural variations as well as socioeconomic status (Lerner, 1992; MacPhee, Kreutzer, & Fritz, 1994). Diversity has increasingly been added to social science courses in many universities (Levine &

Cureton, 1992). MacPhee and colleagues cite attempts to address changing demographics, foster cultural pluralism, and increase critical thinking skills as reasons for the increase in diversity curriculum in higher education. Additionally, research suggests that the effects of increasing diversity in liberal arts curriculum are increased tolerance for, and improved attitudes toward, diversity related topics (Engberg, 2004).

There are many theories and perspectives regarding the discussion of diversity (Cairney, 2000; Cobb & Hodge, 2002; Leeman & Volman, 2001); however, we chose to focus on Brofenbrenner's ecological theory of development as a means of including a diversity perspective in this introductory section of a Lifespan Development course. Some researchers have added to Bronfenbrenner's theory in order to consider the role of culture in child development. In a paper on family psychology and cross-cultural psychology, Szapocznik & Kurtines (1993) stated that to understand a child's cultural framework, each individual must be considered within the context of their family. In turn, they recommended that each family must be considered within the context of their culture. It is important, then, to have an awareness of the cultural variables that can shape development. Typically, parents and children are shaped by multiple cultural forces, which, at a minimum, will include the "family culture" and the "mainstream" US culture. Among immigrant families, racial/ethnic minority families, and bi-racial families, parents and children can be influenced by very different cultural forces as a function of the unique context (both time and place) within which these individuals have lived (Szapocznik & Kurtines, 1993). Ultimately, family members may have vastly different life experiences which can influence human development in a positive way or a negative way.

Although diversity itself has many permutations and variables available for discussion, we have pointed out a few topics in this chapter in the critical thinking and controversial topics sections that we believe would be useful to address in your class. In chapters to follow, we include additional topics that we consider relevant to the chapter content but also provide opportunities to include diversity in your course.

Helpful Resources for Teaching Research Methods for Developmental Psychology

American Psychological Association (1994). *Publication manual of the American Psychological Association (4th ed.).* Washington, DC: Author.
American Psychological Association (APA): www.apa.org.
Future of Children (digital journal): www.futureofchildren.org/.
APA Division 7: Developmental Psychology: www.psy.utexas.edu/psy/div7/div7.html.
The American Psychological Society (APS): www.psychologicalscience.org.
International Association for Cross Cultural Psychology: www.fit.edu/CampusLife/clubs-org/iaccp.
APA Ethical Principles and Codes of Conduct: www.apa.org/ethics/homepage.html.

Chapter 3

Prenatal Development: Labor and Delivery

Teaching material related to prenatal development can be challenging for the novice lifespan development instructor for several reasons. First, relatively few psychology instructors have training in genetics, obstetrics, or pediatrics so the material may seem highly specialized the first few times you teach the course. Second, students are often very interested in prenatal development and they tend to ask questions that are well beyond the scope of the textbook material (e.g., "Can playing Mozart to the fetus increase his or her IQ?"; "What precautions should a mother with sickle cell disease take during pregnancy?"). Third, prenatal development entails a vast array of topics. Nonetheless, prenatal development can be a very rewarding section of the course to teach.

Teaching labor and delivery has its challenges as well. Many of your students are happily oblivious to the process of labor and it can be disconcerting for them to hear about the physical sequella of labor and delivery. You may not have direct experience with labor and delivery so presenting information related to the chapter in a way that is fresh and informative may be a challenge the first few times that you present your lecture. It can be helpful to use visual aids such as video clips for the labor and delivery section but be aware that some students are not comfortable seeing the "blood and gore" that can accompany delivery. In fact, just last semester we had a student faint in class after we watched a video clip of a C-section!

When teaching prenatal development and labor and delivery be mindful that most of the students in your class are future parents (some may be current parents). We approach our lectures as an opportunity to pose questions that stimulate students' thinking about their own plans for parenthood. It is a heady thought, but the information that we teach in these lectures truly has the potential to influence the development of future generations.

In this chapter we summarize the key concepts related to prenatal development and labor and delivery that we believe should be included in a course on lifespan development. We provide examples of class activities and guest speakers that would help to enhance your teaching of prenatal development. Finally, we provide suggestions for videos, Web sites, and local resources that you can use to highlight these key concepts.

Prenatal Development

There are a number of concepts to choose from for your coverage of prenatal development. The concepts that we have included here would be too much information to cover in one class period. Rather, our list of concepts is intended to give you a sample to choose from when planning your lectures. As noted in our last chapter, the amount of information that you will be able to cover in a class period will generally depend on the amount of discussion you are able to generate with the class and the amount of time you devote to in-class exercises and assignments. With these caveats in mind, we consider the following prenatal development concepts to be most important for developmental psychology students to know.

Fertilization

We typically explore the basic elements of the fertilization process with our lifespan development classes because it is the start of the developmental process. At the beginning of our lecture on prenatal development we tell students that our coverage of the biological aspects of prenatal development will be at a very basic level. We also acknowledge that the genetic information that we cover in class may seem extremely basic to the biology and health science majors in the class. Rather than considering our basic coverage to be a weakness of the course, we use this section as an opportunity to request any insight that the biology and health science majors may have to share with the rest of the class. We usually have several students volunteer to share their knowledge of prenatal development and genetics with the class. Another option for your lecture on prenatal development is to find a guest speaker who is an expert in genetics. Such a guest speaker may be a fascinating addition to the course if you have a large number of health-related majors.

We start the didactic part of our lecture by giving our rationale for studying genetics: Students need to have a basic understanding of genetics to understand human development. To illustrate our point, we mention that there are approximately 15,000 human genetic disorders and every individual has genetic mutations that could lead to a medical condition or developmental disorder (McKusick, 1998). Typically these genes are recessive and are not expressed (to the relief of our students) but we all carry the genetic information for at least one disorder.

Although we emphasize the physical aspects of human development during our discussion of fertilization, we also find it helpful to discuss the important social and personality aspects of development as well. You can meet this aim by discussing what life is like for someone with a genetically-based disorder. For example, a genetically-based disorder such as most forms of mental retardation (e.g., Down syndrome, fragile-X syndrome, William's syndrome) can affect an individual's intelligence level and ability to speak, make friends, go to school or gain employment (Goldstein & Reynolds, 1999). Explaining the types of intervention needed by individuals with genetically-based disorders helps to illustrate for the class why it is important for psychologists to learn more about how these disorders develop.

According to developmental psychologists, human development begins at the moment a sperm fertilizes an ovum. As such, most lifespan development texts begin their coverage of human development at conception (e.g., Feldman, 2006; Kail & Cavanaugh, 2007; Santrock, 2007). Our coverage of fertilization typically includes general descriptions of genes, chromosomes, gametes, and zygotes. We also discuss the possibility of multiple births and the difference between monozygotic and dizygotic twins. Depending on time constraints, we like to ask if there are any twins in the class. We usually have at least one twin in our larger sections of the course. Asking about whether they are a monozygotic or a dizygotic twin is an effective way to interrupt lecturing and provide a real-life example for the other students in the class. Aside from the focus on the physical aspects of being a twin, it is a great opportunity to incorporate the social and personality aspects of being a twin. You may also want to ask about how being a twin has influenced this particular student's development. If no one in the class is a twin you can always refer to some well known US dizygotic twins such as the McCaughey septuplets or the Olsen twins (Mary Kate and Ashley Olsen) to generate some class discussion.

Genetics and development

In our course, we like to describe the distinction between genotype and phenotype because it serves as the basis for understanding developmental behavioral genetics and the twin studies that are conducted to tease apart the role that genetics and environment play in development (Segal, 2006). Although we do not require our students to understand the finer points of developmental behavioral genetics, we use our lecture to illustrate that high quality research is conducted by psychologists in the area of gene-environment interactions (Segal, 1993; Segal & Hill, 2005). Some students coming to our course from "harder sciences" may be biased against the softer social sciences. Of course, there are many areas of our discipline that follow rigorous scientific standards and developmental behavioral genetics is one area that we like to highlight.

One short exercise that we use in class to demonstrate genotype, phenotype, dominant traits, and recessive traits is to discuss a simple physical trait such as eye color. You might point out that an individual's eye color is his or her phenotype but that his or her genotype is the genetic information for eye color that they carry. Following our brief definition of phenotype and genotype we like to show the class a slide listing some common dominant and recessive physical traits. Students seem to enjoy noting which traits on the list are expressed by their own phenotype. The list that we show to the class only represents physical traits. However, physical traits comprise just part of the genetic picture for humans in that each individual has inherited physical traits, behavioral traits, and medial conditions (Genetic Science Learning Center, 2008). We end the section on genetics by reminding our students that our coverage of genetics is basic and that we do not cover concepts such as incomplete dominance or multi-genetic inheritance. You may want to direct your students to some helpful Web sites on genetics if they would like to learn more on the subject (we have listed two at the end of this chapter).

We also cover the distinction between homozygous and heterozygous genes using an example of medical conditions. The distinction between homozygous genes and heterozygous genes is the cornerstone to understanding the genetic transmission of phenotypic characteristics. Once we explain the concept of homozygous and heterozygous genes, we typically use phenylketonuria (PKU), cystic fibrosis, or sickle cell anemia as examples of serious genetic disorders that are transmitted through recessive genes (Tercyak, 2003). We have found it helpful to have PowerPoint slides for each possible scenario regarding genetic transmission of the disorder (e.g., neither parent carries the recessive trait for PKU, one parent carries the recessive trait for PKU, or both parents carry the recessive trait for PKU). The general idea that we like students to understand from this discussion is that offspring from two parents with the recessive gene for PKU have a 1 in 4 chance of having a child with PKU and a 1 in 2 chance of having a child who is a carrier of the PKU recessive gene (Pekkanen, 2001). In other words, children with PKU have a homogenous genotype for PKU and express the disorder in their phenotype. Alternatively, PKU carriers have a heterozygous genotype for PKU but do not express the disorder in their phenotype.

As a result of our discussion, we hope that students will have a better understanding of how genetics can influence development following our lecture on genetics. For example, children with PKU have a physical condition in which they cannot neutralize an amino acid called phenylalanine. Thus, these children must follow a very specific diet to avoid toxic levels of phenylalanine from accumulating in their system. If children with the disorder are not identified early enough as having PKU—or if they do not follow the special diet—they are at risk of having mental retardation as a direct result of disrupted brain development caused by high levels of phenylalanine in the body (National Institute of Health, 2006; Pekkanen, 2001). As a simple demonstration of the ubiquity of phenylalanine, we bring a can of *Coca-cola* to class during this discussion: every *Coca-cola* can has a warning on the side that reads, "Phenylketoneurics: Contains phenylalanine."

Often students know someone who has a genetically-based disorder and they are willing to share with the class the accommodations needed by the affected individual. We try to guide the discussion by asking questions that might reveal the physical, cognitive, and social implications of having an inherited genetic disorder. Following the "case study" of an individual with a genetically-based disorder, we then draw upon our experience as pediatric psychologists to emphasize how psychologists might be involved in the individual's care. For example, pediatric psychologists treating a child with sickle cell anemia might help the young patient to manage pain crises, provide intellectual testing to assess for the cognitive effects of stroke, provide support for the patient and his or her family during hospitalizations, or serve as a liaison between the family and the child's school to keep the family updated about in-class assignments as well as inform the school regarding the child's concomitant cognitive difficulties (Lemanek, Ranalli, Green, Biega, & Lupia, 2003).

Stages of prenatal development

When providing the lecture on the stages of parental development, we tend to follow the material in our text very closely. We start with the stages of prenatal development by covering the germinal stage of prenatal development. During lecture we define and explain the importance of the blastocyst, implantation, the placenta, and the umbilical cord. It is helpful to show the class a diagram of the female reproductive system so that you can explain where the structures develop during the germinal stage. In fact, during the lecture on prenatal development and labor and delivery we often refer back to the same drawing of a uterus to help illustrate developmental periods.

For the embryonic stage, we define and explain the importance of the cells that comprise the ectoderm, mesoderm, and endoderm. Following the brief explanation of the embryonic stage we typically show the class an ultrasound photograph (a sonogram) of an embryo. If there are any mothers in the class you can ask for a volunteer to describe what it is like to have an ultrasound. We also take the opportunity to explain how ultrasounds are conducted (Adolph & Berger, 2005). One of us (EBK) has collected quite a few ultrasound photographs from pregnant friends over the years. When asked, these friends happily give permission to show the pictures in class as long as there is no identifying information on the slide. One semester we even had a student bring an ultrasound video of her then-embryo stage niece to class. We find that our students are interested to know the wide variety of physiological structures that are present in the peanut-sized embryo and they enjoy viewing pictures and videos taken during this stage.

The emphasis for the embryonic stage is clearly on physical development. However, there are some junctures during which you can integrate information about social and cognitive development. Most expectant parents become aware of a pregnancy during the embryonic stage. As the mother's body changes, there are discernable signs of her pregnant status that are hard to ignore as the weeks pass. You might choose to discuss the social implications of becoming a parent with your class. For example, an individual's emotional state relative to the pregnancy can vary tremendously. It is easy to consider how specific pregnancy milestones (e.g., having an ultrasound conducted, buying maternity clothes, telling family and friends about the pregnancy) can have different implications for different parents. Indeed, the impending birth of a fetus can lead to varied emotions such as fear, excitement, dread, and happiness.

During our coverage of the fetal stage of development, we describe the age of viability and provide examples of fetal behavioral capacities (for an excellent review of fetal motor development, see Adolph & Berger (2005)). One of our favorite studies to describe the fetal ability to hear is a study on newborn perception of maternal speech sounds (DeCasper & Spence, 1986). The researchers asked expectant mothers to record themselves reading three children's stories, Dr Suess's *The Cat in the Hat* (1957), *The King, the Mice, and the Cheese* (Gurney & Gurney, 1965), and *The Dog in the Fog* (a story created for the study). The researchers then randomly assigned the mothers to one of three groups and asked them to read one of the stories (their assigned target-story) to their fetus twice a day during the last six weeks of pregnancy. After birth, these neonates could activate a recording of their mother's voice by sucking on a non-nutritive nipple. The target-story recording appeared to be more reinforcing for infants because they displayed significantly more sucking bursts in response to the target-story relative to the novel stories (the two stories that were not read to them on a regular basis). Infants exposed to the prenatal target-story also had significantly more sucking bursts in response to their target-story relative to control infants who were not exposed to any prenatal stories. These findings suggested that the neonates remembered hearing their target-story prenatally. We typically bring a copy of *The Cat in the Hat* to class so that we can read a few pages to remind students of the very distinctive rhythm and cadence of this story. Additionally, we show the class an ultrasound photograph of a fetus so they can see the remarkable changes that have occurred since the embryonic stage.

Another social and personality aspect of pregnancy that we occasionally discuss with our students is the parental reaction to having an ultrasound or amniocentesis conducted on the fetus. For example, preliminary research suggests that the anxiety level of mothers increases during the period when they are waiting for the results of amniocentesis (for a review, see Lerman, Croyle, Tercyak, & Hamann, 2002). Similarly, parents anecdotally report a feeling of increased bonding after "seeing" their unborn child for the first time via ultrasound. Another example of the social implications for prenatal testing would be learning that your unborn child has a genetic defect or illness (Lerman et al., 2002). There are some clear emotional reactions that parents may have following such news, but your students may be interested to learn about the new field in prenatal surgery: Some fetal conditions, such as certain heart conditions, can be repaired by surgery while the fetus is in-utero (Makikallio et al., 2006; Quintero et al., 2005; Tworetzky et al., 2004).

Threats to prenatal development (i.e., common teratogens) are an important topic to cover from a developmental perspective as well as from a public service perspective. After defining the term "teratogen," we usually ask the class to generate a list of all the teratogens of which they can think. As students provide examples, we confirm the valid teratogens and provide some background information about why the particular teratogen is harmful for the fetus (e.g., alcohol can lead to fetal alcohol syndrome, mental retardation, low birth weight, and facial abnormalities). As such, it is helpful to know the potential effects of the most common teratogens before going into lecture so that you can speak intelligently about their effects on the fetus. In addition to the material that you read in your developmental text, it will be helpful to consult some outside sources to gain a full understanding of possible teratogens as they should have long-lasting implications for human health—and possible mental health (e.g., Pekkanen, 2001).

Next, we distribute a handout on dangerous teratogens to the class and comment on the teratogens that they were able to generate as well as the dangerous teratogens about which they may not know. Although students often have a general sense that there are some harmful chemical agents to stay away from during pregnancy, they are often surprised to learn the wide array of environmental agents that could be harmful to the developing fetus. The discussion on the effects of teratogens on the developing fetus is also complicated by the dose, timing, and frequency of the prenatal exposure to the harmful agent. We find it helpful to show a graph depicting the sensitive periods in development that provides some general guidelines as to timing of the prenatal exposure to teratogens and their harmful effects.

Labor and Delivery

Much like the prenatal developmental stage, there are many concepts to choose from for your coverage of labor and delivery. The list that we have included here is comprehensive enough that it may take two class periods to cover depending on the amount of discussion and number of videos that you choose to include. Most of the concepts we discuss below are the "nuts and bolts" of the physiological mechanics of labor and delivery. Because of the strictly biological nature of labor and delivery, understanding the process of labor and delivery is our primary goal for our students during our lecture. Time permitting, our secondary goal is to tie labor and delivery to different aspects of social development.

We begin our discussion of labor and delivery by showing two figures from our coverage of prenatal development and reviewing several concepts related to labor and delivery. We show the chart depicting the size of the fetus across the weeks of gestation and the drawing of the female reproductive system. We show the first picture to give students a visual reminder of how far along the fetus has developed over the previous 40 weeks. We use the drawing of the female reproductive system to remind students about the physical structures that are involved in the birth process.

The second activity during our coverage of labor and delivery is to define some key concepts. Many of these terms are medical terms with which many students are unfamiliar. "Neonate," "Braxton Hicks contractions," "uterus," "cervix," "transition," and "episiotomy" are all terms that we define for our students. If you decide to use a chronological approach for describing labor and delivery, these are also the terms that you would first use to describe the birth process.

Stages of labor

After reviewing the two figures and reviewing basic terminology, we describe the stages of labor. We typically use lecture and PowerPoint slides to cover the various stages of this important developmental event. However, you may choose to show the class a video or ask a recent parent of a newborn to talk about the birth process for the class. The more dramatic aspects of labor and delivery lend themselves well to a short video or a guest speaker.

Delivery options

Psychologists have known for some time that pregnant women are less anxious about the birth process if they have more information about what to expect beforehand (Buxton, 1962; Klusman, 1975). Likewise, your lecture on delivery options is an opportunity to introduce the non-parents in your class to common birthing methods. Typically, we discuss vaginal delivery, Cesarean delivery, breech birth, the use of epidurals, and the controversy surrounding the use of episiotomies. We also highlight the pros and cons (i.e., side effects) of using pain medication during delivery so that students have a sense of the factors that are involved when parents make an informed decision regarding whether to use medication during the labor process. Students or guest speakers who have undergone childbirth recently are usually willing to discuss their decisions regarding medication.

We also find it helpful to explain some of the birthing options available to parents in the US. For example, parents can choose to attend delivery preparation classes provided by the hospital. We usually describe what a traditional Lamaze class entails and we provide an in-class demonstration of guided imagery and some of the breathing exercises that might be used during labor preparation classes. Parents also have some options regarding their child's birth. They can choose whether to have the child at home with the help of a nurse midwife, have a nurse midwife attend the birth at a birthing center, or they can choose the more traditional route by having the child in the hospital under the care of an obstetrics team. Many undergraduates have not heard about birthing alternatives so they generally find this information interesting.

Maternal physical changes

There is an obvious physical dimension to childbirth in that the mother's body is altered afterwards. For example, the woman's hips and breasts take a different shape following childbirth. Many mothers undergoing natural childbirth also require an episiotomy, an incision made to increase the size of the birth canal, which can stretch from the vaginal wall to the anus. It would be easy to generate a class discussion on how the mother's physical and hormonal changes following labor and delivery may have implications for the marital relationship. Additionally, there will likely be a change in the woman's body satisfaction after childbirth.

Neonatal appearance

We find that many students are surprised by the typical neonate appearance. Their expectations are likely related to their general lack of experience with neonates and the sanitized version of childbirth that is typically shown in movies and television shows. We like to show pictures of actual neonates to help explain how they often have cone-shaped heads and how they are covered in amniotic fluid and vernix (a thick, greasy substance that covers the skin) soon after birth. Pre-term infants are often covered by lanugo, which is fine hair that develops in utero and covers the entire body by 20 weeks gestation. Coupled with their small size, the fine hair that covers pre-term infants is an aspect of their appearance that may be difficult for parents to see. To be sure, it contributes to the infant looking "different" from what the parents had likely imagined for their unborn child. We remind the class about the disparity between newborn babies as depicted on television and seeing a real neonate, and we reflect on how many first-time parents experience some amazement at their newborn's appearance.

Neonatal assessment

Perhaps because clinical psychologists are notorious assessors of human behavior, we almost always include APGAR scores in our lecture on labor and delivery. The APGAR scale, although the target of some recent criticism, is the first physical measure taken of a neonate and the strength of a neonate's score helps to determine whether he or she needs to have more intensive medical intervention (Aylward, 2003). To provide adequate information about the APGAR, we define the APGAR scale and provide a brief history of it. We also show the class how infants are rated using the APGAR scale immediately following birth. One of us (EBK) had the experience of conducting assessments on clinic-referred school-aged children in a large teaching hospital. If children were born in the hospital, their APGAR scores were included in the file along with their tiny, neonate-sized footprints.

Neonatal psychology

Although the labor and delivery chapter is focused primarily on the physical aspects of development, there are several social aspects that can be included in your discussion of the topic. Due to our pediatric consultation-liaison experience in medical settings, we often include some discussion of neonatal psychology and the role of neonatal psychologists in the neonatal intensive care unit (NICU).

Neonatal psychologists receive specialized clinical training on how to work with at-risk newborn children and their families. Typically, neonatal psychologists are assigned to work in the NICU of a hospital (Aylward, 2003). These psychologists help families to adjust with the stress of having pre-term and/or medically fragile children. We like to give our students a brief description of some of the duties of neonatal psychologists as well as some of the clinical services that they may provide (e.g., helping families deal with the stress of a hospitalization, helping families with the transition of having a child in the hospital, and helping parents to maintain attachment to a child who is confined to a small Plexiglas cubicle). Students are often interested to hear about infant massage and how research suggests that massaging an infant helps to stimulate growth (Field, Diego, Hernandez-Reif, Deeds, Figuereido, 2006). Another application of infant massage is to help parents who have lost custody of their children (e.g., in cases of prenatal drug use) to form and maintain an attachment to their children during weekly supervised infant massage sessions (Porter & Porter, 2004).

Birth complications

If we have time, we try to include some coverage of common fetal complications that might affect development. There are several complications that can arise during delivery, or proximal to the delivery, that adversely affect neonatal development such as anoxia, intraventricular hemorrhage (IVH), and cerebral palsy (Aylward, 2003). Generally, we define these complications and provide examples of how they might have implications for fetal death or later cognitive, social, and personality development. One helpful example is to discuss a family with both typically developing children and a child having a developmental delay. In the past we have used the example of the McCaughey septuplets because they provide a very public example of the developmental challenges that face children with developmental delays. The McCaughey family can serve as a case study for your students because the two children with developmental delays (Nathan and Alexis have forms of cerebral palsy) require additional care and medical treatment relative to their typically-developed siblings (Woodard, 2006).

Critical Thinking Opportunities

We discussed the benefits of including critical thinking exercises in your lifespan development course in the previous chapter; in this chapter we will continue to identify potential topics and ideas for critical thinking with respect to prenatal development and labor and delivery. The format of some of these activities is better suited for small classes, but can be modified to accommodate larger classes without inundating the instructor(s) with extra preparation or grading responsibilities. For example, the evaluation of research studies as an individual assignment with a written end-product is likely to be better suited for smaller classes. However, if that activity is modified to be a group assignment or a class discussion (without an extensive written end-product), then it would be feasible for a larger size class. Some potential topic ideas for evaluating research studies may be:

- Studies related to playing music and/or the use of language to developing fetus (e.g., Al-Qahtani, 2005; Arabin, 2002; Lasky & Williams, 2005)
- Studies related to different types of births (e.g., Caesarian vs. natural birth, and other alternative birth options) (e.g., Sharma, Sidawi, Ramin, Lucas, Leveno, & Cunningham, 1997; Whyte, Hannah, Saigal, Hannah, Hewson, Amankwah, et al., 2004)
- Studies about variables that affect fertility (e.g., stress, fertility drugs) (e.g., Negro-Vilar, 1993; Reddy, Wapner, Rebar, & Tasca, 2007).

In addition to evaluating research studies, other activities may include class discussions or debates in which your students use data-driven arguments to support their position. Again, class size may influence the format of the activity, but the main idea is to pose questions that encourage your students to think critically about how the course material relates to the world outside the classroom. Some topics that encourage critical thinking and are related to current discussions in the community outside of the classroom include:

- What are the benefits, risks and considerations of administering drugs to the mother during delivery?
- What possible consequences exist for the fetus and for the mother in exposing the fetus to specific teratogens (e.g., illicit drugs, alcohol)?

Controversial Topics

In the previous chapter we introduced the idea of using controversial topics to "advance the knowledge of your students" (Guest, 2007). In this chapter, we provide additional controversial ideas related to prenatal development and labor and delivery. Many of these topics can also be used as critical thinking activities in your class. In discussing any controversial topic, don't forget to establish a safe environment in which students feel comfortable exploring the application of course material to sensitive and sometimes confusing topics.

One controversial topic that will likely spark lively conversation is the role of government in determining the right to parent. For example, there have been heated discussions with regard to policy decisions regarding the number of children a parent can or should have (Hardee-Cleaveland & Banister, 1988; Kohler, Behrman, & Skytthe, 2005), and the ability to mandate sterilization (e.g., welfare mothers, drug addicted mothers, developmentally delayed mothers) (Block, 2002; Scott, 1986). These topics can be introduced with articles from scholarly journals, newspaper articles, or from articles in popular magazines. Other sources for introducing this topic to your class may be videos from case studies or segments from popular news programs.

Another controversial topic relates to genetic manipulation. You and your class can engage in a discussion of the benefits and risks of prenatal genetic manipulation. As medical technology advances, so does the likelihood that parents will be able to choose characteristics of their children. Your students will likely have different stances related to the extent to which parents should be able to manipulate the genetics of their children. Potential questions to pose to your class regarding this topic could be:

- What would be the benefits or risks of choosing the gender of your child?
- If you could choose to change the genetic makeup of your child, would you? Why or why not? What would that genetic makeup involve?

A third topic area that is likely to generate multiple reactions from your students is egg and sperm donation. Students may have differing perceptions based on what is donated (e.g., egg vs. sperm) and whether they are freely donated or whether compensation is received. Often, the invasiveness of the procedure for collecting the specimen influences people's perspectives (Cook & Golombok, 1995; Daniels, 2000). There is also a variety of perspectives on anonymity with relation to the donating of eggs and sperm to others than can be explored with your students. We discuss with our students the debate about whether donors can or should be identifiable or anonymous (Brewaeys, de Bruyn, Louwe, & Helmerhorst, 2005). We also discuss the potential implications to donor and recipient of anonymity vs. identified donors.

Developmental Diversity

Diversity is a term used to describe the quality of being diverse or different. Often when we think of diversity we think of race or ethnicity. Although diversity does refer to race and ethnicity, it also refers to all things that make people unique. With regard to discussing diversity in development, we suggest topics that explore all that encompasses diversity such as gender, ability, sexual orientation, age, socioeconomic status, and religion as well as race and ethnicity. You can discuss how the factors that make us unique influence our experiences when it comes to labor and delivery.

There are a number of areas in which diversity intertwines with prenatal development and labor and delivery such as birthing options, complications during birth, and prenatal care. Your students will likely enjoy being introduced to the diverse theories and practices related to having a child that vary by country, religion, or historical context. In our experience, students have enjoyed hearing about the cultural and historical variations on pregnancy. For example, we have shared with classes a variety of pregnancy superstitions from around the world such as women in southern regions of the United

80 Prenatal Development: Labor and Delivery

States as well as pregnant women in Mexico eating clay during pregnancy (Simpson, Mull, Longley, & East, 2000). Other superstitions include a relationship between a mother's heartburn during pregnancy and hair on the baby (the more heartburn, the hairier the baby; Costigan, Sipsma, & DiPietro, 2006).

There are diversity related perspectives and practices for every aspect of childbirth and you have the opportunity to introduce your students to a few of those. For example, students may not be aware of the differences in availability and access to prenatal care (i.e., information regarding a mother's nutrition, birthing options, screening of genetic problems, monitoring of fetal health) for individuals who live in different countries or who are of differing social economic status. Discussing the reasons and potential consequences of lacking or limited prenatal care with your students is a great way to encourage them to think outside their personal experiences and to think about the world around them. Using diversity in prenatal care as a starting point can add more critical thinking activities to your class. Students can research the dietary practices or availability of prenatal care for individuals from different cultures.

In addition to prenatal care, you and your students can explore the various ways in which individuals prepare for childbirth (e.g. Lamaze classes). Once they get a sense of what kinds of services are available to prepare for childbirth, you and your students can begin to investigate the various methods of birthing. For example, you can discuss different settings in which the delivery may occur (e.g., countries, hospital vs. home), how economic resources affect the delivery, and who is assisting with the delivery (e.g., doctor, midwife). One interesting activity you could use to fuse course material with diversity is to have students research the cost of childbirth in their hometown to get a sense of what is available to them and how much it costs to prepare for and have a child. The addition of diversity in the teaching of prenatal development and labor and delivery is likely to increase the critical thinking of your students, broaden their perspectives on what is available, and perhaps increase their appreciation for the complexity of childbirth.

Resources for Your Labor and Delivery Lectures

Occasionally you may find that your lecture could be enhanced by the addition of outside resources. We use guest speakers, professionally produced videos, our own video clips, snippets from television programming, and supplemental readings to help explain lifespan development concepts to our students.

Guest speakers

We highly recommend including guest speakers, especially if you are less than comfortable with the material subject matter experts could cover. Guest speakers can help to keep your course fresh because students typically enjoy having a break from regular lecture. You will also be able to refer to the guest lecturer's information during your subsequent lectures related to the topic. We were very fortunate to locate an instructor associated with our university's School of Nursing who has vast experience as a labor and delivery nurse. Our nurse colleague has provided several guest lectures on labor and delivery for our course over the years. Labor and delivery is a multidisciplinary topic and it has been helpful in our own development as instructors to learn a nurse's perspective towards the topic.

Through trial and error we have discovered some helpful things to consider when inviting guest lecturers to your class:

- Invite your guests to class several weeks or months *before* class to give them enough time to prepare their presentation. It is also a good idea to send guests a reminder e-mail the week before their scheduled presentation to see if there is anything that they need.
- If your guest is from off-campus you will need to provide directions to the classroom and a parking pass.
- Give your guest information about the number of students, the type of course that you are teaching, and the length of the class period. Sometimes guests will want to bring handouts, so it is important to let them know how many students you have in the class. We usually tell our guest speakers that they do not have to talk for the entire class period. In our experience, however, students' questions usually fill the remainder of the class period.
- Some guests may want to see the textbook that you are using so that they can ensure that their lecture compliments the textbook information.
- Advise your guests about the technology that is available in the classroom (e.g., VCR, DVD player, computer with a projector).
- Introduce your guest to the class and be clear to the students about their responsibility for the material (i.e., Should they take

notes? Will this information be on the test? Will the slides be available to them later?).
- Be a good host and have your students sign a thank you note. We usually ask students to sign the thank you note during the class period following the guest lecture. The note does not have to be very fancy, a colored sheet of computer paper will do. Our guest speakers have universally appreciated these thank you notes because students often have very nice things to say about their lectures.

If you are unable to find a guest speaker on labor and delivery, it could be advantageous to include one or more short videos depicting labor and delivery. Videos that are too long tend to bore students. We like to keep students engaged and we have found that short video illustrations with discussion about the footage just viewed works best for our courses. Our inclusion of video depends on factors such as time, extensiveness of class discussion on a particular topic, and how discussion-prone the class tends to be. Some very quiet classes benefit from watching videos because the videos give them a point of reference that often increases class discussion. We often show videos after administering an exam because attendance tends to drop off after an exam: only students who attend class will be able to answer subsequent exam questions based on the video.

Video resources

We like to use McGraw-Hill's two disk CD-ROM *Multimedia Courseware for Child Development* (Patterson, 2000) in our course. This resource has short video clips that can be used to illustrate concepts from conception through adolescence. There are many CDs with video footage currently available for lifespan development and it is just a matter of finding the video clips that fit your lecture best. We tend to use clips from one CD because it can be unwieldy to switch from one CD to another during the same lecture. We use several video clips from Patterson's (2000) CD that relate to prenatal development and the birth process including:

- *Prenatal Development.* The brief film (running time, 1:36) includes footage of the embryonic and fetal stages of prenatal development. At the end of the clip there is a very brief, full-on shot of a vaginal delivery.

- *Childbirth.* The short film (3:37) depicts a mother giving birth in a hospital room. The doctor and nurses are there as well as the neonate's father. In the video the doctor asks the mother to "push" and shortly afterward the neonate's body emerges during the vaginal delivery. The doctor cuts the umbilical chord and the baby is whisked away to a warming table where nurses clean-up the baby boy and administer the APGAR Scale. The video is realistic without invading too much of the mother's privacy.

Television resources

Despite the many negative aspects of television, it can provide information that can be used successfully in a lifespan development course. Given the recent emphasis on reality TV shows in the US, there are currently several TV shows that depict real-life people experiencing issues related to prenatal development and labor and delivery. For example, the Discovery Health Channel has a series called *Maternity Ward* (www.discovery.com) and The Learning Channel (TLC; www.tlc.discovery.com) has a series called *A Baby Story* and *Bringing Home Baby*. We have used video clips from these television shows successfully. Because they are "reality"-based shows, they include a human interest aspect that easily lends itself to class discussion of the social development implications of labor and delivery.

Print resources

Another resource that may be helpful for teaching prenatal development and labor and delivery includes articles from *Psychology Today*, the *APA Monitor on Psychology*, or a resource provided by psychology text publishers. *The Annual Edition on Human Development* (McGraw Hill's annual editions, 2007) is one such resource that we have found helpful in preparing for our classes. Each edition covers a wide range of developmental topics and provides a comprehensive compendium of articles from varied magazines, scientific journals, and public press outlets such as *Newsweek, Young Children, Psychological Science*, the APA *Monitor on Psychology*, and *American Behavioral Scientist*.

We find these articles helpful because they serve as a supplement to most textbook readings. Sometimes when you are a new instructor it is difficult to answer questions beyond the material in the text. We find that reading these resources helps to "fill in the gaps" of our

84 Prenatal Development: Labor and Delivery

developmental knowledge so that we can stay current with the latest media publications related to our course. The McGraw Hill publication is useful for lifespan development because it includes units on conception to birth, cognition, language and learning, social and emotional development, parenting and family issues, and cultural and societal influences.

Helpful Resources for Teaching Prenatal Development

University of Utah's Genetic Science Learning Center: www.learn.genetics.utah.edu.
National Institute of Health's Genetics Home Reference: www.ghr.nlm.nih.gov.
American Academy of Pediatrics: www.aap.org.
The Children, Youth, and Families Education Research Network: www.cyfernet.mes.umn.edu.
National Institute of Child Health and Human Development: www.nichd.nih.gov.
Babyworld: www.babyworld.com.
Children's Nutrition Research Center: www.bcm.tmc.edu/cnrc.
Zero to Three: National Center for Infants, Toddlers, and Families: www.zerotothree.org.
Rutgers Infant Development: www.babylab.rutgers.edu/.
Birthing Naturally: www.birthingnaturally.net/.

Chapter 4

Infant Development

Infant development is a gratifying topic to teach because most students enjoy learning about "babies." In this chapter we summarize key concepts related to infant development and we provide examples of class activities that may help to enhance your teaching of infant development. Finally, we provide suggestions for videos and Web sites that you can use to highlight key concepts.

One of the main challenges to teaching infant development within the context of a developmental psychology course is that there are so many constructs to choose from when developing your lecture material. Although we have taught this material many times, we usually feel as though we do not give the infancy period its "due." Our coverage of the infancy period leans towards the cognitive and social aspects of infancy more than the physical and perceptual aspects. However, we try to cover all these domains at least briefly. If you would like to read more in-depth information about infant development, we recommend several chapters from Bornstein and Lamb's (2005) graduate-level developmental science text.

Consistent with our coverage of topics in previous chapters, the list of important infant development concepts that we provide here is too long to cover in one class period. You may choose to provide more in-depth coverage for the cognitive and physical aspect of infant development if it is your particular area of expertise. With these caveats in mind, we consider the following concepts to be important for developmental psychology students to know regarding infant physical and cognitive development.

Infant Physical Development

It is an exciting time to study infant physical development because of the new technology available to developmental researchers. William James' view that the infant's world could best be described as "one great blooming, buzzing confusion" is long gone (James, 1890). Rather than relying on our limited human faculties to observe infants (i.e., the tools available 50 years ago), researchers can now use computers to monitor brain waves, track eye movements, and measure other physiological functions. The general public appears to appreciate the implications of early infant brain development research as well. From actor/director Rob Reiner's "I Am Your Child" foundation's media blitz of 2001 to a recent *Newsweek* cover story on "Your Baby's Brain" (Wingert & Brant, 2005), issues related to infant development have gained prominence in the public eye. Along these lines, we view our lectures on infant development as an important opportunity to teach undergraduates theories and facts that may help them one day to understand their own children.

Early brain development

We start our discussion of early brain development by describing the basic structures that comprise the central nervous system such as neurons, myelin (aka "fatty sheath") and the cortex. To illustrate the cortex in particular, we usually show the class a CAT scan of an adult human brain. We also show an artist's rendition of how the infant's neural network becomes more complex over time. If you have time and would like to provide a more in-depth depiction of development of the infant's neural network, you may decide to show your class a neural network video clip (e.g., Feldman, 2003). The biomedical science majors in your course also may have knowledge in the area of brain development that they would like to share with the class. Often our biomedical science majors will add information that they have learned in other classes to help illustrate concepts for their fellow students.

Infant brain video

As mentioned in the last chapter, we frequently use videos to illustrate concepts in our course. To start our lecture on infant brain development, we show a video entitled *Infant Brains* (Patterson, 2000). This video clip (running time, 5:01) provides an interview with UCLA pediatric neurologist, Harry Chugani, MD, and presents information related to the complex process of human brain development. During the video, Dr Chugani describes how Positron Emission Tomography (PET scan) has been used with children to chart human brain development and he narrates as the video presents PET scan images of infant brains over time to illustrate the different parts of the brain that develop over time.

In his research, Chugani (1998) found that the pattern of glucose utilization in newborn brains was different from the adult brains he studied in that only the most primitive areas of the newborn brain work initially. However, this pattern of glucose utilization is consistent with the behavior of a newborn. For example, newborns cannot visually track and grab an object. By two to four months of age, the visual tracking centers of the brain (the parietal cortex) are more developed (Chugani, Phelps, & Mazziotta, 1987). Additionally the areas of the brain responsible for motor coordination, the basal ganglia and cerebellar hemisphere, were also more developed in two- to four-month-olds. This brain development helps infants in this age range to track objects—supporting the correlation between increased infant behavioral functioning and brain development. Chugani also found that at seven months of age, lateral and medial portions of the infant frontal cortex have an increase in glucose activity. He suggests that this activity is related to the six- to eight-month period as one of cognitive maturation typical among infants. This brain maturation may be responsible for the "hypothesis forming age" that has been described for this age.

At the end of the video, Chugani relates the emergence of stranger anxiety to brain development. He notes that seven- to eight-month-olds demonstrate stranger anxiety but younger infants do not have stranger anxiety. The burst of complex brain development that corresponds to the seven- to eight-month-old period suggests increased metabolic maturation of the frontal lobe. According to Chugani, the higher cognitive processing associated with stranger anxiety appears to be mediated by frontal lobe activity.

The infant brain development video can serve as a springboard for discussion on how changes in brain function over the first year of life may be responsible for normal psychosocial changes during the infant period. You might also talk about the importance of brain imaging techniques (such as PET scanning and MRI) in expanding our understanding of brain plasticity following neurological injury. Alternatively, you can remind your students about the infant with stranger anxiety depicted at the end of *Infant Brains* when you lecture on infant social development.

Strabismus

To highlight the sensitive period for brain development in humans, we often discuss strabismus, a condition in which individuals have difficulty focusing their vision because of muscle weakness in one eye. Strabismus can be a helpful condition to discuss during your lecture on infant brain development because it provides an example of altered human brain structure. First, we define strabismus and describe how an individual may have difficulty with depth perception throughout his or her life if this condition is not corrected early in life. Next, we ask the students if they know anyone who has strabismus. Students are willing to share what they know about the condition as well as describe how it can negatively impact an individual's functioning—if they happen to know someone with strabismus. Finally, we talk about how strabismus is a naturally occurring "experiment" in that it allows us the ability to see how human visual development is negatively impacted by certain physical conditions. For ethical reasons, one would have to use an animal model to investigate brain plasticity and visual impairment (i.e., we could never randomly assign infants to a group in which their vision was tampered with in order to study the effects on their brain development). Such studies have been conducted, however, with kittens and specially fitted goggles. Students sometimes become very concerned about the kittens in the research conducted by, for example, Hirsch & Spinelli (1970). Nevertheless, this line of research provides valuable information about critical periods in the development of the visual cortex.

Infant states of arousal

Many non-parents do not appreciate the different "faces" that an infant can show during the course of a day. The impressions that young adults have of infants are likely influenced by the media, where infant television characters are typically shown as cooing adorably, smiling as they model disposable diapers, or screaming.

Rhythms To understand infant states of arousal, one must understand that humans are creatures of habit and schedule. These schedules develop during our youth and tend to remain fairly stable over time. One example that we use for our class is the tendency for individuals to have a fairly stable eating and sleeping cycle. To illustrate our point, we engage in a bit of self-disclosure (e.g., Dr. Knight always eats breakfast and needs to eat at least three meals a day. She also requires at least seven hours of sleep to feel rested). If you ask for volunteers from the class, there are sure to be some students who get by each day with eating only one large meal and other students who only need four to five hours of sleep per night to feel rested. These are examples of interpersonal variations—and intrapersonal stability—in rhythms.

Sleep states We typically start describing infant states of arousal by defining the two sleep states of *active* and *quiet sleep*. One question that we occasionally receive from students is how similar is REM sleep in adults to active sleep in infants. Thus, you may want to be ready with an answer and be prepared to tie the concept of active sleep to information from other courses in psychology (e.g., brain and behavior or general psychology). To illustrate the point that infants sleep far more than adults, we show the class a graph depicting both the amount of time infants spend in active vs. quiet sleep.

The graph also shows how the amount of time spent in active and quiet sleep changes over the lifespan. Later in the semester we cover material related to the physical changes of older adults and their decreased need for sleep (i.e., early morning awakening). We comment on the marked decrease in sleep time needed by older adults (an example of how your grandmother starts her day would suffice) to prepare them for the upcoming chapter on older adulthood.

Active sleep Most of your students are not parents and it has probably been years since they had daily contact with infants and/or children. You may need to use an example that is more familiar to them when describing active sleep. Many of the students in our courses have pets, so in addition to giving examples that include infants we also use examples of sleeping dogs to describe the difference between active and quiet sleep. For example, we might say to the class, "Have you ever seen a dog bark, blink its eyes, or move its legs while it is sleeping? In this situation the dog is experiencing active sleep. The same phenomenon occurs with babies (active sleep, not the barking part . . .)."

Quiet sleep There is really not as much to say about quiet sleep. We generally define quiet sleep, give the amount of time that infants spend in quiet sleep, and move on to the transition states between sleeping and waking.

Transition states between sleeping and waking It is fun to describe *drowsiness* and *daze* to our students because they have probably observed children (or dogs, or siblings, or friends . . .) in this state but just did not know the technical term for it. Students are often eager to talk about the daze state and whether they have ever encountered someone who sleeps with his or her eyes open. Students may open a discussion about whether these individuals are truly asleep or if they might be in a daze state. Also, it could lead to a discussion of various parasomnias (i.e., sleep disorders that are especially common in children) if the students ask questions about sleep walking (see the *Diagnostic and Statistical Manual of Mental Disorders* (DSM-IV; American Psychiatric Association, 1994) for a full description of parasomnias).

Awake states Most non-parents see infants when they are in an awake state. During the awake state, the infant can be either crying or alert. To help illustrate these awake states, we show the class a video of a four-month-old infant so that they can evaluate the infant's state of arousal (see the field research video exercise below).

We also provide our students with some clinical anecdotes about working with infants. For example, it is best to test the developmental level of an infant who is calm and in a relaxed state (i.e., in the alert state of arousal). Infants who are alert are able to process information without becoming irritated: Agitated infants are difficult to assess. As a result, psychologists cannot obtain an accurate assessment of a given infant's capabilities if the infant is not in an alert, calm state. To illustrate how quickly an infant can become agitated, we show students a video of an infant who becomes overstimulated and fussy. The video is actually about infant reflexes (*Behavior of the Newborn*; Patterson, 2000) but the end of the video (50 seconds into the clip) demonstrates a brief test of visual stimulation with an infant. During the test, the physician uses a red ball to assess two infants' ability to track objects. The task proves too stimulating for the first infant and she becomes fussy. By contrast, the physician is able to demonstrate how a more calm and relaxed infant (i.e., the second infant) is able to master the same task.

For illustrative purposes, you might describe the different types of crying and how parents learn to distinguish between these types of cries (e.g., the hunger cry, the anger cry, the fussy cry, etc.). On the practical side, you could talk about the best way to soothe a crying infant. Alternatively, you might briefly highlight the findings of some recent studies addressing the response that crying infants elicit in adults (Dinehart, Messinger, Acosta, Cassel, Ambador, & Cohn, 2005; Zeifman, 2003).

The family bed exercise Although the states of arousal are primarily biology-based, there are some social implications that we discuss with our class. For example, there is a great amount of variation regarding sleeping arrangements among families. Some families prefer to co-sleep with their children while other families prefer their children to sleep in separate quarters. The literature on cross-cultural co-sleeping patterns reveals a large amount of variability related to family sleeping patterns around the world (e.g., Ball, Hooker, & Kelly, 2000; Javo, Ronning, & Heyerdahl, 2004; Welles-Nystrom, 2005).

Once we describe the social history of co-sleeping, we refer to a few co-sleeping families as depicted in popular film (e.g., Charlie's grandparents in the movie *Willy Wonka* slept in the same bed (Margulis & Stuart, 1971); a scene from the *Coal Miner's Daughter* (Schwartz & Apted, 1980) depicted Loretta Lynn's parents sleeping in a bed with their younger children). After describing the research on co-sleeping, we draw a "pros vs. cons" chart and record the opinions provided by the class on either the "pros" or the "cons" side of the chart. Using this method, we have had success leading our students in a discussion on the potential merits and problems of parents co-sleeping with their children. As we conduct this exercise, we are mindful of the possibility that individuals in the class may feel very strongly in a positive or negative direction towards co-sleeping. Some of these opinions may relate to whether students in our class were raised in a family that encouraged co-sleeping. For this reason, it is important to stay impartial and allow everyone in the class the opportunity to voice his or her opinion. Your impartial attitude will, hopefully, provide students with a safe environment in which they can share their thoughts. Indeed, our "pros vs. cons of the family bed" exercise is rarely a boring discussion!

"Field research" video A cooperative friend might allow you to video his or her small infant. The advantage of having your own video of a naturalistic observation of an infant is that infant development is constant so you will be able to use the video for a long time. To develop this exercise, we conducted a naturalistic observation by videoing a four-month-old infant for about 20 minutes in her home. We asked the mother to let the child "behave normally" and we taped the child by herself and while interacting with her mother. Typically, we show our students two minutes of video with good sound quality for a naturalistic observation coding exercise.

To set up this coding exercise in class, we describe the video as the result of our own "field research." We tell the class that we would like them to code the video clip so that they can have the experience of coding infant behavior. Next, we give every student an "Infant Behavioral State Coding Sheet" that we developed for the exercise and we briefly describe the operational definitions of infant behavior listed on the coding sheet. We then instruct students to code every behavior that applies during the two minute interval using the coding sheet (Appendix D). As students code the video, we use a stop watch to keep time and tell the class when to move to the next coding segment on their coding sheet (e.g., we say "time 1" at 10 seconds, "time 2" at 20 seconds, etc.).

Because many students become flustered as they code the video, it is a great way to show that it takes practice to learn how to observe behavior and make snap decisions about what you see. Following the exercise, we ask students to raise their hand if they have exactly the same codes as the student sitting next to them. Overwhelmingly, students do not. This exercise becomes an opportunity to describe inter-rater reliability to our students. The critical thinkers in your class will be able to comment on the difficult aspects of the task. They might even discuss the difficulty of providing operational definitions for some behaviors (e.g., determining when a vocalization counts as two vocalizations). We usually end the exercise by asking the class if they observed any behaviors that were displayed by the infant but not reflected on the coding sheet. Asking them to help you refine the coding sheet will provide you with an opportunity to praise them for their sharp observational skill.

Infant Motor Development

Reflexes are an important part of infant development because they can indicate whether the infant's nervous system is intact. To begin this section of the class, we generally define reflexes, give the rationale for why they are important to assess, and describe well-known infant reflexes such as the rooting reflex, the stepping reflex, the palmar grasp reflex, and the tonic neck reflex. There are a few sections in lifespan development during which students will need to memorize a list of concepts and their associated ages. Infant reflexes is one of them. We refer students to the specific table in the text summarizing infant reflexes and we urge them to review it prior to the exam.

Reflexes video

When teaching infant development, there really is no comparison between an instructor explaining infant reflexes and presenting the class with a neonate displaying the same reflexes. Because most instructors do not have access to a very young infant to demonstrate reflexes, a video may be your best option. In the video that we use, *Newborn Behavior* (running time, 1:43), a physician explains infant reflexes, the alert state, and infant imitation (Patterson, 2000). The video has a nice demonstration of the walk reflex; gallant (or swimming) reflex, and grasping reflex. The end of the video has a precious clip of the physician eliciting an imitation of his funny face (tongue thrust) from an infant. The sound quality of the video is good and the infants are so small and cute that the video is a real crowd pleaser. Furthermore, this video can stimulate discussion on a) the function of reflexes, b) when reflexes typically disappear, and c) which reflexes adult humans still display.

Nothing beats watching a video of infants displaying reflexes but in a pinch you could use a doll to demonstrate reflexes to your students. It is also helpful to point out that adults do have some intact reflexes such as the gag reflex and tendency to blink our eyes when an object moves unexpectedly towards our faces.

Milestones of motor development

The milestones of motor behavior are another topic for which students will need to memorize a list of concepts and their associated ages.

We generally show the class a slide depicting the milestones and we indicate the figure number for the slide in their text. Next, we explain the difference between gross motor skill and fine motor skill. We also remind the class about the young infant depicted in our field research video exercise and ask them to guess the age of the infant on the film. You may find it helpful to show your class a video entitled *Early Motor Milestones* (Films for the Humanities and Sciences, 2005). This brief video (running time, 1:12) makes the excellent point that there is a great deal of variability between children in their mastery of motor skill milestones.

Bayley Scales of Infant Development Second Edition (BSID—II) "The Bayley" is a well-standardized test of infant development that can be used to assess infants from birth to 42 months (Black & Matula, 1999). In our course, we use items and stimulus materials from the Bayley test kit to help describe the motor, mental, and behavioral aspects of infant development. The Bayley is often used with high-risk children (e.g., children born pre-term, children born to drug-using mothers) to screen for developmental delay and the need for early intervention services. Items that correspond with the 0–12 month age range are primarily focused on visual perception, auditory perception, attention, gross motor skill, and social skills. Items for children older than 12 months have more emphasis on language development, problem solving, fine motor skills, advanced gross motor skills, and social skills.

Most undergraduate students do not have experience with psychological assessment. For this reason, we show some of the test stimuli to the students and describe what it is like to assess the developmental level of an infant. In addition to describing the clinical uses of the measure, we incorporate specific Bayley items into our lecture on infant development. Because we generally integrate items from the Bayley throughout our lecture, we simply keep the test kit at our feet and describe relevant test items as needed. For example, as we describe the difference between gross and fine motor skill, we use test items from the Bayley to demonstrate how these skills are measured clinically. For example, we illustrate how we assess gross motor skills by showing the class a ring with a string attached to it. To assess a very young infant, the evaluator swings the ring in front of the infant to see if the child will try to grab the ring. We also demonstrate how learning to walk up and down stairs actually follows a developmental progression (e.g., putting both feet on each stair, learning to walk up stairs with one foot on alternating stairs). To demonstrate how fine motor skills are assessed, we show the class a small bottle filled with sugar tablets. A sugar tablet is placed on a table and the evaluator assesses whether the infant is able to pick up the tablet using his or her thumb and forefinger. Of course, the evaluator makes sure that the child does not put the tablet into his or her mouth!

Although the Bayley is a valuable tool for describing infant development, you may want to discuss the major limitation of the measure in that the Bayley items do not correlate well with later measures of child intelligence (Birney, Citron-Pousty, Lutz, & Sternberg, 2005). For example, motor development and early child language ability may not predict later school success as well as some other measures such as specific academic skills, emotional regulation, or social skills.

Our psychology department is fortunate to have a psychology clinic on campus with a well-stocked assessment cabinet. We have permission to borrow the Bayley test kit from the clinic for our lectures on infant development. However, if you do not have a clinical background or if your department does not have a clinic, you might invite a psychologist with infant assessment experience to describe the measure for your class.

Estimating developmental landmarks exercise If you have enough time, you might want to assess your students' knowledge of the social and motor milestones prior to your lecture on this section. The following exercise may be helpful in generating class discussion. In this group exercise, students are asked to estimate the ages, on average, at which children are able to perform certain behaviors (Bolt, 2001). Students should discuss their answers relative to the correct answers provided below:

1) Laugh – social – 2 months
2) Pedal a tricycle – physical – 2 years
3) Sit without support – physical – 5–6 months
4) Feel ashamed – cognitive – 2 years
5) Walk unassisted – physical – 12 months
6) Stand on one foot for 10 seconds – physical – 4.5 years
7) Recognize and smile at mother or father – cognitive – 4–5 months
8) Kicks ball forward – physical – 20 months
9) Think about things that cannot be seen – cognitive – 12 years
10) Make two word sentences – language – 20–22 months.

Infant Sensory Development

We use several techniques to teach infant sensory development. Although we primarily rely on lecture material, we also show videos of infants and we demonstrate items from the Bayley. If you are interested in a short film that provides an overview of infant sensory development, a video entitled *Sensory Capabilities of Neonates* (running time, 2:30) may be a good option (Films for the Humanities & Sciences, 2005).

Visual perception

When presenting infant visual perception, we provide information related to neonatal visual acuity (e.g., binocular vision, distance vision, the ability to track an object, and depth perception). We also provide an example of research on infant depth perception by describing the visual cliff paradigm.

Given that the "visual cliff" is a classic paradigm for studying infant depth perception (Walk & Gibson, 1961), we almost always describe the apparatus and examples of research questions it addresses (Campos & Bertenthal, 1989; Witherington, Campos, Anderson, Lejeune, & Seah, 2005). Although you can describe the visual cliff (i.e., how one side of a Plexiglas sheet is painted and the other side is transparent, creating the illusion of a big drop) watching a video of an infant placed on a visual cliff is far more helpful for understanding the apparatus. In the video clip that we usually show our students, Dr Jospeh Campos and Dr Robert Emde describe a visual cliff study they conducted to explore whether parents, by facial expression alone, could change the behavior of their infant children (Patterson, 2000). Specifically, the researchers examined whether fear of heights is an innate human fear and whether environmental context could influence the development of early emotions.

Infants are actually better than adults in their ability to distinguish several types of visual stimuli (e.g., infant facial recognition skill). Although we do not cover much information related to facial-emotional recognition in infants in our course, this emerging field would be a fascinating area to discuss with students.

Auditory perception

Infants have a well-developed sense of hearing at birth (DeCasper & Fifer, 1980). To illustrate our point, we remind students about the *Cat in the Hat* research conducted by DeCasper and Spence (1986) in which the infants demonstrated that they could distinguish between the stories read by their mothers soon after birth. When presenting infant auditory perception, we provide information related to neonatal auditory perception (e.g., sound localization and sound discrimination). We also provide an example of sound localization by demonstrating an item from the Bayley—we ring a bell while they are writing their notes.

You can ask your students who are studying a new language for the first time about their ability to discriminate sounds in the new language. Sometimes it is very difficult for adult learners of a new language to distinguish among similar sounds in a new language. Infants, however, have keen auditory discrimination skills. Research suggests that infant auditory discrimination skill for languages peaks around six–eight months and then declines as they are exposed to their native language (Kuhl, Stevens, Hayashi, Deguchi, Kiritani, & Iverson, 2006; Sebastian-Galles, 2006).

Smell and taste

For the section on infant smell and taste we describe how researchers determine whether an infant prefers the taste or smell of a food item by evaluating the facial expression of the infant. We also briefly mention research supporting infants' odor preference for their mothers and lactating females (Rattaz, Goubet, & Bullinger, 2005).

Pain and touch

The sense of touch develops prenatally and infants have a well-developed sense of pain and touch at birth. To illustrate the power of human touch, we cite research involving infants and daily massage (for a review, see Field, Diego, & Hernandez-Reif, 2007). Specifically, daily massage appears to stimulate growth hormones for preterm infants. Infants randomly assigned to receive daily massage were larger than control group infants and had higher IQs when evaluated during a follow-up assessment. Another compelling aspect of infant touch is that almost all of the infant reflexes incorporate the infant's sense of touch in some way (e.g., the rooting reflex, the stepping reflex, etc.).

We do not usually have an in-depth discussion on infant pain beyond the information that is in the textbook that we use for the course (i.e., the medical community's initial belief that infants do not experience pain; that circumcisions are typically performed without anesthesia because of possible complications for the infant).

Infant Cognitive Development

Given the (likely) relative inexperience our students have with infants, we like to focus on the amazing abilities that infants have soon after birth. To do these infant cognitive abilities justice, we always cover the basic processes of learning first. In our lectures, these processes of learning include classical conditioning, operant conditioning, and habituation. Teaching these concepts is fairly straightforward, especially if you have taught a general psychology course before.

Processes of learning

Classical conditioning During our lecture on classical conditioning we provide examples of Pavlov's dog and Little Albert to highlight basic principles. You can also use examples from your own pet if you happen to have one. (If you use your own pet as an example, we recommend that you show at least one gratuitous picture. However, don't show too many pictures because students will start sending you e-mails that read like the one that we received recently after showing a picture of our dogs to our class: "Dear Professor, I am sorry that I was not able to make it to class yesterday as my dog was sick. I am sure that as a dog-lover you will understand and not take away any points from my attendance grade. . . .").

We also typically provide a brief history of classical conditioning as well as an example that is easy to follow. You may choose to have students learn all of the technical terms (e.g., the difference between a conditioned stimulus and an unconditioned stimulus) or you may choose to have them understand the general idea underlying classical conditioning. We have had success teaching this information both ways.

We have relied on a CD containing video clips entitled *Video Classics in Psychology* (Prentice Hall, 2002). Just as the name suggests, the CD provides video clips of some classic figures and experiments in psychology. Two video clips that we recommend include a short clip of a dog undergoing a classical conditioning experiment involving electric shock and actual footage from the classical conditioning trials conducted with Little Albert. The video of Little Albert and the dog receiving electric shock really tugs at students' heart strings so be prepared to provide some background information on the very rigorous ethical procedures that must be followed to conduct research with animals and humans. Also, if you use the Little Albert video, be prepared for the question "Whatever happened to Little Albert?"

Operant conditioning To switch gears and talk about operant conditioning we like to conduct an exercise that involves the entire class. We demonstrate the power of positive reinforcement by playing a shaping game that is similar to "hot and cold." The exercise requires one volunteer and assistance from your students. After a volunteer is selected, he or she is asked to leave the room briefly. Next, the instructor leads the class in deciding what the student should perform as his or her target behavior. The behavior should be something relatively easy such as going to the front of the classroom and sitting in a particular chair. Other chains of behavior, such as having the student walk to the front of the classroom and dance or do jumping jacks, are more difficult to shape but we have had success with these behaviors as well. Once the class decides on the behavior, instruct them to click their pens on their desks very quickly as the volunteer becomes "hotter" and not at all as the volunteer becomes "colder." Once you bring the volunteer back into the classroom, just tell them to "follow the clicks." The class will probably follow your lead at first when deciding when to click their pens. Occasionally, we need to give a little hint to the volunteer like, "they want you to do something" or "keep trying different things." Eventually, most volunteers perform the target behavior. We give all of our volunteers a round of applause and two points of extra credit for their effort. Be prepared to guide the students in choosing the target behavior—sometimes students will suggest a behavior that is inappropriate (e.g., have her get on all fours and bark like a dog).

Following this demonstration we describe how our pen clicks reinforced our volunteer because they helped him or her to discern the particular target behavior. Very young infants do not understand language but they are able to alter their behavior based on what happens in the environment as a result of their behavior. We return to our class operant conditioning demonstration when we discuss the behavioral theory for how infants learn language.

One way to describe operant conditioning at work within the parent-infant dyad is to use the example of a crying baby. Babies spend approximately one to four hours each day crying. Infants, especially pre-verbal infants, communicate with their caregivers through crying. Caregivers reinforce crying behavior by responding to the infant when he or she cries. In this scenario, the caregivers positively reinforce the infant by attending to the infant and trying to alleviate the infant's distress through comfort. One could also argue that caregivers experience negative reinforcement because a crying baby can be very upsetting for adults to hear! In all, the baby learns that he or she is a social being and that adults in the environment will respond to their cries.

One key component of operant conditioning is that responses can be strengthened or weakened depending on the environmental consequence that the infant's behavior causes. In the paragraph above we describe the best-case scenario in which a child cries and the caregivers respond immediately. Alternatively, some infants live in homes or orphanages with extreme caregiver neglect. You may want to show your class a video that describes the effect of parental neglect on children. We use a video entitled *Child Maltreatment* (running time, 4:41) that includes a brief clip on the behavior of neglected orphans in impoverished countries (Patterson, 2000). If there is a very low orphan to caregiver ratio, infants will not be fed or diapered on their schedule. Rather, feeding and diapering will be on the schedule of the overworked staff. In these cases, the infants do not cry very frequently because they learn through operant conditioning that it does no good. That is, the infants do not receive reinforcement following their crying behavior so eventually their crying is extinguished.

Another example of operant conditioning in the infant world is sucking a nipple. The sucking reflex becomes a voluntary behavior as a result of operant conditioning. Babies typically receive some reinforcement from sucking on a nipple, be it formula, breast milk, or a recording of their mother reading the *Cat in the Hat* research (if they happen to be participants in the DeCasper and Spence (1986) study). Therefore, their sucking response is rewarded and they are more likely to perform the behavior in the future.

Habituation Habituation is another learning process that is commonly seen in infants. You may want to show your class a video clip of an infant habituating to a stranger (Feldman, 2003). According to this well established mode of infant learning, infants tend to look at an object or event longer when they are surprised (or puzzled or intrigued) by it. In class, we typically use the example of standing in line at a grocery store. Most of us have had the experience of standing behind a child in line. Infants and children often stare at strangers for a couple of reasons. First, they do not yet appreciate the social convention that it is impolite to stare. Second, we are strangers to the children and are, as such, novel stimuli for them. When children stare at a novel adult in their environment they display the *orienting response*. Typically when a child stares at an unknown adult they eventually get bored and look away. Habituation has occurred in these situations. Generally, infants and children will stare longer if the adult is very different from the child's caregivers. You might also want to explain to your class that the process of habituation can involve measuring physical responses other than eye gaze (e.g., heart rate, respiration).

Piaget's theory of cognitive development

Even though many aspects of Piaget's theory of cognitive development have been challenged recently, we still cover his theory in depth because he was—and still is—such an influential presence in the field of developmental psychology. To keep our lecture fresh for this section, we try to incorporate clinical anecdotes and video clips to provide more recent views on Piaget's theory. We cover the sensorimotor stage during our lecture on infant cognitive development and later we return to Piaget during a lecture on the preoperational stage of his theory. However, to provide the class with some context regarding how the sensorimotor stage figures into Piaget's theory, we do show a slide listing all four stages of his theory. We also show a slide depicting the discontinuous nature of his theory and remind the class of our first lecture during which we discussed the debate between continuous versus discontinuous theories of development.

To begin our coverage of Piaget, we provide some biographical information as well as define a few key terms for his theory including scheme, adaptation, assimilation, accommodation, equilibrium, and disequilibrium. The example that we use for assimilation and accommodation is an infant putting blocks into his mouth (assimilation) and that same infant later using the blocks to build a tower (accommodation). Next, we refer the class to a chart in the text detailing the six substages of Piaget's sensorimotor period.

Sensorimotor stage

We start our lecture on the sensorimotor period by giving the students a general outline of what is to come—we will cover the six substages of Piaget's sensorimotor period, we will define each stage, and we will provide some examples to help them better understand the concepts related to each stage. We also tell our students that more recent research evidence suggests that some aspects of Piaget's theory underestimated infant capabilities and we will highlight these inconsistencies as we talk about the substages.

Substage 1 We start our brief discussion of Substage 1 by providing Piaget's explanation of the substage (i.e., reflexes are the infant's mental life) and providing an example. One example that we often use is the case of a one-month-old infant who relies on her sucking schema to relate to the world. If this infant was placed on her father's chest, she would likely start to suck on his chest even though he never breast feeds the child. If the infant was placed near the father's back, she would try to suck his back.

Substage 2 Piaget coined Substage 2 as the Primary Circular Reaction stage because infants will start to vary their actions and anticipate events. For example, an infant during this stage may learn to open her mouth differently depending on whether she is being breast fed or offered a pacifier. Also, an infant may learn that he can put his thumb in his mouth.

Substage 3 According to Piaget, the infant develops an environmental focus during Substage 3. To describe the Secondary Circular Reactions that Piaget proposed to be the main feature of Substage 4, we show a short video (running time, 3:18) detailing work by Dr Carolyn Rovee-Collier with three-month-old infants.

Many adults underestimate the cognitive abilities of infants. As your students will already appreciate, infants have reflexes and perceptual preferences soon after birth. Additionally, experiments with three-month-olds have revealed that infants have a surprisingly complex mind already at work—well before they can speak. In a video detailing Rovee-Collier's research, an infant is placed in a crib with a mobile hanging overhead (Patterson, 2000). The infant's foot is attached to a ribbon but the ribbon is not attached to the mobile. A research assistant counts the infant's kicks to determine a baseline rate of kicking. Next, the researcher connects the ribbon on the infant's foot to the mobile. Three-month-olds cannot crawl or walk but they have enough gross motor skill to control the only leg that makes the mobile work. As a result, the child can control the mobile and can see and hear the consequences of her actions on the environment. Rovee-Collier reports that the infant's rate of kicking tends to double during the test condition, the implication being that the infant can learn to repeat activities that please her.

As we have previously noted, one of our goals for teaching lifespan development is to socialize our students to the process of becoming a psychologist. Therefore, one aspect that we often discuss is the experience of being an undergraduate research assistant (RA). The Rovee-Collier video depicts an undergraduate RA accompanying her to an infant's home. We take this opportunity to see if any students in the class have had the experience of going to a subject's home to collect data. We enjoy talking about this topic because most students in the class do not have the experience of going out "into the field" to collect data. We believe that they should know about the data collection process in psychological science. Additionally, we would like our students to know early in the semester that there are opportunities to work as RAs in different research labs in our psychology department.

Substage 4 To describe this substage, we provide examples of how infants display the goal-directed behavior that is the hallmark of Substage 4. Because object permanence is such a well-known Piagetian construct, we tend to spend some time describing this aspect of sensorimotor functioning. According to Piaget, infants do not fully develop object permanence (the understanding that objects in the world continue to exist, even when they are out of the infant's sight) until after six months of age. First, we explain how the infant coordinates behavior (e.g., gross and fine motor functioning) to execute goal-directed behavior (e.g., pulling a blanket away to reveal a desired toy; reaching for the toy and grasping it). Next, we show a picture that depicts an infant before an understanding of object permanence and after understanding object permanence. We also demonstrate the Bayley item that is used by developmental and clinical psychologists to assess whether an infant has achieved object permanence. The object permanence item involves two coffee cups and a toy rabbit. During the initial administration of the item, the evaluator hides the toy rabbit under a coffee cup in plain view of the infant. If the infant searches for the toy rabbit under the coffee cup, she receives credit for the item—and demonstrates evidence for understanding that the toy rabbit still exists even if it is blocked from sight.

Our final exercise on object permanence is to show the class a video that highlights Renee Baillargeon's research (1994; 1995), which supports the notion that infants may actually develop the concept of object permanence much earlier than Piaget's initial estimate of eight months. We show our students a video entitled *Baillargeon* in order to provide them with a more modern approach to studying object permanence (Patterson, 2000). In the video, Dr. Baillargeon explains how she devised the research design for her experiment on infants' understanding of objects. Based on Piaget's work on object permanence, Baillargeon thought that infants would perform better if they were asked to look at things, rather than search for things. She used the infant learning paradigm of habituation to test her theory. To find out if infants see objects in the way that adults do, Baillargeon developed two different video clips for infants to watch, an "impossible" or "magical" event and a "possible" or "real" event. The impossible or magical event violates a belief that adults have about object permanence. Baillargeon hypothesized that if infants share the same beliefs as adults regarding object permanence, they would find the impossible or magical event surprising. However, Piaget's theory would predict that infants would exhibit no surprise at the impossible video clip, because they do not yet understand object permanence.

Ultimately, Baillargeon found that five and a half, four and a half and many three and a half month old babies looked significantly longer at the impossible event than at the possible event. Baillargeon's research with a computerized visual task found evidence that object permanence seems to be present much earlier than described by Piaget (i.e., at three months of age rather than eight months). At the conclusion of the video we explain that although Piaget was a very influential thinker and theorist, certain aspects of his theory underestimated the abilities of infants and young children. We also like this video because it illustrates that psychology is a constantly evolving science.

Substage 5 and Substage 6 We simply provide lecture and some brief examples for these substages.

If we had more time in the semester, we would cover infant memory and cognitive processing theories in more depth. However, because our course covers the entire life span, we have to make some difficult choices about what to include in our lectures. If you have expertise in these areas, or access to an excellent video or a guest speaker with expertise in these areas, you might choose to cover this information rather than some of the areas that we have detailed in this chapter.

Infant language development

There is a great deal of research on the area of infant language development and the material related to language development can be a lot of fun to teach. Early education majors and communication disorder majors often express interest in language development. In particular, communication disorders majors may have knowledge and information related to language development that they would like to share with their fellow students.

Comprehension proceeds production Language development is one area that many of your undergraduate students currently have in common with infants. Using the example of learning a new language will help to highlight the similarity between many undergraduate students and infants. Most students who have taken a new language can relate to the notion of comprehension before production. If these students were to watch a foreign film in class, they would understand more of the dialog than they would be able to produce if they we were suddenly thrust into the role of actor.

In our course we try to cover information related to babbling, cooing, first words, telegraphic speech, infant-directed speech, under-extension of language, and overextension of language, and language milestones. We also discuss the learning theory approach to language development, the nativist approach, Noam Chomsky's language acquisition device, and the interactionist theory of language development.

To help describe babbling, cooing and first words, we describe how research in this area is conducted. One of us (EBK) has the experience of working as a research assistant for a developmental psychologist who studied language development. As part of our research duties, we coded videos of young infants' early language attempts. Our job was to classify infant utterances as one of four levels of babbling (e.g., vowel sounds only, consonant sounds only, a mixture of vowel and consonant sounds, or an actual word). Our aim in describing our experience to students is to relate how detail-oriented language development researchers must be in their work.

To help illustrate infant-directed speech for our students, we try to point out the unique way that adults speak to infants, children, and pets. Most students know what you mean by infant-directed speech once you describe it, but it can be helpful (and probably entertaining for the students) to hear you demonstrate the construct. Occasionally, there are TV commercials that depict adults using infant-directed language with their children. You could bring a clip of the commercial to class, but if the commercial is played frequently on TV, many students will know the example that you are talking about if you merely describe it.

To help illustrate the learning theory approach to language development, you could remind your class of the operant conditioning exercise that was used earlier to describe infant learning. Alternatively, you could wait until this section on infant language development to use the exercise. One of the more salient methods of illustrating the support for learning theory and language development is to focus on regional accents and how this type of language is likely reinforced by individuals in the environment who speak with a regional accent. As an example, we ask our students if they can think of any words (or pronunciation of words) that may vary as a function of a speaker's region of the country. Students generally have no problem generating good examples for this exercise.

Infant language development is another section that we are not able to cover in nearly the amount of detail that we would like. Generally, we only have time to cover a few concepts and the main theories of language development. However, you might choose to cover this information in greater detail.

Infant Social Development

Ideally, someone in your class will have an infant or you will know parents of a new infant who would be willing to bring their child into the classroom for "show and tell." We typically give extra credit "participation" points to students who volunteer to bring their infants to class. Undergraduates fresh from high school enjoy asking questions about life as a parent and new parents enjoy the opportunity to talk about their experiences. If you are not able to bring an infant to your classroom, you could show a video related to the social development of infants such as *Social Development in Infancy* by Films for the Humanities & Sciences (2005).

We consider the following concepts to be important for developmental psychology students to know regarding infant social development concepts: attachment, separation anxiety, stranger anxiety, social referencing, social smile, and self awareness. In our sequence of teaching infant development, social development is taught last. Occasionally, we do not have as much time to cover infant social development as previous sections due to unforeseen classroom delays. If this unfortunate but common teaching event occurs, we focus on attachment, separation anxiety, and stranger anxiety during our lecture.

Attachment

Have your students ever had the experience of taking care of an infant who will not warm up to them? The responsibility of caring for a baby who is inconsolable because his or her parent is out for the evening can be a daunting experience. On the other hand, it is a positive sign that the baby has a strong attachment to his or her parent. The complex construct of attachment can be a fascinating aspect of infant social development to study—especially given the importance of close human relationships across the lifespan.

Questions regarding attachment have arisen in our own clinical work with children in the foster care system. We often incorporate anecdotes about clinical concerns related to attachment throughout our lectures on infant social development (e.g., the attachment implications for parents who lose custody of their infant children; the disrupted pattern of interpersonal relationships that can occur following a poor parent-child attachment). We have found that providing background information about Harlow's (1959; 1962) surrogate mother research with rhesus monkeys is an excellent place to start our discussion on infant attachment.

The Harry Harlow attachment video (running time, 2:54) presents Harry Harlow's research with rhesus monkeys (Patterson, 2000). Harlow removed newborn rhesus monkeys from their mothers at birth and reared them in an isolated laboratory setting. The newborn monkeys received no physical contact or interactions with other monkeys and very limited contact with humans. Harlow hypothesized that either food or security would become more important for the developing monkeys' attachment. Harlow's observational research revealed that the monkeys would only go to the wire mother for food when he or she was hungry. Alternatively, the monkeys would go to the cloth mother for all comfort needs. In all, the infant monkeys in the study spent 22 hours every day with the cloth mother.

The video we use is quite old but students still respond to the images and sounds of the juvenile rhesus monkeys. We show the video depiction of Harlow's research because it can serve as a springboard for discussion on ethics in developmental research (e.g., could this study be conducted with human children?) as well as the importance of early environment on social development. Harlow's research works well as an introduction to Ainsworth's strange situation research (Ainsworth, 1979; Ainsworth, Blehar, Waters, & Wall, 1978). Also, the monkeys in the video are very cute and sometimes students will ask questions related to the ethical treatment of animals in research after we watch the video.

We spend a good bit of time on Ainsworth's theory of attachment. First, we distribute to the class a handout with the different steps of the strange situation task (Ainsworth, 1979) and then we watch a video depicting the task. We attempt to highlight that researchers look for the balance that the child strikes between an attachment need for his or her parent and the desire to explore the toys in the playroom. The Ainsworth strange situation lecture material also allows us to describe separation anxiety, stranger anxiety, and social referencing. We find that it helps to have a video that depicts all of these constructs so you can refer back to it to illustrate terms as you introduce them to the class.

In addition to the more traditional constructs of social smile, social referencing, and self awareness, you may want to discuss the emerging field of infant emotional development with your class. For example, recent studies on infant empathy (Karrass & Braungart-Rieker, 2004; Leerkes & Crockenberg, 2003; Spinrad & Stifter, 2006) and infant recognition of emotion in others (Montague & Walker-Andrews, 2001) could be of interest to your students.

Temperament

We cover temperament in our course because of its importance for personality and, possibly, certain types of psychopathology. Thus, we describe the classic Thomas and Chess descriptions of Easy, Difficult, and Slow to Warm Up infants (Thomas, Chess, & Birch,

1968). After providing definitions for each of these temperament styles we discuss the importance of *Goodness of Fit* for infants and their parents. We often talk about children with difficult temperaments who later develop school or home behavior problems because these are the children who we see clinically in our work with disruptive behavior disorders. To give your students a look into how different temperaments may look in infancy, a video on infant temperament style can be useful.

For example, the temperament video (running time, 5:16) highlight's Dr. Jerome Kagan's studies on temperamental categories (Patterson, 2000). According to the video, Kagan has been able to predict two temperament styles from a very simple behavioral observation task conducted when children are only four months old. During this behavioral observation, a researcher swings a mobile of toys in front of a four-month-old's face as he sits in a baby seat. Kagan has found that certain reactions in four-month-olds predict future shyness or sociability. A four-month-old who reacts with extreme distress in response to the visual display represents the kind of child that Kagan predicts will later become a shy, timid, and restrained one or two-year-old. The video also shows Dr. Nathan Fox's research on the relation of different brain patterns and temperament. Dr. Fox uses EEG methodology to measure neural activity while the infant is exposed to a stimulating toy. Dr. Fox has found that very shy infants show greater activity in one hemisphere while very outgoing infants show greater activity in the other hemisphere. In average children, both sides of the brain show the same, balanced pattern of electrical activity, suggesting an underlying chemistry and physiology to temperament.

Critical Thinking Opportunities

In discussing infant development with your students, there are many activities that provide critical thinking opportunities. We like to provide as many opportunities as appropriate and available to expose our students to the empirical literature related to classroom topics. We suggested evaluating research studies with your students in previous chapters, and in this chapter we continue to identify additional topics that prove useful for critical thinking opportunities as it relates to infant development. Potential topic ideas for evaluating research studies include:

- Studies related to the sensitive periods for brain development (e.g., Grossman et al., 2003; Stanwood, Washington, & Levitt, 2001).
- Studies related to visual (e.g., Freeseman, Colombo, & Coldren, 1993; Johnson, 2001), motor (e.g., Dewey, Cohen, Brown, & Rivera, 2001), cognitive (e.g., Galler, Harrison, Ramsey, Forde, & Butler, 2000), and/or language development among infants (e.g., Goodwyn, Acredolo, & Brown, 2000).
- Studies related to how researchers study infant memory if the infant is not able to communicate with words (e.g., Rovee-Collier, 1993; Rovee-Collier, & Fagen, 1981; Saffran, Loman, & Robertson, 2000).

Additional topic ideas that we have used to encourage our students to think critically about the material relate to infant development, and how it is associated to the world outside the classroom. For example:

- What experiences influence early language development?
- What things do people need to know about infant development before parenthood?
- How should a daycare center be designed to enhance infant's motor, cognitive, and sensory development?
- In what ways do toys for infants enhance sensory development?
- How can hospital and day care professionals help infants and toddlers deal with separation anxiety?
- How can parents promote attachment with their infants?

Controversial Topics

Infant development is a "hot topic" in society, particularly with respect to what can enhance or deter optimal development (Zeanah, Boris, & Larrieu, 1997). With individuals from all walks of life weighing in on what to or what not to do with regard to infant development, there are a multitude of controversial topics. Some controversial questions that we have raised with our students include:

- Should you be required to get a license to parent?
- Why are there differences in the infant birth and death rates around the world?
- What are the pros and cons of the "family bed"?

- What is the best way to sooth a crying infant?
- What are the pros and cons of infant daycare?
- Are there really critical periods in human development?
- Do infants have the innate ability to make symbolic representations of objects? If so, how does that help them later in life?
- How has parenting changed over the years and what has influenced these changes?
- What are the pros and cons of breastfeeding?
- Can fathers provide the same quality of care that mothers provide?

Developmental Diversity

Opportunities for discussing developmental diversity related to infant development are extensive. We especially enjoy discussing diversity-related infant development topics that expose our students to variations in parenting, attachment, and infants' acquisition of skills. Specific topics that we have discussed with our students include:

- How do attachment styles differ across cultures?
- What are the effects of poverty and malnutrition on specific areas of infant development (e.g., physical, cognitive, and emotional)?
- Are there cultural differences in the acquisition of particular skills?
  - Which skills are acquired at what time and how is that different across different cultures?
  - Are some skills not acquired at all?
  - What factors influence skill acquisition?
- How are developmental delays/disorders defined, measured, and treated?
  - Which developmental disorders are pervasive throughout life?
  - What treatments exist for developmental disorders?
- In what ways do parenting roles differ across cultures?

In many ways, your lectures on infant development may be the most difficult to prepare. Many of your students will lack direct experience with infants and childrearing may not be a part of their immediate life plans. Another challenge related to any lecture on infancy is the great deal of research available for consumption—there is even an entire journal called *Infancy*! Regardless of the challenges, your lecture on the infant development period will set the stage for the rest of your semester—and it just might improve parenting outcomes for the future parents in your class.

Helpful Resources for Teaching Infant Development

American Academy of Pediatrics: www.aap.org.
The Children, Youth, and Families Education Research Network: www.cyfernet.mes.umn.edu.
National Institute of Child Health and Human Development: www.nichd.nih.gov
Babyworld: www.babyworld.com.
Children's Nutrition Research Center: www.bcm.tmc.edu/cnrc.
Zero to Three: National Center for Infants, Toddlers, and Families www.zerotothree.org.
Rutgers Infant Development: www./babylab.rutgers.edu/.

Appendix B

Infant Behavioral State Coding Sheet

Code	Time 1	Time 2	Time 3	Time 4	Time 5	Time 6	Time 7	Time 8	Time 9	Time 10
Indicate the state:										
Alert										
Fussing										
Crying										
Count the number of occurrences:										
Vocalizing (#)										
Indicate motor behavior:										
Grasping										
Leg Movement										

Alert = attentive or scanning the environment. Eyes are open.
Fussing = continuous or intermittent low level cry.
Crying = intense vocalizations occurring singly or continuously.
Vocalizing = cooing, babbling, or making a non-crying noise for attention. (Must have 2 seconds between each vocalization to count as two vocalizations.)
Grasping = attempting to hold/pick up an object.
Leg Movement = vigorously moving/kicking legs.

Chapter 5

Early Childhood Development

Deciding which concepts to cover for the early childhood development period can be challenging because there are quite a few aspects of this topic that could be informative and interesting to students. In order to make our content-related decisions, we tend to think about the needs of the undergraduate students who take our course (e.g., Why are they taking our course? What is it that they need to know about early childhood?) Because this course is intended to meet the developmental psychology requirement for our students, we focus on aspects related to abnormal child psychology, child health, and the academic aspects of early child development. We adopt this strategy because many of our students will need to understand early child cognitive and social development for their careers in psychology, the healthcare field, or education.

Similar to the infant period, there are several high quality videos and resources to use during your coverage of the early childhood development stage. Students seem to relate well to children in the two to six-year-old age range, probably because they either remember going through this developmental stage themselves, because they have younger siblings in this stage, or they have experience working with young children through babysitting or other types of employment. Children in the early childhood age range can be very entertaining to watch and students seem to enjoy watching videos or conducting live observations of them.

Early Childhood Physical and Cognitive Development

During our lecture on early childhood physical and cognitive development, we generally cover Piaget's preoperational stage and Vygotsky's theory of cognitive development. In addition to providing a brief biography of both theorists, we also discuss the trajectory of their careers and the legacy of their theories. Given the number of elementary education majors who take our course, we also compare and contrast Piaget and Vygotsky in terms of the impact their theories have had on the field of early education.

Piaget's preoperational stage

Piaget's theory of cognitive development is a helpful way to conceptualize the preschool and school-age child period. We begin each lecture on the early childhood period by showing our students a slide listing all of Piaget's stages of cognitive development. We show students the same slide that we used at the beginning of our lecture on the sensorimotor stage (infant period) because it lists all the stages and it provides a context for the trajectory of early childhood cognitive development. The following terms are important for a discussion of Piaget's preoperational stage: symbolic function, egocentrism, animistic thinking, conservation, centration, irreversibility, and transductive reasoning. During our lecture on the preoperational stage, we define all of the key concepts and provide examples of the concepts for our students.

Tasks of conservation demonstration If our students remember nothing else about Piaget, we hope that they will remember Piaget's conceptualization of the tasks of conservation. Piaget was interested in children's limitations in thinking at various ages. As such, we recommend that you invite young children to your classroom to help demonstrate Piaget's tasks of conservation. To help demonstrate how young children are limited in their thinking, we ask for student volunteers to bring small children (preferably between the ages of three and eight years) to class so that we can practice the tasks of conservation in front of our students. A live demonstration can be very engaging for undergraduates and nothing illustrates Piaget's theory better than an actual child demonstrating centration. The

Early Childhood Development 119

following are a few tips that we recommend based on our experience with having small children as "guest speakers":

- At the beginning of every semester we ask for student volunteers who are willing to bring children to class. A few extra credit points are usually an adequate incentive for students to bring children to class. Occasionally students bring their younger sibling or their own children; however, students typically bring children they babysit or nieces and nephews to class. Sometimes the parents of these children come to class, but usually the undergraduate will just attend class with a small child in tow. If parents attend class, we try to incorporate them in the experience by asking them questions about being a parent.
- Try to have children of varying ages. If you have several children in class you will have a better chance of finding a child in the preoperational stage for the conservation of liquid task.
- Plan on asking several students to bring children to class. There are usually last minute cancellations when young children are involved. If you invite more than one child you won't be left empty handed if one of them is unable to attend your class. We have had as many as six children in class but this number of children can be somewhat chaotic, especially if you don't have a GTA to occupy the children. Two to three children are ideal for the tasks of conservation exercise.
- Children under the age of three are rarely able to participate in a way that will engage the class. By inviting older children you increase the chances of having a concrete operational stage child in your demonstration as well.
- Make sure that you have something for children to do if you are going to lecture for the first part of the class period. It is helpful to bring age appropriate (quiet!) toys like markers and paper—just be sure to bring enough materials for all of the children. We usually ask the children to draw a picture for the class during the lecture portion of class. Later, we show their pictures to students to highlight the variation in fine motor skills between children.
- There are a few basic supplies that you will need to demonstrate Piaget's tasks of conservation. It helps to have a table at the front of the classroom with chairs for the child, the caregiver, and the instructor. For the conservation of liquid activity, you will need two containers of equal size, two containers of unequal size (one tall and thin, the other low and wide), water colored with food

coloring, and plenty of napkins. For the conservation of number task, you should bring eight wrapped candies or pennies for the children to count. For the conservation of area task, we use eight rectangular and laminated pieces of colored paper. During the demonstration, we usually explain that the concept of conservation is a developmental progression, such that conservation of liquid occurs before most children understand conservation of area, weight, and volume.

- If you have a child available for the entire class period, you could use the time to demonstrate aspects of early child development consistent with Piaget's tasks of conservation (e.g., liquid, number, mass, etc.). In addition to demonstrating Piaget's tasks of conservation, we also demonstrate aspects from Vygotsky's theory of cognitive development (e.g., level of independent performance, level of assisted performance). To highlight physical development, we ask the children to show us what they can do in terms of fine motor (e.g., the itsy bitsy spider) and gross motor skills (e.g., jumping jacks, skipping). Additionally, we ask the children questions to demonstrate their social development (e.g., how many friends they have, what activities they do with their friends, etc.). During subsequent lectures, we often refer to our class guests and use them as examples for concepts that we cover in the early childhood stage.
- Another reason to invite more than one child to your class is that some children refuse to talk once they see a large group of undergraduates. Some children have stage presence and other children are shy. Obviously, it is easier to conduct the tasks of conservation with a child who likes to be the center of attention. If the child is hesitant to speak in front of the class, we start by asking the child to show his or her picture to our students as an ice breaker. We also ask the child's caregiver to sit at the table with the child in an effort to ease any anxiety (on the caregiver's or on the child's part). Some children who are uncomfortable talking in class are more willing to demonstrate their gross motor skills to the class. For a shy child, it can help to have his or her caregiver demonstrate the skill with the child.
- There are some important safety considerations when including a small child in your lectures. Be sure to monitor the child to make sure that he or she is safe during the demonstration. This point may seem like a common sense consideration, but small children can move quickly and they do not have the same sense of danger

that adults have. If you have a small child on a stage, be sure that he or she does not get too close to its edge. If the child is sitting on an adult-sized chair, make sure that he or she is sitting properly on the chair (i.e., don't let the child stand on the chair).
- We recommend timing your lecture so that class ends with the child's "guest lecture." It is very hard to follow a class demonstration involving small children with lecture from a less entertaining instructor!
- It is always wise to have a video backup. We use a video depicting Piaget's tasks of conservation when no students volunteer to bring children to class, when children do not show for class, or when we have a very shy child guest. Occasionally, children will demonstrate an inconclusive mastery of the tasks of conservation.
- We generally use a Piaget video clip from the McGraw-Hill's *Multimedia Courseware for Child Development* (Patterson, 2000). Other video options include an interview with Jean Piaget (*Video Classics in Psychology*, 2002), Prentice-Hall's *The Story of Human Development* (Poole, Warren, & Nunez, 2007), or *Piaget's Developmental Theory: An Overview* (Davidson Films, 1989).
- If you expect students to conduct their own mini-experiment of a developmental phenomenon as a course requirement, you may want to encourage your students to conduct the tasks of conservation with a few small children. To this end, you could remind your students as you interview the child guest that they might want to replicate the in-class demonstration for a class assignment.
- Finally, be a good host. We typically ask all the students in the class to sign a group thank you note for the children who visit our classroom. Guest lecturers of all ages like reading the nice things that our students write on these notes (we use a colored piece of printer paper with a few stickers). In fact, parents have told us that they put the thank you notes on their child's bedroom wall or in a scrapbook for the child to remember their "first day of college."

If there is no way to bring children to class and you can't show a video because of a lack of equipment or audio-visual equipment malfunction, you could have two students (or you and your GTA) play the role of an interviewer and a child in the preoperational stage. A skit with young adults acting like children is not as effective as having an actual child in the classroom but it can effectively break up lecture and it becomes a memorable exercise. In Appendix E, you will find a script that we have used during our in-class demonstrations with students.

Vygotsky's theory of cognitive development

Vygotsky (1962) was interested in how the social environment helps to foster learning. In order to highlight Vygotsky's approach in his theory of cognitive development, the following terms are important to include in your lecture: private speech, zone of proximal development, level of independent performance, level of assisted performance, scaffolding, and cultural tools. If you have time during your lecture on Vygotsky, you may want to show your students the following videos: *Vygotsky's Developmental Theory: An Introduction* (Davidson Films, 1994) or *Play: A Vygotskian Approach* (Davidson Films, 1996). Both videos are quite lengthy so we only show an excerpt or describe part of the video to students.

To start our discussion of Vygotsky's theory, we typically note the different views held by Piaget and Vygotsky towards self talk and private speech. It is easy to use the social stigma related to talking out loud—and some individuals' penchant to talk aloud to themselves—as an example of differing views towards self talk. Private speech can actually be adaptive in structuring our thoughts during difficult tasks, and it is a skill that play therapists often use when working with young children (Carmichael, 2006; Hembree-Kigin & McNeil, 1995). To help demonstrate the value of private speech and play, we describe the skills that we use clinically with parents to help children develop their thinking about play. In our clinical experience, hyperactive and disruptive children become calmer during play when an adult describes the child's play. During a play interaction in which the parent provides a running commentary of the child's activities, the parent provides scaffolding for the child by providing verbal structure to the play interaction. Simultaneously, the child is able to develop a richer sense of things to say during his or her own private speech.

Demonstration of Vygotsky's zone of proximal development If you invite a child guest to your classroom, you may want to have his or her caregiver help him or her with an activity that is slightly beyond the child's ability. This activity can provide a memorable demonstration of the level of independent performance and the level of assisted performance. We have found that asking an adult to provide scaffolding (via helping a child to count objects) can serve as a good demonstration for students regarding the difference between the child's level of independent performance and level of assisted performance. We generally put the objects to be counted on a document camera so that the entire class can see the objects that the child is attempting to count. If you don't have a document camera, having the child sit at a table in front of the class (i.e., the old fashioned way) works, too.

If you are unable to bring a child to your classroom, you can describe situations in which the independent and assisted performance of children can be evaluated. For example, many special education services make use of the level of independent and assisted performance. If a child is learning to read, the reading specialist will help the child by covering part of the word and asking the child to sound out the beginning part of the word, the middle part of the word, and the end of the word. Then the teacher will ask the child to put the sounds together.

All of the scaffolding (i.e., help) that occurs within the context of reading remediation is in direct contrast to the testing methods used to determine if a child needs, or qualifies for, special services in school. The commonly administered intelligence tests and tests of academic achievement are all administered on a one-on-one basis. The psychometricians and licensed psychologists who administer the tests are trained to be unbiased in their administration of the tests—so much so that the evaluator never assists a child who is taking the test. Thus, any testing conducted to evaluate learning disabilities only measures the child's level of independent performance. Occasionally, an evaluator will break from protocol if a child clearly does not know the answer to a question. The evaluator may "test the limits" by providing the child with queries to see if the child may have a shallow understanding of the item being tested. In Vygotskian terms, "testing the limits" provides a measure of the child's level of assisted performance on the particular item.

Generally, college-level exams test a student's level of independent performance. However, one might argue that students who ask for help on an item during an exam are actually turning in their level of assisted performance for that particular exam item. One day when lecturing about the difference between independent performance and assisted performance, we mentioned that well-known psychologist Dr Philip Zimbardo often allows his general psychology students to take exams in pairs (Zimbardo, 1997). Our industrious students immediately asked if they could do the same and, thus, was born our Vygotskian tradition of allowing students to take Exam 2 in pairs. This unconventional testing procedure provides an opportunity for students to test Vygotsky's theory that the scaffolding provided by a partner will result in an improved exam score. It is fun to make predictions before the exam and look to see if the mean scores of the two groups are different. There are, however, several considerations to keep in mind when allowing your students the opportunity to take an exam with a partner:

- We give the option to our students about whether they want to take the exam in pairs. However, all students receive the same exam regardless of whether they take the exam in pairs or individually.
- The exercise works best if you can have two rooms scheduled for the exam. One room can be for students taking the exam with a partner, the other room is for students who prefer to take the exam individually.
- Multiple-choice, matching, and "fill in the blank" exams seem to work best for exams administered to pairs of students.
- We give each student his or her own exam and allow them the opportunity to turn in his or her own answers. This procedure accommodates situations in which the partners disagree about the correct answer for an item.
- We allow students to pick their partner. However, we assign partners if a particular student would like to take the exam with a partner but does not know anyone in the class.
- If a student's partner does not show up for the exam, the student who shows up to take the exam should take it individually—unless an alternate partner is available. Generally, we don't allow groups of three because it leads to more animated discussions which can be distracting for other students.
- All talking should be quiet and only involve the student's partner.
- No assistance is given to students from the instructor or GTA for either group on the exam.

There are some semesters when it might not make sense to allow your students to take an exam with a partner. For example, if you do not have anyone to help proctor the exam, the extra work associated with the exercise may not be worthwhile. Additionally, if you have a critical mass of "problem students" (i.e., contentious students, overly talkative students) the exercise may be more of a hassle than the educational experience that it is meant to be. Having said that, taking an exam in pairs can be a very entertaining exercise for the students (and the instructor—it is a strange experience to have your students talking openly during an exam period). Most students report to us afterwards that they enjoy the experience of taking an exam with a partner. Some have even reported that they learned a great deal during the administration of the test by talking about the concepts with their partner. The downside to the exercise is that some students may perform more poorly on the exam, especially if their partner's level of independent performance was weak on the previous exam!

If you have time to compare Piaget and Vgotsky in class, one helpful resource is a short video clip by Patterson (2000) entitled *Piaget Versus Vygotsky* (running time, 1:27). In this video, developmental psychologist Patricia Greenfield explains the difference between developmentalists Piaget and Vygotsky. According to Greenfield, Piaget viewed the child as an independent learner but Vygotsky viewed the child as a dependent learner, with the child moving to independence during a later developmental stage. Although one might wonder which theory of cognitive development is correct, Greenfield argues that both theories are correct. She further explains that the type of early childhood learning that takes place in a particular situation is a question of the culture and the nature of the task. For example, Piagetian learning occurs in situations in which errors are not life threatening (e.g., imaginative play or a child learning to swing on a swing set). Caregivers allow plenty of trial and error and discovery in these situations because there are generally no life-threatening results of this type of learning. Alternatively, Vygotskian scaffolding is more likely to occur in situations in which life-threatening errors are possible (e.g., a child crossing a busy street). According to Greenfield, young children need to internalize the rules of crossing a busy street before caregivers allow them to perform the activity by themselves. Vygotsky's theory is more accurate for the learning process that adults and children engage in during potentially dangerous situations.

Early Childhood Social and Personality Development

The aspects of infant temperament and attachment that help to shape young child's social and personality development continue to evolve during the early childhood stage of development. There are a variety of early childhood social development concepts that could be useful to cover in your lecture. For example, play style (e.g., cooperative and functional play), sense of self, Baumrind's (1966, 1996) parenting styles (e.g., authoritarian, authoritative, and permissive), and child abuse prevention are all informative areas of early childhood development to cover. As with previous chapters, we suggest more topics than you will be able to cover in your lifespan development class. If we are limited in time and ability to focus on all of the concepts we feel are important for students to learn, we focus on child maltreatment and/or parenting.

Through our teaching, we encourage students to be active citizens in the world. To this end, we attempt to give them tools, based on the course material, to analyze the world around them critically. During our lectures on early childhood development, we highlight our research interests in parenting, child abuse prevention, and parenting interventions. We also use examples from our clinical work to highlight concepts that are especially relevant to life outside the classroom, such as child maltreatment and the influences of parenting practices on children's development.

Parenting

Parenting is a major life event in which most individuals in the world participate (Dion, 1985), including many of your students. Even if you have students who decide not to be parents in the future, we have all experienced parenting in one form or another. During our lecture about parenting, we expose our students, even if briefly, to the extensive research on parenting. We discuss how parenting research provides interested parties with information regarding practices that are beneficial and practices that could be deleterious to children. We discuss with our students the areas in which parenting researchers are interested, such as which aspects of parenting increase children's problem behavior as well as those practices that are likely to reduce problem behaviors (Thompson, Raynor, Cornah, Stevenson, & Sonuga-Barke, 2002). We also discuss how parenting under stressful conditions can be particularly difficult and, at times, result in child abuse (Medora, Wilson, & Larson, 2001). To end on a positive note, we also discuss the prevention of child abuse by identifying parenting attitudes and behaviors that predict future risk of abuse (Medora et al., 2001).

Darling and Steinberg (1993) defined parenting practices as "specific, goal-directed behaviors through which parents perform their parental duties" (p. 488). Because parenting practices have been repeatedly linked with disruptive child behavior problems, we identify the dimensions of parenting practices (e.g., monitoring, supervision and parent involvement) that have emerged as the most substantial and consistent influences on child behavior (Shelton, Frick, & Wootton, 1996). The most concise way to describe parenting attitudes, parenting practices, and corresponding discipline strategies is to highlight Baumrind's classification for parenting.

Parenting styles and discipline practices According to Baumrind's (1966) observational research, there are three styles of parenting that vary according to beliefs and practices of parental control: authoritarian, authoritative, and permissive. To begin our discussion of the parenting styles, we ask our students to think about the way that they were parented as children and adolescents as we describe Baumrind's three parenting styles. After we define the parenting styles, we try to guide the students in a recollection of the discipline strategies and parenting engaged in by their parents and other caregivers they encountered during their youth. Another way to illustrate the parenting styles is to ask the class to identify movie or television "parents" who seem to fit the different styles. For example, many father characters with a military background are depicted as authoritarian (the military dad in *American Beauty*). The parents on the 1980s comedy sitcom *Cosby Show* (with re-runs on *Nick at Nite*) are good examples of authoritative parents. Permissive parents place too few limits on their children, such as the parents on MTV's *My Super Sweet Sixteen* show.

We identify authoritarian parents as those individuals who "attempt to shape, control, and evaluate the behavior and attitudes of the child in accordance with a set standard of conduct, usually an absolute standard" (Baumrind, 1966, p. 890). You could ask your students to generate examples of parents in television or the movies who seem to fit the authoritarian category. Most likely, the parents described by your students will correspond to research findings that authoritarian parents tend to discourage child autonomy and value child obedience. Additionally, the children raised in authoritarian homes tend not to argue with parents, but rather consider what the parent says and does as correct (Baumrind, 1966).

As a counterpoint to the authoritarian parenting style, we discuss how current viewpoints on the goal and direction of parenting in the US are generally inconsistent with authoritarian parenting practices (Baumrind, 1966, 1996; Darling & Steinberg, 1993, Hill, Bush, & Roosa, 2003). Specifically, we discuss how authoritarian parenting practices tend to be viewed as less effective than authoritative parenting practices in general (Darling & Steinberg, 1993). Authoritative parents attempt "to direct the child's activities in a rational, issue-oriented manner" (Baumrind, 1966, p. 891); they have a tendency to encourage a bidirectional discussion surrounding conflict, and share their reasoning behind making decisions. We explain that the authoritative parent appears to be open to hearing the concerns of their child when conformity is not achieved. The authoritative parent tends to value both "autonomous self-will and disciplined conformity" (Baumrind, 1966, p. 891), which they encourage through the affirmation of their child as well as limit setting and setting standards of expected behavior (Baumrind, 1966).

As we discuss authoritative parenting, we identify the discipline practices that are characteristic of the authoritative parenting style, which include the use of reasoning, power, and shaping through structure and reinforcement (Baumrind, 1966). We discuss how for authoritative parents, obedience is not sought for the sake of obedience, but the parent sets realistic and meaningful limits and standards based on reasons that they are willing and able to communicate to their child (Carter & Welch, 1981). We discuss the fact that the goal of authoritative parenting appears to be to teach children a balance between "pleasure and duty, and between freedom and responsibility" (Baumrind, 1966, p. 891). Additionally, we hope that our students understand that authoritative parenting practices have been demonstrated to be most effective in developing "an instrumental competence characterized by the balancing of societal and individual needs and responsibilities" in comparison to permissive and authoritarian practices (Darling & Steinberg, 1993, p. 487).

Permissive parents "attempt to behave in a non-punitive, acceptant, and affirmative manner toward the child's impulses, desires, and actions" (Baumrind, 1966, p. 889). We explain that according to Baumrind, these parents allow children to regulate themselves as much as possible and encourage the child's input in making decisions about rules. The discipline practices of Baumrind's permissive style are generally inconsistent in nature. We discuss how by definition, the permissive parent does not insist on a specific type of behavior from the child and tends to avoid having to be in control; the permissive parent tends to use "reason and manipulation, but not overt power" (Baumrind, 1966, p. 889), in order to get what they want. Most importantly, permissive parents tend not to follow through on requests if their methods of achieving what they want are unsuccessful.

Influence of discipline practices on children's behavior

Once we have identified and explained the different parenting styles and the discipline practices that tend to be associated with each style, we discuss the impact that particular discipline practices have on children's behavior. We use research studies to show links between punitive and inconsistent parenting practices and oppositional and aggressive behavior in children (Danforth, Barkley, & Stokes, 1991; Hart, Ladd, & Burleson, 1990; Kuczynski, Kochanska, Radke-Yarrow, & Girnius-Brown, 1987). We also discuss with our students how inconsistency has also been linked with child oppositional and aggressive behavior (Wahler & Dumas, 1986). Although some discipline practices are linked to poor child behavior, others are linked to better child outcomes. For example, warmth/involvement has been identified as an inverse predictor of oppositional behavior (Stormshak, Bierman, McMahon, Lengua, & Conduct Problems Prevention Research Group, 2000) and parenting strategies consistent with authoritative parenting, such as parental warmth, inductive discipline, non-punitive punishment practices, and consistency have been associated with positive child outcomes (Lamborn, Mounts, Steinberg, & Dornbusch, 1991).

Good supervisor/bad supervisor exercise

One way to highlight the importance of positive parenting skills is to conduct the good supervisor/bad supervisor exercise. Russell Barkley (1997) developed this exercise for clinical use with parents presenting for treatment of child disruptive behavior disorders or child maltreatment. Often parents who are referred for treatment from an outside entity (e.g., teachers, child protective services) are unwilling to accept their role in the parent-child dynamic that has developed in their home. Barkley uses the good supervisor/bad supervisor exercise as a way to address an individual's core beliefs about parenting without eliciting the defensiveness that many parents have about their parenting. The exercise is an excellent way to initiate an honest dialog about parenting with caregivers who prefer not to talk about their own parenting.

To conduct the good-supervisor/bad-supervisor exercise, start with a piece of paper that has a lengthwise line down the middle and the words "bad" and "good" written at the top of the paper on either side of the line. Tell your students that you are going to show them an exercise that is helpful when working with parents and that you are going to take a "step back" from your discussion on parenting styles. Next, ask your students to tell you about the worst boss that they ever had and write their responses on the paper. Students usually have no problems generating an extensive list for the qualities of their worst supervisor such as constantly nagging employees, blaming employees for problems around the store, or playing favorites. If your students have never had a bad supervisor, they can use their worst teacher as an example (hopefully not you). After the bad supervisor list has been generated, ask students to describe the qualities of their best supervisor. In the past, our students have given examples such as providing praise following a job well done, flexibility, and good communication. Once the list is generated, we tell students that parents are like supervisors for their children. When we work clinically with parents we ask them to complete the good-supervisor/bad-supervisor exercise (thinking of their employment history) and then we make a shift by asking parents to think about the type of "supervisor" that they are for their children. Parents are usually caught off guard by the exercise because it forces them to evaluate the type of supervisor/parent that they are to their children. Most parents will admit that they have qualities of both the good supervisor and the bad supervisor. When using this exercise clinically, it is our hope that parents will be motivated to develop more "good supervisor" qualities. To make it more applicable to your student's lives, you could ask them to think about what type of supervisor their parents were—or what type of supervisors they hope to be in the future. Another option would be to tie this exercise into your discussion of Baumrind's parenting styles by picking out the good supervisor and bad supervisor qualities associated with each parenting style.

We enjoy allowing students to discuss variations in parenting and discipline strategies as well as what may influence their parenting behavior in the future. It is interesting to hear the students' rationale for why they believe particular discipline strategies to be effective or not. We also like to have students combine their life experiences and information from the text to think critically about what it means to parent and what they think *they* would do as a parent. As instructors giving our students access to multiple discipline strategies and the evidence that supports the use of those strategies, or that identifies a particular strategy as harmful or ineffective, we allow them to become informed consumers and make informed decisions about their future parenting behavior.

Child maltreatment

Because we have training in the area of child maltreatment, we almost always include child maltreatment as a lecture topic for the early child developmental stage. All students are potential reporters of child abuse—and some of them might even become mandated reporters of child maltreatment as a function of their future profession (e.g., teachers, physicians, dentists, psychologists). Thus, understanding the characteristics, physical signs, and behavioral indicators of abuse can have important public safety implications.

One key aspect of this lecture is dispelling the myth that child sexual abuse comprises the majority of calls to investigative services. Although child sexual abuse currently comprises 12% of the actual substantiated cases of child maltreatment (US Department of Health & Human Services (US DHHS, 1996, 1998, 1999, 2000, 2001, 2003, 2004), most lay people would estimate that the percentage is much higher. (Anecdotally, the students in our last class on child abuse guessed that sexual abuse comprises 63% of all child maltreatment cases.) This overestimate is primarily due to the sensational nature of child sexual abuse and the large amount of media coverage that the issue has received in the last 15 years. Another key aspect of this lecture is to introduce students to the different types of child maltreatment (e.g., physical abuse, sexual abuse, neglect, and psychological maltreatment), the indicators of abuse (both physical and behavioral), and contributing factors that have been identified as risk factors for abuse (e.g., family characteristics, child characteristics, and parent attributions). Time permitting, we also discuss theories related to risk for abuse (e.g., cycle of violence hypothesis) as well as consequences and prevention of abuse.

Field trip to local Child Advocacy Center

We have had a wonderful opportunity to work closely with the Child Advocacy Center (CAC) that is near our university. The National Child Advocacy Center (NCAC) is "a non-profit organization that provides training, prevention, intervention and treatment services to fight child abuse and neglect" (www.nationalcac.org) that was established in 1985. It offers education, training, and professional services; prevention; intervention; and therapy. There are over 500 CACs in the United States and there is increasing international interest in the programs that the NCAC has to offer. Occasionally, we invite the forensic interviewer from our local CAC to speak to our students. This guest lecture allows students to hear first-hand about the process of investigating allegations of child sexual abuse. Most CACs are non-profit agencies with brochures, videos, and other promotional resources describing their resources to share with your students. Most students are unaware that such an organization exists and they ask the lecturer questions about the CAC for the reminder of the class period. We have found that bringing speakers or materials into the classroom from agencies in the community helps to link course material to "real world" settings. Indeed, we have been able to send student volunteers to the CAC. Most recently, the lecture on child maltreatment and the CAC helped to bring into focus a career path for one of our undergraduate students. This student is currently applying to Marriage and Family Therapy programs to help families dealing with child maltreatment and substance abuse issues.

Behavioral parent training

After discussing the effects of negative parenting (particularly child physical abuse) in detail with our students, we reassure them that there is ample research evidence to suggest that parents can learn effective ways to interact with their children (Arnold & O'Leary, 1997; Chaffin et al., 2004; Eisenstadt, Eyberg, McNeil, Newcomb, & Funderburk, 1993; Hood & Eyberg, 2003). Admittedly, this part of the course is one of our favorite sections to teach because it provides us with an opportunity to discuss how our clinical research is related to previous discussions on lifespan development. We discuss how, given the relationships between parenting practices and child behavior problems, many clinicians choose to focus on parenting practices in the course of treatment of child behavior problems. We tell our students that there are many effective parent-training interventions in existence that focus on teaching parents to use more consistent, moderate and firm discipline strategies (Brestan & Eyberg, 1998; Chambless & Ollendick, 2000; Forehand, Wells, & Griest, 1980; Webster-Stratton, Kolpacoff, & Hollinsworth, 1988).

One parent-training intervention that both of us use clinically is parent-child interaction therapy (PCIT). PCIT was developed by Sheila Eyberg, a professor at the University of Florida's Department of Clinical and Health Psychology, as a treatment for behaviorally disturbed preschool children and their families (Eyberg & Robinson, 1982). It uses a two-phase treatment approach, which uses operant conditioning within a behavior family therapy model. PCIT involves teaching parents behavioral management techniques within a play-therapy context and uses a combination of didactic, modeling, and interactive coaching techniques (Gallagher, 2003). Clinicians focus on parent-child relationships by increasing positive interactions between parents and children but the ultimate goal of therapy is to increase child compliance and teach parents sound discipline techniques. Because we use PCIT clinically, we often incorporate either a role play of some therapy techniques with students or we demonstrate PCIT techniques with our child visitors. Depending on your interest in the topic, you may choose to show a portion of a video that demonstrates the two phases of PCIT and the treatment goals associated with those phases (University of California at Davis, 2003). Our goals for providing information about PCIT during lecture is to introduce our students to the basic principles of PCIT and its structure, to demonstrate an example of applied developmental psychology, and demonstrate how Baumrind's parenting styles might translate into a therapy context.

Critical Thinking Opportunities

In discussing early childhood development with your students, there are a variety of activities that provide critical thinking opportunities. We like to provide as many opportunities as appropriate and/or available to expose our students to the empirical literature related to classroom topics. In previous chapters we have suggested evaluating research studies with your students. Providing a review of empirical research can be a useful critical thinking opportunity in the area of early childhood development as well. In this section we outline several possibilities for classroom demonstrations and activities for the early childhood development stage. These activities have been selected with an eye towards emphasizing active learning and critical thinking.

Potential topic ideas for evaluating research studies may be:

- Studies related to visual (e.g., Atkinson et al., 2001), motor (e.g., Rosenbaum et al., 2002), cognitive (e.g., Grantham-McGregor & Ani, 2001), and/or language development (e.g., Botting & Conti-Ramsden, 2001; Scarborough & Dobrich, 1990) among children.
- Studies related to gender identity in children (e.g., Bartlett, Vasey, & Bukowski, 2005; Taylor, 1996).
- Studies related to racial awareness in children (e.g., Hughes & Chen, 1997; Quintana, 1998).

Additional topic ideas that we have used to encourage our students to think critically about the material related to early childhood development, and how it is associated to the world outside the classroom, include:

- What factors help promote resilience during the early childhood stage of development?
- What do first friendships look like? What is the nature of first friendships?
- Describe typical play behavior of children.
- How is self-concept developed in children? How can we help children develop a positive self-concept?
- How can we increase prosocial behavior, while reducing aggression in children?
- How is gender socialized in children?
- Evaluate research studies using participants from the early childhood development stage. What do we gain by these studies and how are they flawed?
- Have students describe their opinions on optimal parent-child interactions before you lecture on early childhood development. After your lecture on this topic, ask students to review their answers and describe whether their understanding of parent-child interactions has changed.
- Have your class conduct a live or videotaped observation of preschool-aged children playing with their parents.

- *The Legacy of Piaget*. In this short, take home assignment developed by Goodwin (2002), students write a short essay on the following questions regarding early child cognitive development:
  - Does cognitive development proceed through stages, or is it a more gradual process?
  - What is the role of nature and nurture in Piaget's theory?
- Compare and contrast Piaget and Vygotsky in terms of their impact on education. Students could include the following aspects in their answer to the question "How would you structure a classroom using Piaget's or Vygotsky's theories?"
  - the role of the teacher
  - the role of peer collaboration
  - the structure of the classroom
  - emphasis on discovery learning vs. assisted discovery
  - sensitivity to children's readiness to learn
  - acceptance of individual differences

Controversial Topics

Becoming a parent and raising a child are responsibilities that most adults take very seriously. As a result, there are some aspects of parenting young children that have become the subject of much debate. In this section we highlight a few topics that may promote lively discussion during your coverage of early child development.

- What are the benefits and pitfalls to home schooling?
- Does providing children with frequent praise negatively impact their intrinsic motivation?
- Should children eat low sugar, low fat diets?
- What are the benefits and pitfalls of different discipline practices (e.g., spanking, timeout)?
- Is TV viewing related to violence/aggression in children?
- Should children only have toys that are specific to their gender? What are the possible consequences of a child playing with toys designed for the opposite gender?

Developmental Diversity

Opportunities for discussing developmental diversity related to early childhood development are far-reaching. We especially enjoy discussing diversity-related early childhood development topics that expose our students to variations in parenting, social behavior, and children's acquisition of skills. Specific topics that we have discussed with our students include:

- Do parenting styles differ across cultures?
  - Is there variation in parenting styles within cultures?
  - What factors affect parenting styles?
  - Should immigrants to the US change their parenting practices to adapt to their host culture? See Thirumurthy (2004) for a discussion on this issue.
- How do collectivist and individualist societies differ with regard to their expectations for early childhood?
  - How are a society's expectations expressed through their parenting behaviors?
- What is the definition of child abuse?
  - Are there differences in what is perceived as child abuse in different cultures?
- Do gender differences in aggression exist? If so, what would account for these differences?

Appendix A

Piaget Conservation Task Script

How old are you?

We're going to play a game. I'm going to pour some colored water into this measuring cup up to this line.
[Pour liquid into one measuring cup]

OK this is mine. Now I'm going to pour one for you. You watch and make sure that we have exactly the same amount of liquid.
[Pour liquid into the other measuring cup]

Are they the same? You make sure because we can add some if they're not.
[Let child determine if they are the same amount]

OK, so we have the same. This one is mine and that one is yours.

OK, I want you to pour yours into there and I'm going to pour mine in here.
[Let child pour her liquid into tall container while experimenter pours liquid in shallow container]

Where is your drink?

Where is mine?

Do we both have the same to drink or does one of us have more?

Why do I/you have more? *Or* Why are they the same?

If child says they are the same: But isn't there more in here since this one is taller?

Who would have more if I poured mine back into my measuring cup and you poured yours back into your measuring cup?

Chapter 6
Middle Childhood Development

Middle childhood is a time of tremendous developmental growth, particularly socially. During the early school years, peers become extremely influential as children spend more time away from parents. Because children have more independence, they start to make their own decisions when faced with morally ambiguous situations. School-aged children also begin to evaluate their abilities and self-worth. Many self-appraisals are based on their perceived physical traits, cognitive abilities, and social status. In our coverage of the middle childhood period, we focus on topics such as attention-deficit hyperactivity disorder (ADHD), intelligence testing, moral development, self-esteem, and the stages of friendship. We discuss these topics because we believe that they are relevant to the career paths of many students. These topics also happen to be the very issues about which many parents are concerned with regard to their own children.

Middle Childhood Physical and Cognitive Development

Good looks, athletic prowess, and academic success are highly valued attributes in our society. If you were to ask young adults about their hopes for the qualities of their future children, academic success would probably be near the top of the list. However, a variety of issues constrain academic ability (e.g., genetics, trauma to the brain, impoverished environment) and the difference between the "ideal child" and the "real child" can be a difficult issue for parents, teachers, and children to resolve. To highlight the difficulty faced by many families in the academic arena, we focus on the cognitive development of children in the middle childhood stage. We start by discussing attention-deficit hyperactivity disorder and then the process of intelligence testing.

Attention-deficit hyperactivity disorder (ADHD)

We start our first lecture on middle childhood development by asking our students to rate themselves on a checklist. We do not tell the students that the checklist is usually given to parents or that the items list the core symptoms of ADHD (see Appendix for a copy of the checklist). Rather, we simply ask students to rate themselves on a scale of 0 to 3 for the severity of each symptom. It is probably a testament to the widespread press received by ADHD that most of the students know which disorder the checklist refers to by the end of the exercise.

Occasionally, students will ask for the cut-off score on the checklist to find out if they might have ADHD. We make it a practice not to give information regarding the checklist cut-off score because we are not in the business of diagnosing our students! Instead, we meet privately with students who approach us about ADHD and we provide them with referral information to our student clinic as a first step in the assessment process.

To help clear any misconceptions regarding the disorder, we provide a brief history of ADHD by describing the changing thought regarding the etiology of the disorder that has occurred over the last 30 years. We also explain how many people refer to ADHD as attention deficit disorder (ADD) when, in fact, ADHD is the current diagnostic label according to the manual used by psychologists and psychiatrists to diagnose psychopathology (Diagnostic and Statistical Manual of Mental Disorders – Fourth Edition Text Revision (DSM-IV-TR); American Psychiatric Association, 2000). ADHD was called ADD in the DSM-III (American Psychiatric Association, 1980), an earlier version of the DSM. Many laypeople still refer to the disorder as ADD; however, children who display the core criterion areas of impulsivity, inattention, and hyperactivity likely meet the diagnosis of ADHD. Although the DSM-IV-TR describes various subtypes for ADHD, we do not require that our students know the difference between the subtypes. Instead, we ask the students to know the core features for ADHD.

The majority of our ADHD lecture regards the prevalence, symptoms, and co-occurring problems common among children with ADHD. We use items from the ADHD checklist as a framework for our coverage of ADHD symptoms. For example, we describe how children act when they are impulsive, inattentive, or hyperactive. We also provide clinical examples for how these symptoms may manifest in school-aged children and detail some diagnostic criteria for ADHD that most lay people do not know (e.g., symptoms must be present for at least six months, symptoms must be present before seven years of age, and symptoms must be observed in more than one setting; American Psychiatric Association, 2000). Finally, we detail disorders that must be ruled out when diagnosing a child with ADHD. Admittedly, ADHD is a good fit for our teaching style because it allows us to provide clinical examples for the ADHD diagnostic criteria. If you do not have clinical examples to share with your class, a video depicting a brief interview with parents of a child diagnosed with ADHD can be just as compelling (e.g., Patterson, 2000).

One crucial aspect related to having ADHD that you might highlight for your students is how having ADHD can affect an individual's development. For example, symptoms related to ADHD can have a negative impact on one's academic functioning, occupational functioning, social relationships, or self-esteem. Depending on time constraints, we mention relevant research findings that apply to children with ADHD (e.g., Kenneth Dodge's research on the hostile social perceptions of aggressive children; Crick & Dodge, 1996; Dodge, 2006). Despite the potentially negative aspects related to having ADHD, we always attempt to describe individuals with ADHD in a sensitive manner because some of our students may have ADHD.

Occasionally, you will have students with ADHD who are comfortable talking about their experiences with the disorder. It can be wonderful to have a student contribute background information, but you will need to be cautious of the student's right to privacy. There is also a balance between keeping discussion alive, and providing a student support group. Although we try to offer encouragement to any students who decide to share their story with the class, we try not to dwell too long on any one student's story in an effort to keep the momentum of the class.

Treatment for ADHD

Drug therapy and behavior modification are the treatments with the most empirical support for treating ADHD (Pelham, Wheeler, & Chronis, 1998; Pelham & Waschbusch, 2006). During lecture, we typically start by describing drug therapy (e.g., methylphenidate, amphetamines, pemoline, or atomoxetine) for children diagnosed with ADHD (see Brown (2003) for a layperson-friendly description of child-focused drug treatment). We attempt to provide an even-handed coverage of available treatments by covering both the positive and negative aspects of drug treatment. Typically, we engage our students in a discussion about why a parent may have strong negative feelings about medicating young children. Although there are several compelling reasons why parents may not want their children to start drug therapy (e.g., side effects such as loss of appetite and facial tics), we also point to research suggesting that a combination of drug therapy and behaviorally-oriented family therapy leads to the best outcome for children with ADHD (MTA Cooperative Group, 1999).

Behavior modification Behaviorally-oriented family therapy is often an effective ADHD treatment because child clients and their parents learn new skills to use at home (Barkley & Murphy, 1998). Typically, behavior therapy also targets school functioning and teachers become important corollary sources of information about the child's on-task and off-task school behavior. It may be enlightening for your students to watch a short video about behaviorally-oriented parent training. Laypeople often have the misconception that treatment for child psychopathology involves talk therapy during which the child discusses his or her feelings with a therapist. Although a focus on emotional functioning may be part of a treatment for children with ADHD, this discussion usually comprises a very small part of the therapy hour. Rather, the majority of treatments for ADHD focus on parents (much to their surprise). Your students may find it interesting to see some of the materials that are used in a behavior therapy protocol designed for children with ADHD, such as a home behavior chart or a school daily report card (Barkley, 1995; Barkley & Murphy, 1998). If you do not have clinical expertise, a clinical child psychologist may be an ideal guest speaker for your course.

Our students are often interested in gaining more practical hands-on experience with an ADHD population. We typically direct them to a Summer Treatment Program (STP) for children with ADHD modeled after William Pelham's program (Pelham & Hoza, 1996). Several similar programs around the country provide STP to school-aged children during the summer and they can easily be found on the Internet by conducting a search on "Summer Day Treatment Program for ADHD." Each program relies on the help of undergraduate counselors to provide the intensive behavior modification therapy to children with ADHD. Although the location of available programs may be prohibitive for some of your students, those students serious about graduate school may be able to arrange some way to work for class credit at a Summer Day Treatment program location.

Individual differences in cognitive abilities

Just about everyone knows that someone with a "high IQ" is very smart. However, few laypeople could tell you what an IQ quotient actually represents. One way to start a discussion about IQ testing is to ask students what it means to be "intelligent." Historically, many different views about the nature of intelligence have been proposed (for a review, see Birney, Citron-Pousty, Lutz, & Sternberg, 2005). It is likely, therefore, that your students will generate several descriptors for intelligence (e.g., verbal ability, problem solving, numeric operations, spatial reasoning). Notably, the standardized tests that psychologists currently use in clinical practice to measure intelligence do not assess all cognitive abilities (e.g., creativity, social skills) that predict success in life. Your students would probably be interested to learn that the main criticism of the IQ tests widely used today is that these tests predict academic achievement, not how successful people will be in their future career. In response to the notion that intelligence reflects more than one aspect of human functioning, Howard Gardner and his colleagues proposed that there are as many as seven types of intelligence: musical intelligence, bodily-kinesthetic intelligence, logical-mathematical intelligence, linguistic intelligence, spatial intelligence, interpersonal intelligence, and intrapersonal intelligence (Gardner, 2004; Kornhaber & Gardner, 2006). Our purpose for discussing these "multiple intelligences" is to illustrate that having an average score on a traditional intelligence test may not reflect important strengths possessed by a specific individual (for example, the ability to execute an excellent jump shot or the ability to negotiate a purchase using a second language). Rather, true intelligence may be a variable construct that represents a range of both academic and non-academic abilities. Whatever your own personal beliefs about the nature of intelligence, this is an opportunity to explain that our discipline currently includes several theories on the subject of intelligence.

In addition to the current prevailing thought regarding the nature of intelligence, we provide our students with some background information on the history of intelligence testing (e.g., Alfred Binet's work in France) as well as the constructs of chronological age, mental age, and the equation for the IQ score (Wechsler, 1958). We also provide a brief demonstration of how IQ testing is conducted by discussing the Wechsler Intelligence Scale for Children Fourth Edition (WISC-IV; Weschler, 2003), a widely used assessment measure of child intellectual functioning. Although the ethical code of psychology prohibits us from showing our students the exact items on the WISC-IV, we cover the broad abilities tested by the WISC-IV (verbal and visual-spatial) and provide a brief overview using mock examples provided by a development text. To supplement our lecture on the structure of the WISC-IV, we describe the process of intelligence testing for children in the middle childhood age range. Undergraduate students rarely have an opportunity to observe psychological testing, so a brief description of the training required to conduct psychological assessments and some mention of what testing "looks like" can be helpful information to place intelligence testing into context for your students. Typically, we borrow a WISC-IV testing kit from our university psychology clinic so that we can show students the flip-book style manual and the briefcase that is used to transport the WISC-IV. We also describe the way that assessment rooms are often configured and how parents are occasionally allowed to observe testing through a one-way mirror. If you do not have clinical expertise, psychological assessment is another topic that a clinical child psychologist may be able to discuss with your class.

Many of your students would like to pursue a career in education or communication disorders. Understanding how and why psychological testing is used to diagnose learning disabilities could be a beneficial introduction to students who plan to work with children in the near future. If you have time, you might cover the procedure for assessing learning disabilities using the WISC-IV and measures of academic achievement such as the Woodcock-Johnson tests (WJ-R; Woodcock & Johnson, 1989) or the Wechsler Individual Achievement Test (WIAT-II; 2002). You can find a fairly complete description of learning disorders in the DSM-IV-TR. Research regarding learning disabilities can also be found in the *Journal of Intellectual Disability Research* or the *Journal of Intellectual Disabilities*.

Another area that can be discussed with regard to the assessment of middle childhood cognitive development includes the broad implications psychological assessment may have for social development. For example, a child who qualifies for gifted classes at school has more options available for an enhanced curriculum—and possible higher self-esteem in the academic arena. Conversely, a child who is not able to master class work may be placed in special education classes and develop poor academic self-esteem—especially if other children tease the child because of his or her academic placement. Parents who obtain psycho-educational testing for a child who is struggling in school may advocate for the child to receive needed services at school. The child in this scenario could have a very different academic trajectory relative to a child whose parents do not have the resources, or ability, to advocate for the educational needs of their child.

Middle childhood social and personality development

Middle childhood social and personality development contains a variety of concepts that we find enjoyable to discuss. Our training in child clinical psychology provides us with the opportunity not only to discuss concepts that are relevant to current events but also to discuss how certain issues could be attended to in a therapeutic environment. We find linking current events, developmental concepts, and therapeutic activities to be consistent with our teaching style and the goals we have for our students to be able to apply what they learn in the classroom to how they view and interact with the world around them.

We consider moral development and social functioning, as it relates to self and peers, to be important for developmental psychology students to know about middle childhood social and personality development. We tend to teach social and personality development after physical and cognitive development, so we often have limited time to discuss a multitude of topics. However, many of the topics that we choose to discuss are particularly relevant to "hot button" issues in society because they relate to increased awareness of bullying and incidents of school violence.

Moral development

The development of moral judgments, as defined by making judgments that are in accord with what society considers "right" or "good," is arguably one of the most important areas in which humans develop. Some theorists posit that individuals progress through stages of moral development throughout their lifetime (Gilligan, 1982; 1987; Kohlberg, 1984; Colby & Kohlberg, 1987). Middle childhood is about the time that children are first cognitively able to reason through scenarios and make judgments based on their sense of justice. In introducing the concepts related to moral development, we find it important to discuss the different theories about the stages of moral development and the descriptions of the different stages.

We generally begin our discussion of moral development with Lawrence Kohlberg's stages of moral development, which we often introduce with the "Heinz dilemma" (Kohlberg, 1984; Colby & Kohlberg, 1987). Although there are different scenarios associated with the "Heinz dilemma" we tend to either read, or give our students a copy of, the following scenario:

> Your spouse is near death from an unusual kind of cancer. One drug exists that the physicians think might save them—a form of radium that a scientist in a nearby city has recently developed. The drug, though, is expensive to manufacture, and the scientist is charging 10 times what the drug costs him to make. He pays $1,000 for the radium and charges $10,000 for a small dose. You have gone to everyone you know to borrow money, but you can get together only $2,500—one quarter of what you need. You've told the scientist that your spouse is dying and asked him to sell it more cheaply or let you pay later. But the scientist has said, "No, I discovered the drug and I'm going to make money from it." In desperation, you consider breaking into the scientist's laboratory to steal the drug for your spouse. Should you do it?

After we read and discuss the "Heinz dilemma" we discuss how Kohlberg's theory about the stages of moral development is based on a person's responses to the dilemma. We discuss the different stages that Kohlberg posited and examples of responses at each of those stages. We then ask students to generate similar dilemmas that would require a moral judgment and could also produce a variety of responses. We encourage students to generate their own examples to examine further the intricacies and diversity with which one makes moral judgments. This exercise also helps students to identify the kind of reasoning present in middle childhood since many of them will likely be further along in their moral reasoning than children.

After spending some time discussing Kohlberg's theory of moral development, we encourage our students to analyze critically his theory and identify areas in which it may not account for what we as a class observed in the discussion of moral reasoning. We then go on to discuss an alternative theory about moral development, particularly as it relates to gender differences in moral development. Carol Gilligan (1982; 1987) posited an alternative theory that suggests that the socialization of boys and girls in our society leads to differences in moral reasoning and behavior. Discussion of Gilligan's theory allows us to have students identify where the alternative theories overlap and where they differ; it also opens up the discussion about gender role socialization. We particularly like to discuss Gilligan's argument that males tend to view morality in terms of justice and fairness whereas girls view morality in terms of responsibility to others, self-sacrifice, and compassion (Gilligan, Lyons, & Hammer, 1990; Gilligan, Ward, & Taylor, 1988; Gump, Baker, & Roll, 2000). We enjoy providing students with the opportunity to examine more than one theory or perspective about a concept because we feel it encourages our students to be critical in their analysis of theory and to form their own opinions about what the data represent. Once we discuss moral development, we often like to discuss how children function socially.

Social functioning

When we begin to discuss social functioning as it relates to middle childhood, we want our students to acknowledge how children's representation of self influences their social functioning as well as to understand the nuances of peer relationships at this stage of development. Often our students can remember aspects of their middle childhood and we encourage them to think back to this time period to help them connect to the material and make connections from the text to "real world" scenarios.

Self

One of the objectives we have for our students is to differentiate between social competence, self-esteem, self-concept, and self-efficacy. We find these terms to be particularly relevant when we are discussing how they interact with the child and the environment. We often discuss the self-perpetuating cycle that low self-esteem has on competency and self-concept. We also find it extremely important for our students to recognize that children in middle childhood are better able to compartmentalize their abilities and can list multiple attributes in their identities (Marsh & Ayotte, 2003; Marsh, Ellis, & Craven, 2002; Sotiriou & Zafiropoulou, 2003). The ability of our students to recognize specific characteristics children use at different ages to form their self-concept is also important to us as instructors. We emphasize to our students the importance of having children develop a sense of competency in at least one area of their life in order to combat areas in which they struggle.

In addition to being able to differentiate different aspects of the self, we discuss with our students how children tend to evaluate their competency in particular areas. One method of evaluation used often by children, and adults, which we discuss with our students is downward social comparison. Downward social comparison is the tendency to compare oneself to others who are similar, but noticeably less proficient or successful (Aspinwall & Taylor, 1993). We discuss why people use downward social comparison and encourage our students to identify both costs and benefits to using downward social comparison as a method of self-evaluation.

Peer relationships

The discussion of social functioning in middle childhood would not be complete without including relationships with peers as a factor. Middle childhood is a time in which peer groups begin to become increasingly important in children's sense of self, and how they function in society (Collins, 1984). One of the most important aspects of peer relationships is friendships (Gifford-Smith & Brownell, 2003).

Friendships As children age and develop, their friends influence their development in many ways. Friends help to provide children with perspectives of the world that may be different from those they are exposed to within their families. Friends, particularly those at school, spend an enormous amount of time together and thus are a great source of emotional support (Berndt, 2002). Friendships also provide children with an opportunity to practice communication and interactions with others who may or may not respond in a manner similar to what the child experiences at home (Harris, 1998; Gifford-Smith & Brownell, 2003; Nangle & Erdley, 2001). Just as play is important in helping children hone their abilities and practice for "real world" scenarios, friendships also provide similar opportunities.

Friendships unfold throughout development; William Damon proposed a series of stages through which a child's view of friendship passes (Damon, 1977; Damon & Hart, 1988). Although we describe these stages, we often do not have enough time to go into a lot of detail. We invite our students to discuss the nature of the friendships they had during middle childhood and we encourage them to compare their friendships in middle childhood to their friendships at earlier and later stages of development.

Peer status Status is an interesting phenomenon in the school setting. The hierarchies that develop tend to begin in middle childhood and persist throughout high school. Peer status categories include popular, rejected, and neglected, but many schools have their own terminology to group children in social hierarchies. We often encourage our students to talk about the peer status categories that were present in their schools and to identify the hierarchy that reflected those categories. We also encourage our students to think about potential relationships between social hierarchies and instances of bullying and school violence. Often our students are able to recount anecdotes about instances of bullying or violence that were between students of different status categories. Recently, more of our students are able to recall the high profile cases of school violence and hypothesize about their relation to social hierarchies.

The horrific acts of violence that occurred at Columbine High School have spurred discussion about school violence in many households. The media's portrayal of incidences of school violence represents an increasing pattern of violence among the youth of today. Although violence in schools does exist, many schools have programs aimed at reducing the incidence of violence. Programs aimed at preventing school violence are often in the form of conflict resolution or peer mediation. These programs aim to reduce physical aggression as well as verbal aggression (i.e., bullying; Ridley, 2005).

Some research being conducted is aimed at understanding who is liked and who is not liked in a classroom or school setting. Often this research involves a sociometric measure called "peer nomination." Peer nomination includes asking students to identify the peers they would like to spend time with—and the peers they would rather not have as friends. The peer nomination method is useful because researchers can identify the popular, rejected, and neglected students in a classroom simply by conducting a survey with the students (Maassen, Goossens, & Bokhorst, 1998). One particularly valuable aspect of peer nomination research is that the methods have been used to identify children at risk for later maladjustment such as high school drop-out and juvenile delinquency (Maassen et al., 1998).

There are intervention programs available to address self-esteem and peer relationship issues in childhood. During lecture, we often discuss peer status categories, the consequences of these categories on children, and solutions designed to prevent the negative consequences of being part of an at-risk group (i.e., rejected children). We like to highlight local activities that are focused on helping children so we often describe a peer mediation program in our community that was designed to address bullying and peer conflicts among school children. As part of the peer mediation program, graduate students trained a select group of elementary and middle school children to serve as conflict mediators. These children served as peer mediators throughout the school year and were supervised by teachers and the graduate students. The ultimate goal of the program was to decrease school-based bullying, peer violence, interpersonal conflict, in- school suspension, and disciplinary actions (Ridley, 2005). If you do not have a local peer mediation program to describe, you may be able to find a social skills program for children in need of developing interpersonal skills. Students seem to appreciate our efforts to provide meaningful links between the text, their experiences growing up, and local child-based programs. They also appreciate any information related to disruptions in development and how child problems can be addressed by parents, teachers, and therapists.

Critical Thinking Opportunities

In discussing middle childhood development with your students, there are many activities that provide critical thinking opportunities.

Consistent with previous chapters, in this section we identify topics relevant to middle childhood development that provide useful opportunities to encourage your students to think critically. Potential topics to foster critical thinking may be:

- What factors help promote resilience during the middle childhood stage?
- What is the "best" way to decrease bullying in the middle school environment?
- Outline steps that need to be taken to prevent and address school violence.
- Discuss the development of wisdom in children (for a review, see Birney et al., 2005).
- How can independence in children be fostered? What are the pros and cons of independent children?

Controversial Topics

There are many topics being discussed in today's society that relate to middle childhood development, many of which are highly debated. Some controversial topics that we address with our students include:

- Should drug therapy be used for ADHD treatment? When is drug therapy beneficial? When is drug therapy harmful?
- What impact do parents really have on their children: Do parents really matter? (see Belsky, 2006) Are children always better off with two parents at home? With married parents? With a father and a mother?
- Are parents becoming too overprotective? Why or why not?
- What are the pros and cons of intelligence testing (Belsky, 2006)?
- There are many constructs related to intelligence that we do not evaluate regularly in children. Should we assess EQ, wisdom, creativity, etc. during child assessments?
- Are all "extra-curricular" activities good for children? At what point is it too much? Popular media has discussed the phenomenon of "overscheduled kids" (see Larsen, 2001; Quindlen, 2002), what are the potential consequences of overscheduling a child's day?
- What are the benefits of encouraging early specializations (e.g., sports, music) in children? What are the potential risks of encouraging such specializations?

- Which is better public or private school? What factors make one better than the other?
- Identify the pros and cons for "gifted" programs in school.
- Does the current school system favor girls?
- Should children be taught by computers instead of teachers?
- How much should a parent monitor and supervise their children's use of technology (e.g., TV, Internet)? Should children be allowed to play violent video games and watch violent television?

Developmental Diversity

The middle childhood period is no different from other developmental periods in that there are many opportunities to address diversity as it relates to development. We often choose topics to discuss with our students that are relevant to their future professions and/or their future experiences as parents. We often spend time addressing issues of culture-free measures of intelligence, particularly if such a thing exists. We recently spoke to a child psychologist who practices in the South Caribbean. When assessing a child using a standard intellectual assessment measure, the psychologist asked the child to name the seasons of the year. Given that the child lives in a tropical, resort area, the child's response that there are two seasons of the year (high and low season) seemed perfectly reasonable. However, the child received zero points for this answer because it was incorrect in the context of the assessment measure, which was developed by researchers in the more temperate climate of the US (R. Rosen, personal communication, February 24, 2007). Additional topics we have discussed with our students include:

- Is child aggression adaptive in some environments?
- Describe the interface between culture and parenting in the middle childhood period.
- What is the best way to promote gender equality in young children?
- What is the role that culture and race play in friendship development?

Appendix A

Rate yourself (0–3) for how often you do the following:

Never or rarely	*Sometimes*	*Often*	*Very often*
0	1	2	3

1. Fail to give close attention to details or make careless mistakes in job tasks or schoolwork.
2. Have difficulty sustaining attention in tasks or leisure activities.
3. Do not seem to listen when spoken to directly.
4. Do not follow through on instructions and fail to finish work.
5. Have difficulty organizing tasks and activities.
6. Avoid tasks (e.g., job tasks, schoolwork) that require mental effort.
7. Lose things necessary for tasks or activities.
8. Easily distracted.
9. Forgetful in daily activities.
10. Fidget with hands or feet or squirm in seat.
11. Leave seat in situations in which remaining seated is expected.
12. Move about excessively in situations in which it is inappropriate.
13. Have difficulty engaging in leisure activities quietly.
14. "On the go" or act as if "driven by a motor".
15. Talk excessively.
16. Blurt out answers before questions have been completed.
17. Have difficulty awaiting turn.
18. Interrupt or intrude on others.

Adapted from the DSM-IV-TR (APA, 2000) diagnostic criteria for ADHD.

Chapter 7

Adolescent Development

When does adolescence end? Pose this question to your class and you are likely to receive at least a few different answers. For example, does adolescence end when an individual reaches the "age of majority" in the US? Perhaps it is when the individual graduates from high school? Maybe we should consider adolescence officially over when an individual can legally buy alcohol or when he or she graduates from college? Some people argue that the adolescent period ends when a young person is completely self-sufficient and independent from parents—which might place many of your students squarely within the adolescent period. Defining the time frame for adolescence with your class could be the starting point for your lecture on the adolescent period of development.

Similar to our previous chapters, we have distilled a variety of lecture options for the adolescent period to focus on a few topics. In this chapter we describe physical and cognitive aspects of adolescence such as puberty and adolescent thinking styles. We also discuss social and personality concepts related to the adolescent period such as body image, anorexia, bulimia, teenage depression, and suicide prevention.

Adolescent Physical and Cognitive Development

There are some sensational aspects of physical and cognitive development that one could choose to cover for the adolescent period. For example, adolescent drug use, alcohol use, and sexual activity can be quite engaging as lecture topics. However, we typically cover less sensational concepts when we lecture on the adolescent period of development: adolescent cognition and puberty. We prefer to cover broad issues related to adolescent physical and cognitive development because almost all of our students will have personal or professional contact with adolescents going through puberty.

Puberty

Puberty is a natural starting point for your first lecture on the adolescent period because there is general consensus among researchers that the growth spurts, bone age, and hormone activity related to puberty marks the onset of adolescence (e.g., Tanner, 1999). During our initial discussion of the adolescent period, we provide definitions for puberty and we discuss the social implications of reaching puberty early relative to one's peers (i.e., precocious puberty). One goal that we have for our students is for them to know that puberty occurs, on average, two years earlier for females than for males (Kail & Cavanaugh, 2007). Although we do not highlight all of the physical changes that occur during puberty, you might find it helpful to teach the physical milestones (e.g., development of secondary sexual characteristics) associated with the onset of adolescence. We tend to discuss the social implications of puberty for young people by sharing the results of survey research conducted with young people who experience precocious puberty and young people who enter puberty later than their peers do (Celio, Karnik, & Steiner, 2006; Feldman, 2006). Occasionally, students in your classes will want to share their recollections about a younger brother or sister who was an "early maturer." You may need to guide the discussion towards the social implications of being an early maturer for the young person—as well as for his or her family (for a parent's perspective on the subject see O'Sullivan & O'Sullivan, 2002). Interestingly, we have never had students share stories about being a later maturer—perhaps reflecting the negative social stigma related to being a "late bloomer."

Adolescent cognition

When you lecture on the infant stage, early childhood, or middle childhood stages, you might be able to bring actual children to class as guest speakers. To date, we have not attempted to bring adolescents into our course for "show and tell" because finding adolescents willing to speak to our classes would probably be a difficult task. Instead, we typically show a video to highlight the cognitive processes that illustrate the adolescent stage. One way that we encourage class participation for the topic of adolescent cognition is to ask our students if they have examples to share of any younger siblings (or former room mates) in the adolescent period. For confidentiality sake, we usually check to make sure that any former room mates in question are not in the class before we use them as an example!

The topic of adolescent cognition includes several aspects that can be interesting for lecture material. We believe that the key concepts related to adolescent cognition should include formal operations (i.e., the last stage of Piaget's theory of cognition), meta-cognition, adolescent egocentrism, the imaginary audience, the personal fable, and body image. The best way to illustrate these concepts for your students is to describe how an adolescent may operate in the world as a result of these cognitive styles. For example, an adolescent who speeds though red lights or frequently drives a car after consuming large amounts of alcohol probably operates under the personal fable—the belief that nothing tragic could happen to him. Or, an individual influenced by the notion of an imaginary audience may spend hours making a wardrobe schedule to ensure that no outfit is worn twice within the same two-week period (because everyone is watching...). Of course, there are everyday occurrences that remind us of our very own imaginary audience—what is the first thing that you do when you trip and almost fall in a public setting?

Davidson Films produces several high-quality videos that we have used in class (see www.davidsonfilms.com for an alphabetical list of their lifespan development videos). As previously mentioned, our inclusion of video in class depends on factors such as time, extensiveness of class discussion on a particular topic, and how discussion-prone the class tends to be. We often show videos after administering an exam because the students enjoy having a break from lecture. Because attendance tends to decrease after an exam, only students who attended the class period after the exam will be able to answer questions based on the video. For the adolescent period, we typically show our students a portion of Adolescent Cognition: Thinking in a New Key (Davidson Films, 1999; running time, 32:30). Although we like all of the information presented in the video, we usually do not show the entire video due to time constraints. During the portion that we show to our students, developmental psychologist David Elkind presents information related to the unique thinking patterns typically seen during the adolescent period. In particular, he discusses the imaginary audience, personal fable, and meta-cognition in depth. Our usual procedure when showing a film is to give our students a list of terms to look for during the film. After we show the video with pertinent information related to adolescent cognition, we provide lecture and discussion related to the concepts in the video.

Following our discussion of the personal fable, imaginary audience, and Piaget's formal operations stage, we turn to the notion of adolescent body image. As a course instructor, it can be challenging to start a genuine discussion about body image with students. Indeed, body image is a sensitive topic that many individuals typically do not want to talk about in front of others. However, to evaluate critically the environment that adolescents operate within, it is necessary to discuss both the proximal and distal correlates of adolescent body image development. We have had good success with our body image discussion as a by-product of the Beautiful People Exercise that we developed for our lifespan development course.

As is the case with many effective class exercises, we developed our Beautiful People Exercise out of necessity. One day we did not have quite enough course material for our lecture on the adolescent stage. To fill some time, and possibly start some discussion, we decided to "wing it" by asking the class to describe what beautiful people look like according to the US media (i.e., print magazines, motion pictures, television shows). During the exercise, we asked the class to generate a list of the physical qualities seen among attractive males and females in the US media. The final, and arguably most important, step of the exercise was to ask our students to estimate the percentage of female and male high school students who meet the ideal physical type portrayed by the US media. Typically, our students estimate that 3 to 10% of their classmates met the cultural ideal of a thin and toned body during the high school years. Students responded very well to the exercise (we were recently asked to reprise the lecture on the campus radio station) and we have used the exercise as a launching point for our discussion of adolescent body image every semester.

When conducting our body image exercise we are mindful of several things. First, we try to avoid comments such as "OK, now it's time for the ladies to say what is attractive in a male." Because some comments may negate the possibility that same-gender students could have opinions to share, we encourage the entire class to participate in the male and female parts of the exercise. Second, we are very aware that students in the course may have issues with their own negative body image so we are careful not to say anything negative about unattractive people. Additionally, there could be some students who actually do meet the ideal body image and who make very concerted efforts to meet the ideal (e.g., students who compete in beauty pageants). Thus, it is important not to make any value judgments about individuals who do, or do not, spend a great deal of time on their appearance. Finally, some students may mention some attributes that are not typically viewed as attractive (shapely ear lobes, beer bellies, and the like). These offbeat attributes may not be portrayed frequently by the media as attractive, but we welcome these comments as they indicate that our students feel comfortable discussing sensitive topics in class.

Most undergraduate college students can empathize with the desire to appear attractive and, as consumers of the popular media, they can generate a good bit of discussion around the correlates of adolescent body image. The purpose of the body image exercise is to look objectively at the physical qualities that are valued by mainstream US culture and think about how these images may impact adolescent body image, self-esteem, and social functioning. Of course, one by-product of the exercise is that our students likely evaluate their own body image and the implications that body dissatisfaction may have on their own lives. To be sure, the best way to decrease class resistance towards a sensitive topic is to talk about the topic from an outside perspective (instead of asking, "What don't you like about your body?" ask "What is the ideal body for males and females? Why might adolescents have difficulty meeting this ideal?").

Eating disorders

In our experience teaching lifespan development, we have found that most students know someone who is struggling with serious eating problems. As a result of the widespread prevalence of dysfunctional eating patterns on our campus, our students seem interested in learning about the diagnostic criteria, physical symptoms, and social implications of eating disorders. Additionally, some of your students will become educators or healthcare providers who will have contact with adolescents who are high-risk for developing eating disorders. Any information that you cover related to eating disorders has the potential to help your students better understand adolescents in their environment.

As noted, the adolescent mind has frequently been described as egocentric. Part of adolescents' tendency to over think most aspects related to themselves results in extreme concern for how others see them. Physical appearance is one area where adolescent self-absorption manifests itself and it is no coincidence that eating disorders tend to develop during the adolescent years, rather than during later stages in life (American Psychiatric Association (APA), 2000). To begin our discussion of eating disorders, we relate the development of eating disorders with typical adolescent cognitive style. For example, the belief that everyone in your environment is critically aware of your appearance (i.e., the imaginary audience) and the belief that eating very little food won't negatively impact your long-term health (i.e., the personal fable) can lead to distorted thinking patterns and disordered eating habits.

Depending on the amount of time that you have to spend on the lecture, you may decide to show students the amount of food consumed by an individual with anorexia or bulimia and detail the diagnostic criteria as described in the DSM-IV-TR (APA, 2000). We often provide our students with an in-depth discussion of eating disorders and how problems related to self-esteem, distorted body image, depression, and an irrational fear of becoming fat, work in concert to contribute to disordered eating behavior (Stice & Bearman, 2001). We have also found it helpful to discuss the similarities between anorexia and bulimia, the differences between them, the common contributing factors to body dissatisfaction, and the typical treatment for eating disorders (APA, 2006).

Discussion of anorexia and bulimia also could easily fit within the scope of adolescent physical and cognitive development. However, there is a good deal of overlap among the physical, cognitive, social, and personality aspects of eating disorders. As such, we do not feel comfortable limiting our discussion of adolescent eating disorders in one section. Rather, a thorough discussion of eating disorders should include the physical, mental, and social development aspects of adolescence. For the physical domain, you could describe the symptoms of eating disorders. For the cognitive domain, you could explore how adolescent thinking regarding body image likely places teens at risk for eating disorders, depression, and substance use (Stice & Bearman, 2001; Stice Presnell, & Bearman, 2001).

Following our lectures on anorexia and bulimia, students have approached us with an interest in talking to future classes about their own struggles with eating disorders. We have found peer-guest speakers to be very powerful and, when available, we include them as a supplement to our own lectures on anorexia and bulimia. Obviously, when asking a former student to speak to a class about his or her experiences you will want to avoid placing a fragile individual—or someone who has not yet completely "come to terms" with their problems—in front of a class. For this reason, we have asked only a few students to speak to our classes and we screen students to include only those who have had some success in treatment.

If you don't have a guest speaker available for your class, you could show a video on anorexia and bulimia. We like a film entitled Dying to be Thin (2000; running time, 60 minutes). The NOVA film can be viewed in its entirety, along with possible activity items, on the NOVA Web site. One industrious GTA of ours put together "Swiss cheese" notes for this film using the transcript available online (the notes are in bullet form and pertinent facts are omitted in the notes. Students listen along with the video and fill in the blank spaces on the Swiss cheese notes as the film plays). We often distribute the Swiss cheese notes to our students because there is a good deal of information in the film and the notes help students to structure their note taking during the video.

Some of your students may be engaged in a current struggle with eating disorders. Other students may know of someone with an eating disorder and seek help from you to learn how to assist an individual in need of intervention. We are mindful of the potential that our lecture on anorexia and bulimia may trigger negative emotions for some of our students. To address the possibility that our lecture may elicit negative feelings for our students, we usually end our lecture by directing students to our student counseling center on campus if they know of someone struggling with eating issues.

Adolescent Social and Personality Development

Given the widespread belief that adolescents are "sullen and angry," we typically address the "stress and turmoil" stereotype associated with the adolescent period for our lecture on adolescent personality development. We specifically discuss the nature of clinical depression and how it is very different from the depressed state that characterizes some adolescents. In our view, it is important for our students to know the warning signs of severe depression and suicide so that they can take appropriate measures when they encounter high-risk teens in future private or professional contexts.

Depression

Students typically have little knowledge about the criteria for clinical depression. We discuss how depression as a disorder has minimum criteria based on duration, severity, and impairments in functioning (APA, 2000; Dumas & Nilsen, 2003; Mash & Wolfe, 1999). We often discuss the symptoms of major depressive disorder as well as dysthymic disorder. We discuss the ways in which depression is assessed and treated. The discussion of treatment options often leads us to a discussion of antidepressants and the controversy surrounding the prescription of medication to adolescents. We enjoy bringing real-world significance to this lecture by showing the class a few examples of items from the Beck Depression Inventory (BDI; Beck, Steer, & Brown, 1996). Because we have an obligation to protect testing materials, we do not pass out copies of the BDI; instead we direct students to a Web site for depression if they would like to learn more about the illness (www.nimh.nih.gov/publicat/depression.cfm).

One key developmental psychopathology concept that we discuss with the class is the notion that depression can look different in children and adolescents than in adults. In particular, the DSM-IV diagnostic criteria for major depressive disorder in which the clinician assesses for two weeks of sad mood could be expressed as an irritable mood in children and adolescents. To add to our discussion of the differences in the clinical presentation of depressed adolescents as compared to depressed adults, we identify how age and gender can present different symptom clusters for depression. For example, we discuss how, although children and adolescents tend to exhibit similar symptoms, adolescents appear to display more melancholic symptoms (Birmaher et al., 2004). Additional differences in symptom presentation include increased frequency or severity of symptoms as an individual gets older (Marcotte, Fortin, Potvin, Papillon, 2002). Specifically, symptoms of melancholia, psychosis, suicide attempts, suicide completion, and impairment of functioning tend to increase with age (Birmaher et al., 1996). Additionally, the presence of anhedonia, hypersomnia, loss of appetite, and decreased ability to concentrate tends to be more common in 12 to 13-year-olds where feelings of worthlessness and symptoms of oppositional defiant disorder are more common in 8 to 11-year-olds (Sorensen, Nissen, Mors, & Thomsen, 2005).

As instructors, we try to highlight why depression could be an important consideration for our students' personal lives (e.g., the risk of post-partum depression, the possibility that a friend may disclose depression) or professional lives (e.g., if they work with adolescents in a school setting). Given the increased attention to depression in media, we provide our students with basic information about depression as well as options for treatment.

Suicide

Much like the sections on prenatal development and child maltreatment, we are mindful of the "service course" designation for our lifespan development course when teaching information related to depression and suicide. In light of statistics indicating that suicide is the third leading cause of death among adolescents (Centers for Disease Control, 2005; Cutler, Glaeser, & Norberg, 2000; Healy, 2001), many of your students will know someone who has attempted or completed suicide. Thus, the information that you present could have an important impact on their ability to address crisis situations in their future personal or professional lives. In this lecture we focus on the clinical picture of suicide and talk about some real-world examples related to suicide.

We discuss the gender gap in suicide, both in the means used in suicide attempts and the completion rate. Specifically, we point out that although more adolescent females attempt suicide, adolescent males are the more frequent suicide completers. We explain that this discrepancy in attempts and completions is arguably due to adolescent females' tendencies to use less lethal means of suicide (e.g., drug overdose) and adolescent males' tendencies to use more lethal means of suicide (e.g., gunshot wound, hanging) (Brent, Baugher, Bridge, Chen, & Chiappetta, 1999; Gelman, 1994; Joseph, Reznik, & Mester, 2003). Additional explanations for the gender gap in adolescent suicide relate to differences in risk factors for suicide. For example, Brent and colleagues (1999) found that adolescent males with co-occurring mood, substance abuse, and disruptive disorders are at high risk for suicide. Additionally, adolescent males appear to be more vulnerable to the stress caused by legal or financial problems and interpersonal loss. Adolescent females with mood disorders and past history of a suicide attempt are at a great risk for suicide. With respect to adolescents in general, family history of psychopathology and adolescent history of abuse are also significant risk factors for suicide.

Anecdotally, we have found that students enrolled in psychology classes have friends who tell them their problems because they are psychology majors. Obviously, simply taking a few psychology courses is not enough training for the challenging task of working with a suicidal individual. For this reason, we stress to our students that they should seek help from the campus student counseling center if someone they know discloses thoughts of suicide (i.e., suicidal ideation), the desire to commit suicide (i.e. suicidal intent), or a plan for committing suicide.

If you cover material related to adolescent depression and suicide in the same day, there is a chance for the class to seem morbid. We try to end this lecture on a positive note by giving the class examples of what "to do" should they encounter an individual contemplating suicide. We typically finish our lecture on suicide by providing a handout on the "Danger Signals of Suicide" to the class. The handout was originally developed as part of an instructor's guide for Robert Feldman's Development Across the Lifespan text (Feldman, 2006). Providing suicide prevention information may someday help one of our students faced with a challenging situation.

Critical Thinking Opportunities

In discussing adolescent development with your students, there are many activities that provide critical thinking opportunities. As with previous chapters, we encourage you to bring empirical literature into the classroom and allow your students to evaluate the developmental literature related to adolescence. Potential topics to use to foster critical thinking may be:

- What stereotypes do adults have about adolescents?
- What factors help promote resilience during the adolescent stage?
- How can we improve an adolescent's body image?

- What challenges are raised by childhood obesity?
- What are the social consequences of being an early maturer? What gender differences exist relative to the social consequences of being an early maturer vs. a late maturer?
- What effects might cyber-friendships have on adolescent development?
- Is teen violence on the rise?
- Should teens who commit serious offenses be tried in courts of law as adults?
- When does teenage rebellion become delinquent?
- What tips would you give parents of a teenager to help them navigate the adolescent period?
- What is the best way to allow an adolescent to gain autonomy?

Controversial Topics

As we have already observed, there are many topics discussed in the media that are related to adolescence. Some controversial topics that you may choose to address with your students include:

- Should adolescents use antidepressants?
- What is the role of a parent of an adolescent: Are they parent or friend?
- How much should parents monitor their teens' use of the Internet (e.g., myspace, AIM)?
- Teenage sexuality
  - Should all female adolescents receive the HPV vaccine?
  - How should sexual identity be discussed in adolescence?
  - How does teen "dating" affect development?
  - How do "double standards" in sexuality affect adolescents?
  - In sex education, what are the pros vs. cons of abstinence education vs. providing condoms in schools?
  - Should teens have access to birth control without parental consent?

Developmental Diversity

Adolescence is a period in which there are a multitude of opportunities to address diversity as it relates to development. We often discuss topics with our students that are relevant to their future professions and/or their future experiences as parents. Specific topics we have discussed with our students include:

- How do history and culture affect variations in puberty timetables (Belsky, 2006; Tanner, 1999)?
- What are the cultural variations in the role of, and goals for, adolescence?
- Culture and body image
  - What factors influence the concept of the ideal body type?
  - Do males worry about achieving the "ideal" body?
  - What differences exist in the social standard for body image among males and females?
  - Compared to women around the world, young women in western cultures are more at-risk for eating disorders. What aspects of the US culture (and other western cultures) might be responsible for the increased prevalence of eating disorders in the US?
- Gender and eating disorders
  - Although the majority of individuals with anorexia and bulimia are female, eating disorders also exist among young males. You could lead students in a discussion of the variations in eating patterns that are related to gender. For example, are there any differences in the way that eating disorders develop or are maintained among males? Are certain groups more at risk for developing anorexia or bulimia (e.g., athletes, models)?
- Gender and depression
  - Why do more female patients report depression relative to male patients?
  - Which social, cultural, and biological factors differentially influence the prevalence of depression among males and females?

Chapter 8

Young Adult Development

Most of your undergraduate students will be able to relate well to young adult development. Concerns related to academic performance, physical conditioning, dating, mate selection, and career selection are topics that many undergraduate students encounter daily. In our coverage of this section, we acknowledge that our students are the "experts" because they currently experience the young adult stage of development. We see our task for this section as presenting research that relates to adult cognition, factors related to college enrollment, mate selection, and career selection.

Early Adulthood Physical and Cognitive Development

There are several theories that highlight current perspectives on young adult cognition. Unlike previous sections of the course that deal with the cognitive functioning of adorable newborns or charming toddlers, we find that adult cognition can be a tough sell for an engaging lecture. In our experience, including examples that students may encounter themselves helps to increase the interest level in early adult cognitive development. Before we lecture on the theories of adult cognition, we distribute a handout listing the theories and their corresponding stages in detail. The theories that we believe are important for a sound understanding of young adult cognition include Piaget's formal operations stage (Piaget, 1972), Labouvie-Vief's theory of adult cognitive development (Labouvie-Vief, 1992), Perry's theory of adult cognitive development (1970), and Schaie's theory of adult cognitive development (Schaie, 1994). We have found that it often takes the majority of a class period to outline these theories and provide examples. Although we tend to focus on cognitive development in the young adult period, a discussion of physical conditioning and the range of physical abilities of individuals in the young adult period could work just as well.

We stay fairly close to the text for the material related to young adult cognitive behavior but we also attempt to infuse some examples to help illustrate the theories. For example, to help illustrate the abstract reasoning that highlights Piaget's formal operational stage, we bring a yo-yo to class. The yo-yo is our visual aid to help illustrate the hypothetical-deductive reasoning needed to answer the question "What makes a pendulum swing faster?" Although a yo-yo is not the best device to use (you cannot easily add weight to a yo-yo), it helps the class to visualize the question. We typically end our discussion of Piaget—which at this point has spanned the majority of the semester—by discussing the criticisms of his theory.

Labouvie-Vief's theory of adult cognitive development is an excellent counter-point to Piaget's theory. We typically describe her theory and define the term *post-formal thought* for the class. To help illustrate the notion of post-formal thought, we often read our class a few short vignettes that challenge individuals to use post formal thought. In one example, a young woman is married to a man with a drinking problem (Feldman, 2006). She tells him that she will leave him if he comes home drunk one more time. As you can imagine, the man comes home drunk several days later. We then pose the following questions to our students: "What should the young woman do?" "Why would she decide to stay with her husband?" Another example that we use to illustrate post-formal thought refers to a young woman who is a staunch feminist and a career-driven individual. If this woman were to marry, have a child, and become a stay-at-home mother, how would she interpret the situation if she were operating under the post-formal thought stage? How would someone interpret the situation if he or she has not yet reached post-formal thought? Hopefully, your students will be able to generate some answers to such questions that reflect post-formal thought: real-life dilemmas are rarely straightforward (i.e., no right or wrong answer) and that there can be room for re-interpretation of a dilemma depending on an individual's perspective.

William G. Perry's (1970) theory of adult cognitive development is important to describe as part of the young adult period because it purports to describe the process of cognitive development experienced by most undergraduates. We typically describe Perry's sample and define the constructs of dualistic thinking and multiple thinking. Next, we read examples of how a student in the dualistic thinking stage would describe a psychology course—and how a student in the multiple thinking stage would describe the same course. Interestingly, students in the same undergraduate course may represent both concrete and relativistic thinking styles (see Hood & Deopere (2002) for a more recent evaluation of Perry's theory). The differences in thinking style between students may become frustrating for instructors —and for fellow students—to appreciate, especially with respect to the questions that more concrete thinkers may ask. Another point that we try to make is that individuals in the multiple thinking stage understand that a theory can have shortcomings but still be important for the advancement of a field (you can use Piaget as an example —and all of the criticisms of his work that you may have recently discussed). If you decide to take a diversity slant on Perry's work, you could discuss the limitations of his sample (Harvard University undergraduates in the 1960s to 1970s) and the implications they pose for Perry's theory.

We like describing Schaie's theory of adult cognitive development because it is a theory that provides specific predictions for how individuals differ cognitively across the lifespan. Schaie's theory could be described during a later lecture of older adulthood, but we like how it provides a bridge from the young adult period to the older adult period. When lecturing on Schaie's theory, we find it helpful to show a time line with all of Schaie's stages listed (e.g., achieving stage, responsible stage, executive stage, and reintegrative stage). The best example that we have developed to describe Schaie's theory of cognitive development is the notion that family reunions often have a large number of individuals in attendance and various family members will fall into different cognitive stages depending on their life stage (e.g., teenagers are typically in the achieving stage, the grandparents are typically in the reintegrative stage, etc.).

College life

Presenting information on college life is a bit like conducting a self-study and it can be fun to share data with your students that actually includes them as part of the sample. During our coverage of college life we typically discuss the demographic background of US undergraduates, the most often cited benefits of college attendance, factors related to a positive college experience, the financial benefits of attending college, data related to gender and grades, data related to gender and salary, and often cited reasons for attrition from college.

The data on students enrolled in college-level coursework can easily provide a focus on developmental diversity. In the course of teaching aspects of college life we find ourselves comparing the national data on student demographics to our local university. Depending on your type of institution, you may find that your university or college does not quite mirror the national data. For example, there has been quite an increase in the number of female undergraduates and students from racial/ethnic minority backgrounds enrolled in college nationwide but an increase in a diverse student body has been slower to develop at our particular institution. We make a point of presenting the racial/ethnic and gender breakdown of US undergraduates as well as the trends for enrollment that have been observed at other universities over the past decade. You might find it interesting to compare these figures with your university undergraduate body and the US census data for the racial/ethnic background of individuals living in your state. It is easy to find undergraduate statistics for your institution—they should be posted on your institution's home Web page. Comparing the national demographic data with the demographic data for students at your own institution can be a compelling exercise. In our case, it allows us the opportunity to discern whether our student body reflects the demographics of our home state and discuss reasons for any discrepancies.

One point of interest regarding college life for faculty, students, and administrators is attrition. It may be sobering for your students to learn the statistics related to the percentage of students who graduate in four years (again, this statistic will depend on the nature of your institution). We typically make a point of illustrating the demographic background of students who *enroll* in university courses and the demographic background of students who *graduate* with undergraduate degrees. With respect to the racial/ethnic breakdown of students who drop out of college and the larger number of women graduating from college, we return to this information during the subsequent lecture on mate selection as there are some important implications for the educational background of potential mates.

Academic disidentification, the notion that some undergraduates are disenfranchised from the academic process because they have difficulty finding academic mentors, is of particular concern (Cokley, 2002; Osborne, 1997). Because students who do not feel "connected" to the academic process are at risk for school failure and dropout, we try to both teach and *prevent* academic disidentification in our course. We work towards this goal by spending some time in class explaining the construct, reviewing risk factors, and describing some of the on-campus programs available to help prevent students from feeling disconnected. For example, we often describe the student success center (a campus unit where students can receive free tutoring), the career counseling services, and the minority peer mentoring programs that exist on our campus. We also try to de-mystify the experience of going to a professor's office to talk about a class problem as the majority of our students do not make contact with professors outside the classroom. A little bit of self disclosure—that we were intimidated by well-known and accomplished professors when we were undergraduates, too—appears to normalize the reaction for our students. The downside of providing this information and encouragement to our students is that we probably create more work for ourselves after the class (those endless letters of recommendation!). Hopefully, our efforts help to identify a potential problem for our students as well as offset academic disidentification in our department in some small way.

Clearly, your students will understand the reasons why an individual would choose to attend college. To provide students with another perspective, we offer data regarding the financial aspects of having an undergraduate degree. It is easy to include a chart in your lecture that highlights the small number of college graduates who live in poverty relative to those with a high school degree. The financial data related to college graduates lends itself well to a discussion on diversity-related issues, particularly if you provide data regarding gender and racial/ethnic background.

One fun way to explore gender differences in salary is to start with gender differences in undergraduate academic majors. During our *Gender and Undergraduate Major* exercise we typically ask our students to provide their opinions regarding the majors that tend to attract male and female students at our institution. Not only do our students provide their impressions for the more male-dominated or female-dominated major areas of study, they also cite the number of males or females in their other classes. For example, there are currently no male students majoring in fashion design at our institution and there are very few majoring in communication disorders, social work, or nursing. Conversely, only a few female students on our campus major in building science, forestry, or agriculture. There are some majors that attract both males and females but predominately attract one gender over the other (most of the business and engineering majors are male, most of the psychology and English majors are female at our institution). The next step that we take in this exercise is to explore which majors typically lead to lucrative careers. Sometimes there are differing opinions regarding the majors that lead to lucrative careers but it can still be an engaging exercise. The *Gender and Undergraduate Major* exercise also can be informative for the instructor—we had no idea that there was a major at our institution called Building Science before teaching this course!

The purpose of our *Gender and Undergraduate Major* exercise is to help explore some reasons why women, on average, make less money than men. Obviously, one common-sense reason is that many female students may decide to major in fields that traditionally do not make a great deal of money. Although we do not typically present data related to graduate school enrollment, it could be an informative addition to the exercise.

Often we turn to gender and faculty jobs as an extension of a discussion of gender and the workplace. Remembering our own ignorance as undergraduates on how one becomes an academic, we typically take this point in the course to share with our students the process that it takes to become a psychology professor at a university. For example, most students do not understand the distinction between an assistant, associate, or full professor and they may not recognize the difference in rank among some of their professors and instructors. It is possible to bring the discussion to diversity in higher education by investigating the gender breakdown of full professors in your institution to provide some perspective for your students. Indeed, one of us (EBK) had the experience of being one of only two female psychology faculty members in a department of 19 faculty members for one year (being the only female at faculty meetings and program meetings was not uncommon at the time). For us, revealing the gender distribution of faculty members to our students often leads to a discussion as to why the academy does not attract more female faculty (particularly in psychology, with our pool of predominately female undergraduate and graduate students).

Because our university is a state institution, all of the salaries for our faculty and staff are posted on the university home Web page as a matter of state record. You may not want to conduct the following exercise for a few reasons, but it can be helpful for you as an instructor to get a feel for the salary breakdown of professors as a function of their rank, gender, and age at your institution. We definitely do not recommend revealing salaries to your students (they probably don't reflect individual take home pay anyway if you factor in consultation work, etc.) but you can speak of the general trends in base salary that you find. Many students are brought up with the notion that hard work and perseverance will lead to equal pay for equal work and it can be interesting to consider some of the documented reasons for variations in faculty members' salaries (US Department of Education, 1999; Bradburn & Sikora, 2002).

Early Adulthood Social Development

After addressing cognitive and physical development of early adulthood, we move on to discuss social development. We acknowledge that there are many concepts worthy of discussion, but we tend to discuss mate selection and career selection. We find that our students are quite interested in both mate and career selection because as early adults they are currently facing or will soon face these topics.

Mate selection

To teach research findings related to mate selection to an audience of young adult students is to teach with the "wind in your sails." We find that the Southern, conservative, traditional-age students in our course are very interested to learn the material related to mate selection. Based on the number of dating shows on TV and Internet dating services available, students outside our locality would probably be highly interested in the topic of mate selection as well. Our simple introduction to the mate selection topic is to generate students' opinions regarding whether research supports the notion of "birds of a feather flock together" or "opposites attract" in the dating world. This question typically provides an easy transition into the relevant social psychological research on relationships. In particular, we discuss the importance of similarity (that people are drawn to others who have attitudes and values that are similar to their own) and proximity (people form relationships with others who live in close proximity to them and with whom they have frequent contact) of individuals in forging relationships (McCaul, Ployhart, Hinsz, & McCaul, 1995). Although somewhat dated now, it can be fun to describe the classic social psychology research conducted by Festinger, Schachter, & Back (1950) on proximity because the subjects in this study were randomly assigned to apartments. You might pose the question of whether your students would be willing to participate in such a comprehensive relationship study!

Although our students often acknowledge the importance of similarity when queried about the factors that play into their current relationships, they tend not to articulate proximity as an important aspect of their close friendships. One way to assess this dichotomy in your course is to ask your students (a) Are you still friends with anyone that you met during your first year at school? (b) How did you meet these friends? and (c) Are you still in contact with high school friends "back home?" Typically, new friends will be individuals who lived near your student and these new friends will be closer than high school friends (who no longer have proximity). There are exceptions, of course, but this line of rhetorical questioning can encourage students to evaluate whether the research findings on proximity and similarity hold true in their experience. The opposite situation, having proximity but no similarity, can be an interesting experience to explore as well. Just ask your students if they have ever had a room mate situation gone sour. With a few well placed questions, you will probably find that the "room mate gone bad situation" was due to a marked lack of similarity—and too much proximity!

We move from our discussion of relationship formation to mate selection by discussing with our students what they look for in a romantic partner. If you have time it might be beneficial and fun to have students communicate the attributes they look for in the form of a personal ad (see Isbell & Tyler, 2005 for more detail on this activity). The personal ad activity can give your students an opportunity to articulate, in a semi-structured manner, the traits and characteristics that they offer and those that they are looking for in a partner. Additionally, Isbell and Tyler found that students enjoyed the activity and it increased their knowledge about interpersonal relationship research.

The short-cut approach to the personal ad exercise is to enlist help from your students to develop a list of desirable qualities in a mate. As qualities are mentioned by students (e.g., commitment, achievement orientation, sense of humor, etc.), we comment on the presence—or absence—of research to support the qualities they cite. It can be interesting to tie-in research by "love labs" such as the one headed by Robert Sternberg (1986, 1987). Next, we lead the students in a comparison of the qualities mentioned in the text about mate selection and the list that they generated in class. Invariably, there are some differences between the two lists that can be discussed.

If you would like to highlight a diversity-focused aspect of mate selection, a discussion on arranged marriages can be interesting. We start the topic of arranged marriages by asking students to raise their hands if they would be willing to enter an arranged marriage. Virtually no students in our classes raise their hands in response to this question—probably because they have been socialized to look to marry someone with whom they are "in love." In the past, we have included guest speakers from cultural groups that encourage arranged marriages (e.g., East Asian Indian) to conduct a brief guest lecture in our class. When no guest speakers are available, we relate information that we learned from interviewing individuals awaiting arranged marriages. Our majority-culture students appear very interested in learning about the process of arranged marriages and they often have questions about the process. To foster critical thinking in your students, you could present data related to the low divorce rate found among couples in an arranged marriage and ask them for their explanation for the data (religious reasons, cultural sanctions, cognitive dissonance, etc.). On a side note, we have heard from our students about arranged marriages between European-American individuals in our home state. These marriages appear to be both extremely rare and arranged by sets of parents who want to keep large land holdings within their family.

We expand our conversation about mate selection to discuss theories of love. How would your students define love? You could remind your students about the long-ago lecture on research methods and how all good research questions start with a solid operational definition for a construct. It can be helpful to have students provide an operational definition of love and then compare their definition to the definitions used by current researchers in the field.

For example, the definitions of passionate love and companionate love (Hecht, Marston, & Larkey, 1994; Hendrick & Hendrick, 2003; Lamm & Wiesman, 1997) or Sternberg's Triangular Theory of love (Sternberg, 1986, 1987) could serve as good counterpoints to the student-generated definition. It can also be helpful to remind your students that love is not a static state, but that relationships progress through stages, as highlighted by Murstein's stimulus-value-role theory (Murstein, 1987). To round out our discussion on mate selection and love, we also talk about marriage and the variables that people use to filter potential mates. We believe that the term *homogamy* and its relation to the similarity concept we discussed earlier (Suro, 1999) is an important concept for students to understand.

Undergraduates are in a unique period of their lives because they are surrounded by individuals who are, more or less, their same age. After college, most young adults are in contact with a wider age range of potential mates. In both situations, however, the marriage gradient, or tendency for women to marry men who are slightly larger, older, and higher in status occurs (Bernard, 1982). To provide examples of the marriage gradient, we usually ask students to recall the marriage trends of celebrities—do older women tend to marry much younger men or do older men tend to marry much younger women? We use celebrity examples because most students recognize these individuals, but examples of non-celebrities would work as well.

The next step is to evaluate whether the class-generated examples follow the marriage gradient definition. It also helps to ask the students to generate examples of "cream of the crop" women (i.e., women who do not have any men of higher status to date) and "bottom of the barrel" men (i.e., men who do not have any women of lower status to date). Our final note on the marriage gradient is to discuss the implications that the marriage gradient has for highly educated women, particularly women of color (see Kiecolt & Fossett, 1997; Tucker & Mitchell-Kernan, 1995; Willie & Reddick, 2003 for discussion of these issues).

Time permitting, we explore some historical trends related to marriage. Specifically, we discuss trends in the age of first marriage, why people choose to marry, and the trend for people to live together before marriage. We supplement this discussion with data from the US Census Bureau and recent research (Fields & Casper, 2001; Martin, Martin, & Martin, 2001; Smock & Manning, 2004; US Bureau of the Census, 2001; White, 2003). A discussion of the historical trends of marriage can lend itself well to a diversity-focused lecture. For example, you could address gender and cultural differences in mate selection (e.g., cultural differences in the primary characteristics for choosing a husband or wife). We discuss data from cross-cultural studies of people from around the world that found significant differences in primary characteristics of people from the United States, China, and South Africa (Buss, 2003; Buss et al., 1990). We also discuss gender differences in preferences for romantic relationships. In discussing gender differences, we identify particular gender differences in preferred characteristics that are similar across cultures such as men preferring physically attractive mates and women preferring mates who are ambitious and industrious (Sprecher, Sullivan, & Hatfield, 1994). An introduction to the evolutionary theory for mate selection and the current debate about this explanation (e.g., not testable and possible similarity in gender stereotypes across cultures) could be used here as well.

Career selection

The desired end result of attending college is a college degree and ultimately, for most, a job. As academics, we hope that students gain a comprehensive fund of knowledge and well-honed critical thinking skills with their degree. However, attaining financial independence and stable employment is the main goal for many students. To this end, we have found that some discussion of the research related to career selection is welcomed by most students.

Selecting a career can be a stressful process for some students and our coverage of career selection provides us with an opportunity to present some relevant data and theory related to this milestone. We tend to use Vaillant's theory of career consolidation (Vaillant & Vaillant, 1990) and Ginzberg's theory of career selection (Ginzberg, 1972) to describe the process by which individuals decide on a vocation. We begin with Vaillant's theory because it provides the framework for linking adult development and career selection. Next, we discuss Ginzberg's theory because it describes specific stages that an individual progresses through when selecting a career. One novel aspect of Ginzburg's theory is that it provides us with a rare opportunity to describe some differences across the lifespan in the same lecture. For example, the way that a child views his future career is very different from the way that an adult might view her day-to-day work experience. A young child in the fantasy period may dream of becoming a firefighter one day, despite having severe asthma that is triggered by smoke! Discussing Ginzberg's stages also helps to normalize feelings many of our students may currently experience.

John Holland's theory of personality types can also be a helpful framework to present (Gottfredson & Holland, 1990; Holland, 1973). His coverage of personality types is similar to our focus on personality traits and individual difference in other classes. We also enjoy discussing Holland's theory of personality types because it encourages our students to think more realistically about those occupations for which they may be well suited. To provide a supplement to the in-class discussion of Holland's theory, you could include a guest lecturer from your campus career services office. In our experience, career advisors enjoy describing the services offered by their office and chances are that they use a measure based on Holland's theory to help students determine an appropriate career path.

Time is short when teaching young adult social development and we typically run out of time before we have a chance to discuss all of the topics that we would like to cover. We chose to cover mate selection and career selection because we believe the class would benefit most from lecture on these two topics. Although we do not often discuss topics such as parenthood, marriage, divorce, and changing male and female work roles, these could all be very interesting and informative topics to address with students. Additionally, data related to the trends of dual-income families, stay at-home fathers, the stress of work-place lay offs, fertility problems, and adoption rates could all be fascinating constructs to cover during the young adulthood period.

Critical Thinking Opportunities

In discussing early adult development with your students, there are many activities that provide critical thinking opportunities. As with previous chapters we encourage you to bring empirical literature into the classroom and allow your students to evaluate the developmental literature related to young adult development. Potential topics to use to foster critical thinking may be:

- How do you know when you are an adult? What are the religious, sexual, social, educational, and economic milestones that could be related to becoming an adult?

- What is the best way to promote career selection and prevent college drop-out?
- Is there a link between adult attachment styles and childhood attachment? Do you think that attachment style can change?
- What are some stereotypes that we have about relationships? Are there different stereotypes for singles, couples who cohabitate prior to marriage, married couples, or homosexual couples?
- Has the institution of marriage always been the same? An article by Coontz (2004) suggesting that our modern concept of dating and marriage is relatively new could help to generate discussion on the topic.
- Does cohabiting prior to marriage lead to a more successful marital relationship?

Controversial Topics

There are many topics discussed in the media that are related to early adulthood, many of which are highly debated. Some controversial topics that you may choose to address with your students include:

- How has technology changed the "dating game"? See Rosen (2004) for a discussion on Internet dating.
- Have gender roles changed or stayed the same over the past few decades? See Paludi (1986) for methods and activities to generate discussion.
- What is the appropriate role of a parent in the life of a young adult? Are hovering parents (e.g., parents who call college professors, parents who call potential employers) taking their parenting role too far?
- Can and should we use scientific advances to boost intelligence, expand memory, etc.? What are the long-term ramifications of such use?

Developmental Diversity

Adulthood is a period in which there are a multitude of opportunities to address diversity as it relates to development. Specific diversity-related topics to discuss with students that are relevant to their future experiences and choices include:

- What are the historical and cultural variations in dating and mate selection? For example, what do men and women in China look for in a mate? The Zulu culture? India and Pakistan? Discuss the differences between these cultures and the US (see e.g., Buss, 2003; Buss et al., 1990).
- What are some historical and cultural variations in marriage?
- What are some historical and cultural variations in work and family roles?
- Describe some important issues related to lesbian and gay relationships, marriage, and parenting.

Chapter 9

Middle Adult and Older Adult Development

It is an exciting time to teach middle adult and older adult development, in large part because the notion of middle age and older adulthood is currently being redefined by the "baby boomer" generation that is now reaching the 60-year-old age milestone. Local publications for mature adults such as *Forever Young Living on the Coast* (Barone, 2007) feature articles on the best way to maintain long distance connections with grandchildren and advice on how to be an "aging hipster." Additionally, the depiction of older adults has changed dramatically in films. Just think of the difference in portrayal of "dad" in the 1950 version of *Father of the Bride* (Berman & Minnelli, 1950) starring Spencer Tracy and Elizabeth Taylor and the 1991 version of *Father of the Bride* (Baum & Shyer, 1991) starring Steve Martin and Diane Keaton. The writer and producer of the 1950 version probably never would have considered a *Father of the Bride* sequel in which Spencer Tracy's wife becomes pregnant again; however, the 1991 version had just such a sequel in *Father of the Bride Part 2* (Baum & Shyer, 1995). The concept of becoming a new father at 50 is no longer a far-fetched concept!

Another fascinating aspect of older adulthood is the sheer number of older individuals living in the US today. The increase in older adults is due partly to population trends and partly due to advances in modern medicine. For example, it is projected that by 2050, a full

25% of the US population will be over the age of 65 (US Census Bureau, 2005). Most texts indicate that the middle adult period lasts from 40 to 60, but can include 35 to 65-year-olds as well. Even admitting that one is "middle aged" is quite possibly a milestone in itself as most people in the beginning stage of the middle adulthood period do not consider themselves to be middle aged (just ask your nearest 36-year-old). However, the human body has a definite expiration date and although most 60-year-olds might describe themselves as middle-aged—there are very few 120-year-olds alive today.

Another interesting aspect of teaching the older adult development section is the field of gerontology and its focus on the oldest old—individuals who are 85 years of age and older. The oldest-old segment of the population has doubled in the last two decades and it is still increasing (US Census Bureau, 2005). The implications of the large number of older residents in terms of life expectancy, health expectancy, and financial planning are immense. Indeed, an entire housing industry including retirement communities, independent-living facilities, assisted-living facilities, and nursing homes have emerged in response to the growing needs of the oldest-old members of our population.

There are many interesting topics to choose when developing your lectures on the middle adult and older adult period of development. The first decision that you have to make is how to manage this vast amount of information. If you have a good bit of time to devote to middle age and the older adult period, we recommend presenting the information over four class periods: middle adult physical and cognitive development, middle adult social and personality development, older adult physical and cognitive development, and older adult social and personality development. Breaking the information into four separate lectures gives you adequate time for each section. If you are pressed for time, you might consider consolidating middle adult and older adult physical and cognitive development into the same lecture as many of the physical systems that start to decline in middle age continue to do so in later adulthood. We often consolidate the middle and older adult physical and cognitive lectures during abbreviated summer sessions. However, because the social and personality development of middle and older adulthood is rather distinct, we prefer to lecture on these two stages separately.

Middle Adult Physical and Cognitive Development

During middle adulthood, many individuals first become aware of physical changes that are the first signs of aging. Muscle strength, firm skin, and eyesight are all physical aspects that can change by the time an individual reaches his or her mid-30s. Perhaps for this reason, we also like to point out that some individuals who take care of themselves and lead a healthy lifestyle are in better physical condition than younger individuals without healthy life habits. Indeed, one of the important features of physical and cognitive development is that some aspects of aging can occur at different rates for different individuals.

One way to start your discussion on the physical and cognitive aspect of middle adulthood would be to ask your students to think about the large array of prescription and non-prescription medication that is currently advertised for middle-aged individuals. Taken together, these medications reflect the types of physical problems experienced by many of this target group. In a related exercise, you could ask a group of students to review the commercials that are shown during television programming targeting an older demographic group (e.g., news television shows, financial television shows). To provide a counter point, another group of students could review television commercials that appeal to a younger market (e.g., dating shows, reality television shows). Advertisements for drugs related to erectile dysfunction and bladder control problems will likely be included in your students' reports of commercials from the middle-aged demographic shows whereas feminine hygiene products, Internet dating services, and early pregnancy tests will likely be highlighted in the shows targeting a younger demographic.

Physical appearance

We typically begin our lecture on middle adulthood by describing some of the salient physical changes that occur during middle age including decreased bone density, the "middle-age spread," and a decrease in muscle strength. Although many of the physiological changes that occur in middle-aged adults may not be readily apparent to the outside observer, the development of wrinkles, graying hair, and a lack of muscle tone are more noticeable. In class, we often talk to our students about what it means to look older in our society, which one could argue is clearly a youth-oriented culture. Aside from the inconvenience of aging and the change in appearance, an older individual must also endure ageism, or the pervasive negative perception of older individuals often displayed in the US (Nelson, 2002; Nelson, 2005). One example of ageism that we describe for our students is the gender double standard in our culture—that older women are described in unflattering terms whereas aging and maturity enhance a man's status. To describe the double standard in terms of physical appearance we share with our classes an anecdote about trying to find pictures of attractive older women to show in class. Many advertisements that show women with gray hair actually depict them as having a trim body and very few wrinkles. On the other hand, it is very easy to find pictures of attractive older men on the Internet and in magazines. It is also much easier to think of examples of seasoned male actors with young love interests (e.g., most of Sean Connery's latest films) relative to examples of mature female actors having much younger love interests.

If you prefer to present more empirical evidence on ageism, you could describe some scales that measure age-related attitudes (e.g., Rupp, Vodanovich, & Crede, 2005) or recent research conducted with young adults in which participants reported ageist attitudes towards service providers and employees (e.g., Duncan & Loretto, 2004; Kalavar, 2001). Alternatively, you could ask students to watch a film on the subject of ageism and the double standard for women. During the documentary film *Searching for Debra Winger* (Arquette, 2002), female actors describe the pressures from the movie industry to look youthful and the personal slights they must face to stay in the business. (For a list of other films related to physical appearance and aging, please refer to our section on developmental diversity at the end of this chapter.)

Physical changes

In addition to the details related to the decrease in bone density for women, middle-age spread, and the decrease in muscle strength, we also describe the changes in vision and hearing that start to occur during the middle adulthood period. During our coverage we stay rather close to the textbook information. However, we discuss the implications of hearing and vision problems on the social and work lives of adults. You may consider asking a communication disorders specialist to give a guest lecture on the hearing tests that are used to determine if someone is losing his or her hearing. During your subsequent lecture on older adulthood you, or your guest speaker, could describe how hearing aids work, why some individuals are resistant to using a hearing aid, and the best techniques for talking to an older individual with hearing loss (e.g., turn off the television, have face-to-face contact when you speak, avoid crowded restaurants and noisy environments, etc.).

Osteoporosis The majority of our students are female so we tend to include information related to osteoporosis in our lecture on middle adulthood. Osteoporosis is a female-dominated condition in which bones become fragile and thin. A lack of calcium, poor exercise habits, family history and a poor diet have all been linked to the development of osteoporosis (Saladin, 2007). We describe for our students what it is like to have a bone density test (it is not at all painful or invasive) and we provide them with a risk checklist to complete on their own. In the past, we invited an instructor from the School of Nursing to talk to our students about the dangers of osteoporosis and the best way to prevent the disease. This guest speaker described a research study conducted at our university that targeted osteoporosis prevention in young adults. Following our colleague's lecture, we were able to link the discussion of her study to our previous lecture on research methods and help our students discern the hypotheses of the study, the dependent variable, and the independent variable.

Menopause An important change that occurs for most women during middle age is the female climacteric, or the transition from fertility to infertility. The female climacteric typically begins around 45 years of age and ends with cessation of menstruation and menopause (Poole, Warren, & Nunez, 2007). Medical findings, however, suggest that signs of approaching infertility are apparent during perimenopause, which can begin during a woman's early 30s. Notably, the fluctuation in hormone production associated with perimenopause can lead to depression and a difficulty becoming pregnant before full-blown menopause begins in some women (Freeman, Sammel, Lin, & Nelson, 2006). Although psychological problems are often associated with menopause, Freeman et al.'s research suggests that the rate of depression actually drops during the years associated with menopause and that women experience the highest risk for developing depression during perimenopause.

To highlight the social aspects related to the perimenopause and menopause experience, we sometimes mention a recent controversial book, *Creating a Life*, in which the author argued that media exposure related to fertility treatments and the success rate of the fortunate minority of women who benefit from these pricey medical interventions are providing a misleading picture for young women (Hewlett, 2004). Indeed, many young women are unaware of perimenopause and the extent to which their fertility decreases each year from their mid-twenties through midlife.

Another aspect of menopause that we describe for students is the controversy surrounding hormone replacement therapy—HRT (Manson & Bassuk, 2006). Although some research suggests that there are some risks related to taking HRT during late menopause, many post menopausal women currently take HRT—some of them may even be the mothers of your students! We typically begin our discussion on HRT by asking students if they know of anyone taking HRT. Next, we describe the pros and cons of treating women with HRT. Notably, there is a vast literature—and at least one medical journal, *Maturitas*—completely devoted to the topic of menopause. If you are interested in presenting a more detailed lecture on perimenopause, menopause, or HRT, a brief literature search will yield a large amount of potential material for your lecture.

The female climacteric and menopause are both physical changes that occur for women but they are also very much tied to social and cultural factors as well. For example, not being able to bear children can be a very distressing issue for a woman who decided to delay childbirth in favor of a career. On the other hand, many women report a renewed sexual satisfaction once the threat of pregnancy is no longer present (Feldman, 2006). Furthermore, quite a bit of research has focused on potential ethnic differences related to the frequency of symptoms, severity of symptoms, and the distress that women report as a result of going through menopause (e.g., Melby, 2005; Winterich, 2003). Contrary to the negative connotations that menopause holds for women in the US, East Asian Indian and Mayan women report positive feelings related to no longer being able to bear children and very few negative symptoms related to menopause (Feldman, 2006). Japanese women report a very low rate of hot flushes, a common symptom described by women in North America (Melby, 2005). Taken together, the body of cross-cultural research on the female climacteric suggests that menopause symptoms may not be biologically universal!

Chronic illness One of the benefits of modern medicine is that many infectious diseases that plagued humans in the past (e.g., influenza, pneumonia, TB, diptheria) are much less deadly as a result of the powerful antibiotics that are now available (Brannon & Feist, 2007). The end result of our improved ability to fight infection is that people are living longer and living with chronic illness for longer periods of time. You might choose to cover some of the chronic illnesses that typically begin during the middle adult period such as arthritis, hypertension, heart disease, cancer, and stroke. If you decide to cover chronic illnesses in detail, we recommend using a health psychology textbook as a resource as these texts often provide a great deal of information on chronic illness. You could also invite a nurse or physician to your class as a guest speaker. In the past we have asked the women's health physician from our campus medical clinic to speak to our class. She was very committed to improving student health outcomes and was always willing to come and speak to our students about a topic for a few minutes—as long as our class time did not conflict with her clinic schedule.

The field of health psychology is vast and it can be challenging to choose just one or two areas to cover during your lecture on middle adulthood. If you are limited on time, you may consider talking about heart disease and cancer because they are both so widespread and potentially deadly. Heart disease actually comprises a collection of problems that include both the myocardium and the circulatory system and can include hypertension, stroke, myocardial infarction, and congestive heart failure, to name just a few of the potential heart problems that can surface during middle age (Taylor, 2006). In our experience, talking about the high prevalence of heart disease and how it is the leading cause of death in the US can be a very eye-opening lecture for students (most students would guess that cancer is the leading cause of death). If you decide to lecture on cancer, we recommend that you focus on lung cancer, colon cancer, or skin cancer because they all have strong behavioral components.

Although it can be challenging to master the medical terms and physiological explanations for a lecture on heart disease and cancer, we really enjoy teaching about these two chronic conditions. First, many students know an individual with heart disease or cancer so they are able to contribute anecdotes about the people that they know during lecture. Second, because heart disease and many cancers have strong individual behavior and lifestyle components, teaching students about the importance of avoiding certain activities and substances (e.g., cigarette smoking, sun exposure, multiple sexual partners, a high fat diet) could have a positive long-term effect on their health. The potential to help your students avoid risk factors for deadly diseases can be extremely rewarding. It is especially gratifying when a former student tells you that he or she decided to change a bad health habit as a result of your lecture!

If you choose to focus on diversity and health, you might consider exploring the compelling factors related to ethnic and gender variations in health. For example, ethnicity and gender are both related to life expectancy (Brannon & Feist, 2007). There are reported health disparities in which people with lower incomes and less education in the US have poorer access to healthcare and adequate health insurance (Shi, 2001). Survey research also suggests that racial disparities exist with regard to health insurance access (Hargraves, 2004; Saver, Doescher, Symons, Wright, & Andrilla, 2003).

Middle Adult Personality and Social Development

After addressing cognitive and physical development of middle adulthood, we move on to discuss personality and social development. We acknowledge that there are many concepts worthy of discussion, but we tend to discuss only a few, such as personality in midlife and changes in family structure. Our students appear quite interested in these topics, perhaps because their parents and/or grandparents are currently facing these issues.

Teaching material related to middle adulthood can be fun because we have the chance to lead our students into periods of development that they have not personally experienced. Up until now, our students have been able to relate their own personal experiences to the course material. However, for the remainder of the course they will have to look to the experiences of others (i.e., parents, grandparents, and neighbors) to connect the course material to their daily lives. Often our students have a preconceived notion about what the middle adulthood period of their lives will entail with regard to personality and social development. As with the previous topics that we encounter in the course, we encourage our students to share their ideas and beliefs about the middle adult years before moving into the text material. One way to start the discussion is to pose questions such as: When does personality stop developing? Do all adults experience a midlife crisis? What three words or ideas come to mind when you hear the terms "middle adulthood" or "midlife?" Students' responses to these questions may represent a range of perspectives and provide a solid foundation from which to continue the discussion.

Personality development in midlife

We often begin our discussion of personality development in midlife by having students predict (either out loud or in a short journal exercise) which aspects of their personality will be the same or different 30 years from now. We also ask them to think about someone they know who is currently in middle adulthood, and to think about whether the individual's personality has stayed the same or changed since young adulthood. Once our students consider personality and whether they believe the construct is stable or changes over time, we provide background information on two personality theories from the field of developmental psychology: the normative-crisis model and the life events model of adult personality development.

The normative-crisis model of adult personality development is generally the perspective with which most of our students are familiar and their responses to our questions at the beginning of this section often reflect that familiarity. This perspective suggests that people move through a fixed series of stages, each of which are closely tied to age. The stages are related to "crises" (intense periods of questioning and psychological turmoil) that each individual encounters in life. We remind our students about Erikson's theory of psychosocial development and how he predicted that people move through a series of stages and crises throughout life. After briefly discussing the normative-crisis model with our students, we challenge them to think about factors that could have influenced the development of the model. Additionally, we identify some criticisms of the normative-crisis model, such as the rigid and uniform social roles that were in place when the model was developed (i.e., the traditional view that men work to support their family while women stay at home and take care of the home and children).

To supplement our discussion on the normative-crisis perspective on personality development, we also cover Erikson's stage of generativity vs. stagnation in middle adulthood. In this stage, Erikson argued that an individual's time is spent either in generativity (e.g., making a contribution to family, community, work, and society) or in stagnation (e.g., focusing on the triviality of their own activity; questioning their contribution to society). We point out those individuals who Erikson would identify as generative focus beyond themselves and anticipate continuing their lives through others

(McAdams & de St. Aubin, 1998; Pratt, Danso, Arnold, Norris, & Filyer, 2001; McAdams & Logan, 2004). The individuals Erikson would classify as generative often seek new experiences and new careers, while others get frustrated and bored (Feldman, 2006). After providing definitions for Erikson's theory, we attempt to illustrate the continuum between stagnation and generativity by asking students for examples of some specific activities that could be associated with the theory. Volunteerism, advocacy work, and holding high-powered leadership positions can all be examples of the generative stage. Students sometimes have difficulty generating examples for stagnation but regular café patrons who complain loudly about every aspect of their dining experience on a daily basis are likely experiencing stagnation.

Depending on the time that you have available for personality development in middle adulthood, there are several additional normative-crisis theories that you may cover in your course. Because some of them are quite similar to Erikson's theory, you might decide to compare and contrast the theories. For example, Vaillant's (1977) theory that middle adulthood involves keeping meaning in life vs. rigidity has both similarities and some important differences from Erikson's theory. Gould's (1978, 1980) theory corresponds with the normative-crisis model, but it specifies different stages and corresponding ages.

Contrary to the normative-crisis model, the life events model of adult personality development suggests that particular events, not age, determine the course of personality development (Helson & Srivastava, 2001; Helson & Wink, 1992; Roberts, Helson, & Klohnen, 2002). Levinson's (1986, 1992) seasons of life theory is one such life events model. We like to cover Levinson's theory because his description of the midlife transition allows for a fantastic opening to the concept of a midlife crisis. If you ask your students how people act when they are having a midlife crisis, they will be able to generate a plethora of examples (i.e., men start exercising more and buying red sports cars, women start dating younger men, etc.)—perhaps because movies like *The First Wives Club* (Rudin & Wilson, 1996) and *American Beauty* (Cohen, Jinks, & Mendes, 1999) portray the midlife crisis so frequently. We discuss reasons for the widespread belief surrounding midlife crises, such as media and poignant examples that are around us. Students are often surprised to learn that there is some controversy surrounding the notion of a midlife crisis, such as a paucity of supporting research for Levinson's first study describing the construct and the relatively tranquil and rewarding lives that the majority of people in midlife experience.

After discussing the models of personality development in middle adulthood, we return to the questions we posed to our students at the beginning of the section, and discuss the aspects of personality that are stable throughout life, and those that change. To provide a counterpoint to the theories that predict personality change in middle adulthood, it can be helpful to discuss research on the stability of the "big five" personality traits of neuroticism, extroversion, openness, agreeableness, and conscientiousness (McCrae & Costa, 2003; Srivastava, John, & Gosling, 2003).

We often show a brief video clip on personality development. Listening to individuals talk about their lives can give your class a fresh perspective and ample examples for the material related to adult personality development. Even though the individuals in the video are in the older adult stage (and not middle age) we like to show clips from *In Their Own Words: Widowhood and Integrity vs. Despair* (Magna Systems, 2002, running time 28 minutes). We typically do not take the time to show the entire video but a short clip that highlights one or two of the personality theories may help to supplement for your lecture.

Following a video presentation or your description of the various theories, you can question your students as to which model they believe best describes adult personality development. In an effort to foster the critical thinking skills of our students, we readily point out that there are conflicting theories about adult personality development and that criticism abounds for almost all current psychological theories. Although it is difficult to determine which perspective is the best descriptor of adult personality development, we also point out that most theorists agree that individuals continue to grow throughout middle adulthood. Rather than focusing on the inconvenient fact that psychological theories for human behavior are incomplete, we tend to highlight that there is much empirical work to be done in the area of personality development—and that some student in our course may be the very psychologist to conduct future ground breaking research!

Changes in family structure

After discussing the models of personality development and the stability and change of personality, as time permits, we discuss the changes in family structure that may occur during middle adulthood. Typically students' parents experience the very changes in family structure that we discuss in lecture. Many students are able to look beyond themselves but sometimes they forget that, as they transition into early adulthood, their parents encounter life changes as well. Of the many changes a family can experience, we discuss those most common for individuals in middle adulthood, such as the empty nest syndrome, boomerang children, and the sandwich generation.

As part of the paper requirement that we include in our course, many students choose to interview their parents and write papers on the empty nest syndrome. Because the empty nest syndrome is a popular topic for our students, we have read many accounts of how mothers and fathers deal with the empty nest syndrome. The concept of the empty nest syndrome is one that your students will recognize as they recall the difficulties that many parents undergo when adult children leave home to attend college. Research suggests that some of the difficulties parents feel include unhappiness, loneliness, worry, and depression (e.g., Lauer & Lauer, 1999) and our students have reported very similar reactions among their parents. We encourage an open discussion with students about how their parents responded after they left home to attend college, how their parents differed in their responses from each other, and whether their parents' responses differed from what the students expected. To highlight the gender factors related to the empty nest syndrome, we typically discuss the research that examines the empty nest syndrome and its general focus on women (e.g., Antonucci, 2001; Crowley, Hayslip, & Hobdy, 2003).

The natural progression from a discussion on the empty nest syndrome is a discussion on boomerang children, the phenomenon of adult children who leave the family home and then return to live with their middle-aged parents after graduating college, ending a relationship, or following economic difficulties (Bianchi & Casper, 2000; Lewin, 2003; Mogelonsky, 1996). We discuss the pros and cons of adult children returning to the family home from the parent and the child perspective with our students. A recent popular movie titled *Failure to Launch* (Aversano & Dey, 2006) may even provide you with some examples to use in class.

The sandwich generation is a term used to describe individuals in middle adulthood who find themselves having to care for their children as well as their aging parents. We discuss factors that may have accounted for this recent phenomenon including adults marrying later in life, becoming parents at an older age, and the increased longevity of older parents. We encourage our students to discuss their experience with their own parents caring for grandparents and/or their perspective on this practice.

A discussion of boomerang children and the sandwich generation can offer a wonderful opportunity to bring in material and discussion of the role culture plays in living with and caring for extended families (Ho, Friedland, Rappolt, & Noh, 2003; Kim & Lee, 2003). Additionally, there are clear financial implications of caring for younger and older members of a family simultaneously that you could discuss with students.

Middle adulthood is a wonderful stage in life to teach because of the vast amount of material available for lectures. Additional topics that you may choose to cover for middle adulthood include work satisfaction, stereotypes of older workers, changing careers, career burnout, the health effects of having a Type "A" personality, family violence, divorce, and second marriages. At times, we are disappointed that we cannot include more topics during our lectures. The upshot of having so many choices, however, is that you can incorporate different topics for middle adulthood if your lectures start to feel stale.

Older Adult Physical and Cognitive Development

Admittedly, one of the things that we love about the section on older adult development is providing examples of the following concepts through the stories of people we know (mostly our rich extended family of grandparents, great aunts, and great uncles). Despite the wisdom and perspective that older adults can offer to young adults, many students do not have a great deal of contact with older individuals. At our institution, undergraduate students live in something akin to a youth-oriented biosphere. Instructors are the oldest individuals with whom they come into contact on a daily basis—which can create a strange dynamic for young instructors (admittedly, there was something of an adjustment period for EBK when she started her career as an assistant professor and suddenly became the "old" person in the room at 28). We often start our lecture on older adult development by evaluating some of the stereotypes that people have for older individuals.

How are older characters depicted in cartoons? Several years ago, some students in our research lab investigated the manner in which older adult and child characters interacted during adult and child-oriented cartoons (Park, Klinger, & Brestan, 2003). As part of the study, the students discovered that older characters were often depicted in stereotypical ways. Question students about the manner in which older characters are depicted in cartoons and they are likely to generate a sizeable list of attributes: gray hair, wrinkles, glasses, thinning hair, a cranky attitude, needing to use a cane, and having a shaky voice, etc. We gently remind our students that many of the older characters depicted by the media are done so in a not-so-flattering light. At worst, many of the images of older cartoon characters are a sign of ageism.

Another introduction for your section on older adult development could include a discussion of the products that are currently marketed towards older adults. This exercise can be fun because numerous products are available to help older adults navigate their environments. For example, current SUV designs, rhinestone-studded reading glasses, and ergonomically correct eating utensils are all marketed in catalogs and on Internet sites catering to older adults. Some of the products such as eye droppers, bibs, and walkers can be a reminder to students that old adulthood often brings along some unavoidable physical infirmities.

Physical disorders

Following our introduction on products targeting older adults, we define gerontology and launch into a discussion of the physical and cognitive changes that accompany older age. The decrease in visual acuity such as presbyopia, cataracts, glaucoma, and age-related macular degeneration are all important changes to cover. Many students have probably had the experience of trying to talk to an older individual with hearing loss and it can be informative to cover the reasons why hearing loss occurs in older individuals. For example, presbycusis can occur as a result of hair cell loss in the inner ear and loss of elasticity in the ear drum. Environmental factors, such as loud occupationally-related noises can also have a detrimental effect on older adults' hearing. To help illustrate the impact of having poor hearing, you could ask students to respond to the following experiential exercise: Imagine that your husband of 55 years has just died and you need to move into an independent living facility. Because you are new to the facility, you do not have any friends in the dining room and the staff do not know where to seat you for dinner. During your first week at the facility, you are seated with a husband and wife couple. The wife is completely blind and your hearing aid is not working well enough for you to hear clearly. How will you communicate with your new friends?

Poor eyesight and poor hearing are common signs of old age that are familiar to most of our students. However, many students are unaware of the link between the decrease in taste buds and possible malnutrition found among older individuals. Indeed, individuals do not eat as much food as they age. The decrease in food intake is related to a reduction in metabolism and a phenomenon in which an older individual's olfactory bulbs shrivel. Without an acute sense of taste, older individuals may have difficulty tasting their food and decrease their food intake even more. Some older adults may also over-salt their food because their sense of taste is less discriminating. Have your students ever eaten a meal at an independent or assisted-living facility? If so, they can probably speak of the small portion size and lack of sodium that characterize most of the food options.

Aging theories

Your lecture on older adulthood could also include a discussion on the current theories of aging as well as the current anti-aging interventions that are in vogue. We usually describe the programmed theories of aging and the wear and tear theories of aging. With regard to anti-aging interventions, we cover telomere therapy, anti-oxidant drugs, caloric restriction, and organ transplantation. Most of the anti-aging interventions have little empirical support for use with humans. For example, caloric restriction has been found to increase the lifespan of rodents but not humans (Weindruch, 1996). Additionally, the notion that we can simply replace the worn out organs of older adults generates some important ethical questions: Will *Medicare* pay for these transplantations? Who will decide whether an older adult should go on an organ recipient list? Where will all the extra organs come from given the current shortage of organs for medically needed transplantations?

Adult intelligence

The information related to intelligence in older adulthood is rich and we believe that lectures on adult intelligence should include a discussion of fluid intelligence, crystallized intelligence and the effect of age on episodic memories, semantic memories, implicit memories, and short term memory. To account for memory loss in older adults, you could also describe the various reasons for memory loss including environmental factors, information-processing deficits (speed and inhibition difficulties), biological factors, and sensory-motor changes.

The notion that intelligence declines with age is a misconception. Rather, research suggests that overall intelligence remains fairly stable. Previous research has found that adults had stable, and even increasing, IQ scores until mid-30s and, for some individuals, until their mid-50s (Schaie, 1994). However, results of IQ testing are complicated by physical performance subtests, which are often timed. Reaction time slows with age so any decrease in intelligence scores may actually reflect results that are impacted by physical change rather than decreases in cognitive ability (this point could be an excellent tie-in to the cohort effects that you may have discussed during a previous research methods lecture). We typically end our discussion of adult intelligence by covering two theories related to the gradual slowing of reaction time observed in older adults: the peripheral slowing hypothesis and the generalized slowing hypothesis.

Aging and memory

Most students have heard of dementia and Alzheimer's disease (AD) but very few of them know the medical definitions for these memory disorders. In addition to providing more specific information about these diseases, we like to present information related to our favorite research on the topic. David Snowdon and colleagues (Riley, Snowdon, Desrosiers, 2005; Mortimer, Snowdon, Markesbery, 2003) have published a series of retrospective and longitudinal studies conducted with 678 Catholic sisters (aka the nun study; Lemonick & Mankato, 2001). Snowdon et al. obtained autobiographical essays written by the elderly nuns when they were in their early 20s. Together with interviews of the elderly nuns, cognitive evaluations, medical record review, and data from brain autopsies, Snowdon and colleagues have presented a number of interesting findings. For example, they found that more complex writing style (i.e., high idea density writing) during early adulthood was related to a lower risk of developing AD in later life (Riley et al., 2005). Another study found that nuns with higher education and a larger head circumference were at lower risk for developing dementia (Mortimer et al., 2003). Finally, they also found a link between high positive emotional autobiography content and longevity (Danner, Snowdon, & Friesen, 2001). The Danner et al. study on positive emotions and longevity could provide a nice segue into a discussion on the stability of personality.

Information related to aging and memory can be dense with technical information so we find it helpful to incorporate video clips in our lecture. Although you can try to describe how an fMRI machine works, what a CAT scan image looks like, or how to conduct cognitive remediation for stroke victims, it is much better to show video footage of these cutting edge techniques. *The Secret Life of the Brain* (Public Broadcasting Service, 2001; running time 60 minutes) is a five-episode series that can offer great supplemental information to any discussion on the brain. In particular, Episode 5 titled, *The Aging Brain: Through Many Lives*, provides a nice overview of aging, memory, stroke, and AD.

You also may consider bringing an expert on aging and memory to provide a guest lecture. If you are located near a large medical center or a teaching hospital, you may be able to invite a neurologist or neuropsychologist to discuss issues related to memory and aging. We are fortunate to have a Center on Memory and Aging located near our university. The director of the program is a faculty member in the School of Nursing. She provided a few guest lectures for our department that were very well received by students. During one lecture, our colleague described some of the early signs of memory loss, the methods used by her center to help caregivers of individuals with AD disease, and practical ways to help individuals with memory loss. When you invite an expert to speak to your class, it is possible that valuable future collaborations will arise. One of the happy by-products of arranging a guest lecture on memory and aging was that we were able to send a few psychology majors to work as supervised interns at the Center. It was truly a win-win situation for both the students (who gained valuable field experience) and for the center (which was in need of volunteers to work with patients).

Live expectancy vs. health expectancy

The possibility of knowing how long we have left to live is intriguing—and the plot line for many books, ghost stories, and horror movies. Although we cannot provide a very accurate prediction for students, we can critically evaluate the current data related to life expectancy. To highlight the section on life expectancy for students, we bring to class a chart listing the estimated life expectancy for individuals based on gender, race, and the year they were born. Each semester we ask for a few volunteers and point out the life expectancy for the year that they were born (this exercise can be sobering for the instructor as you become older ... you mean I was in college when you were born?). Currently, the life expectancy for an individual born in 1980 is 74 years (Brannon & Feist, 2006). We find it helpful to define life expectancy (e.g., it is based on the average lifespan for individuals born in the same year and includes infant mortality), outline the factors that are related to longer life expectancy (e.g., being female, moderate to light drinking, exercise, higher education, being married, rural living, etc.), and describe the factors that are negatively associated with life expectancy (e.g., being male, a history of heavy drinking, urban residence, divorced, never married, etc.). One of our teaching goals is for students to understand the difference between life expectancy and health expectancy as they are different concepts.

Older Adult Personality and Social Development

Again, following the discussion of physical and cognitive development in older adults, we move on to discuss issues related to social and personality development. As we are getting to the end of the course and likely have limited time available, we choose a select number of topics from the abundance of options available to discuss with the class. Often we choose to discuss successful aging and work and retirement with our students. We find that these topics are interesting and eye opening for our students because they often have not thought about these issues.

Successful aging

Having discussed human development from conception to adulthood and the growth that comes through those periods, students often become somewhat disheartened when we begin to discuss the later stages of life when growth is slower and our bodies begin to show their mortality. We find that discussing successful aging helps to keep students engaged in the material and lifts their spirits. We begin our discussion by asking students to think about an individual (that they know personally or have seen in the media) who they feel is aging successfully. We then ask students to list the attributes or factors that they feel contribute to this individual's successful aging. We use the list of attributes and factors later to link the students' responses to the theories we discuss.

In discussing successful aging, we cover three major theories: disengagement theory, activity theory, and continuity theory. Disengagement theory suggests that successful aging is characterized by an individual's gradual withdrawal from the world, physically, psychologically, and socially (Cummings & Henry, 1961). The withdrawal is a mutual endeavor and is not necessarily negative. When we discuss disengagement theory, we encourage our students to express their perspective on the theory and what costs and benefits individuals and society might experience from withdrawal.

Activity theory suggests that successful aging occurs when people maintain their engagement with the world. Activity theory grew from inconsistent results in studies examining aging. Although research suggests that some people age successfully by withdrawing (Carstensen, 1995; Settersten, 2002), research also suggests that others who remain active and involved are just as happy, and sometimes happier, than those who withdraw (Bergstrom & Holmes, 2000; Charles, Reynolds, & Gatz, 2001; Consedine, Magai, & King, 2004; Crosnoe & Elder, 2002). The variable results of studies examining successful aging suggest that one method does not work for everyone. We discuss with students that the current view of successful aging—continuity theory—is a compromise between disengagement and activity theories.

Continuity theory suggests that people should maintain a level of involvement in society that maximizes their sense of well-being and self-esteem (Atchley, 2003; Whitbourne, 2001). We return to our students' responses about the attributes and factors that they identified as contributing to successful aging and try to identify where they fit in terms of the different theories. Often we have attributes and factors that fit in each of the theories, which helps to accentuate our point that one's activity level and engagement with society and the world and the link to successful aging is quite personal and varies, based on an individual's needs. We end our discussion of successful aging by giving students a list of keys to successful aging that include:

- good physical and mental health;
- financial security;
- a sense of autonomy and independence;

- a positive outlook;
- choices (i.e., ability to reduce demands of life);
- optimization (i.e., highlighting your skills);
- compensation (i.e., making up for slowing down).

Work and retirement

After discussing successful aging, we move our discussion of social and personality development of older adults to work and retirement. Because many students are in the early adulthood phase of their lives and have not yet begun a career, it is hard for them to imagine how to wrap up a career. However, some students' parents are in the beginning stages of, or will soon be facing, retirement. We find it helpful to discuss the risks of retirement, how to retire successfully, the proposed stages of retirement, and how to plan for retirement.

As the semester winds down and students become more comfortable talking in class, we encourage them to participate in more discussion. We open the discussion of retirement with questions about when people should retire, the pros and cons of retirement, how far in advance one should think about retirement, and the sorts of plans one should have before retiring. Once we have our students thinking about retirement in a broad sense, we list some risks that are related to retirement such as unexpected health problems, risks to pension and benefits, outliving resources, having no husband, timing of retirement, and poor investment luck. Students may be able to think of some other risks that are associated with retirement. Although we feel it necessary to point out some risks related to retirement, we have a difficult time staying with the negative outcomes that could occur. To help lift students out of the negative view of retirement, we discuss some tips on how to manage retirement successfully. Some of the tips we have identified are paying off your home, working longer than you may have planned, managing your expenses and standard of living, managing your children, calculating the expenses of retirement, managing your assets to last for life, and consulting a financial planner.

Once we have discussed tips to avoid some of the risks, we discuss what retirement looks like. We remind students that mandatory retirement is illegal and has been since the late 1970s, with the exception of certain public safety jobs such as police, firefighters, prison guards, and pilots. We then go on to discuss the stages of retirement suggested by Atchley (1985; Atchley & Barusch, 2004). Atchley suggested that retirement may begin with a honeymoon phase where individuals participate in a variety of activities, such as travel, which they were not able to do when they were working. After the honeymoon period, individuals experience disenchantment because retirement is not meeting their expectations, they may be missing the stimulation and companionship they got from their jobs, or may be having a difficult time staying busy. Following disenchantment, individuals become reoriented with retirement and begin to consider their options and find new, more fulfilling activities to fill their time. This reorientation, if successful, often leads to a retirement routine, where the realities of retirement are acknowledged and the activities in which the individual is engaged are fulfilling. The last phase is termination, which can occur in one of two ways, an individual can return to work or they experience major physical deterioration and are unable to function independently.

We acknowledge to our students that not all individuals go through all the proposed stages of retirement nor is the sequence of stages the same for everyone. We encourage our students to think about and identify factors that may influence a person's reaction to retirement. We also reiterate that retirement is just like aging and is dependent on the individual.

We end our discussion about retirement by discussing some important things people should consider when planning their retirement. Gerontologists suggest several tips for retirement planning such as planning ahead financially, tapering off work gradually, exploring interests prior to retiring, discussing views and expectations of retirement with spouse or partner, consider living arrangements, determining the advantages and disadvantages of downsizing the current home, and planning to volunteer (Kreitlow & Kreitlow, 1997; Rowe & Kahn, 1998). Although the majority of our students are far from thinking of retirement, we find discussing retirement important because they may be able to help their parents through retirement.

Critical Thinking Questions

In discussing middle and older adult development with your students, there are many activities that provide opportunities for critical thinking. As with previous chapters, we encourage you to bring empirical literature into the classroom and allow your students to

202   Middle Adult and Older Adult Development

evaluate the developmental literature related to middle and later adulthood. Potential topics to use to foster critical thinking may be:

- Do you think that personalities change across the lifespan? Why or why not?
- Outline the possible threats (financial and otherwise) to a "good" retirement.
- What is the best way to accommodate someone with dementia?
- How would you depict an elderly character on TV?
- What stereotypes do we have about young-old adults and old-old adults?
- Describe the pros and cons of independent living, assisted living, retirement communities, nursing home care, and staying at home.

Controversial Topics

There are many topics discussed in the media that are related to middle and later adulthood, many of which are highly debated. Some controversial topics that you may choose to address with your students include:

- Should the very old be permitted to drive? Why or why not? What criteria should be used to determine who can drive?
- Should companies have a mandatory retirement age?
- Who should care for aging individuals?
- What are the pros and cons for the increased number of older adults?

Developmental Diversity

Middle and older adulthood are periods in which there are a multitude of opportunities to address diversity as it relates to development. Specific diversity-related topics to discuss with students that are relevant to their future experiences and choices include:

- Cultural differences in the way that younger individuals treat people in late adulthood. What aspects do these cultures have in common?
- Do Asian societies really revere old age? If so, what factors may account for the cultural propensity to revere older individuals?

You might assign students to watch a documentary film titled *Acting Our Age* (running time, 30 minutes; NAATA). The film features older South Asians in a retirement facility and the various cultural and generational issues they encounter. Another documentary film that focuses on gender roles and aging within the family context includes *Half the Sky: The Women of the Jiang Family* (running time, 50 minutes; Bullfrog Films). This film examines gender roles in China through the story of four generations of women in the Jiang family.
- What are some cultural variations in grandparenting, widowhood, and retirement?
- Is there a relation among gender, SES, and aging?
- The documentary film *Beauty Before Age: Growing Older in Gay Culture* (running time, 22 minutes; New Day Films) explores the attitudes held by a diverse group of gay men about the aging process.
- The documentary film *The Silver Age* (running time, 24 minutes; Bullfrog Films) explores aging and longevity in Japan, India, and Tunisia.

Appendix A

Helpful Websites for Teaching Older Adult Development

Adulthood and Aging, Division 20 of the American Psychological Association
  http://aging.ufl.edu/apadiv20/apadiv20.htm
National Institute on Aging – National Institutes of Health
  http://www.nia.gov/
Erik Erikson's 8 Stages of Psychosocial Development – Department of Psychology, SUNY-Courtland
  http://snycorva.cortland.edu/~ANDERSMD/ERIK/WELCOME.HTML

Chapter 10

Death and Dying

Providing a lecture on death and dying can be a daunting task. Admittedly, teaching a section on death and dying was extremely challenging for us as new instructors but it became easier with more teaching experience—and death-related life experiences. As beginning instructors, we were concerned that our lecture would be too somber and that we did not have adequate death-related experience to give the subject its due. To be sure, talking about the process of death, embalming, and purchasing a casket can create a serious atmosphere in the classroom! The more teaching experience we obtained, however, the more we have come to enjoy teaching material related to death and dying. We have grown to like teaching about death because it is one of the few life experiences that we can say with 100% certainty that all of us will eventually experience (unlike marriage, childrearing, attending graduate school, etc.). Indeed, teaching about death and dying will provide you with the opportunity to remind your students about an inevitability that they probably do not consider regularly. Also, when describing individual differences in dealing with death, your students may experience some emotions that do not typically surface during a regular lecture. In some way, it can be satisfying to see that a lecture can affect your students—that they are, in fact, listening to it and not dozing! Another (admittedly selfish) reason that we enjoy teaching the topic of death might be that it is the last chapter of the book. Teaching about death always signals the end of our journey through the lifespan with our students.

If you are extremely uncomfortable teaching material related to death and dying, you may want to include a video or ask a guest speaker to cover this lecture. For example, an individual who recently experienced the death of a loved one, a hospice worker, a palliative care physician, or a funeral home director could be excellent supplements to your lecture. Before we felt that we had adequate experience to teach death and dying, we had a guest speaker lecture on her personal knowledge related to the stages of grief. Hearing the experiences of our guest speaker helped us to formulate a significant portion of our lecture on how to help someone who has experienced the death of a loved one. You may also want to read some of the available literature on the topic of death and dying to prepare for your lecture. There are many excellent resources available on the subject of death. The two-volume edited text, *The Handbook of Death and Dying* (Bryant, 2003) contains an amazing compendium of information related to death and dying on everything from reincarnation to physician-assisted death. The non-fiction best sellers *How We Die* (Nuland, 1993) and *When Bad Things Happen to Good People* (Kushner, 1981) also provide very helpful perspectives on death.

We find that organization is the key to a successful course and giving a rushed lecture on death and dying is not the optimal way to end the semester. When teaching about death, we find ourselves taking a slightly slower tempo to present information. Our students may influence our slowed tempo because they seem to be fascinated by the death-related information that we present at the end of the course. Another reason for our slowed pace may be that students have anxiety about the end of the semester and we like to make the learning environment as calm as possible to help allay student fears about the final exam. To be sure, the fact that we are teaching about death may have something to do with the down-beat atmosphere as well. In retrospect, our more successful lectures on death and dying have included the human element—anecdotes of how people we know have responded to the news of a loved one's death, how parents (and we) have dealt with the death of chronically ill children in the hospital setting, and memories that we have of our own experiences with death as children. We find that an honest lecture about death infused with a little bit of appropriate humor is the best recipe for the end of our course.

Some important thanatological constructs to cover for the death and dying period include the definitions of death, developmental differences in understanding death, common reactions to grief in childhood, factors related to death across the lifespan, Kubler-Ross' (1969, 1995) stages of dying, hospice, the difference between bereavement and grief, and how to help someone who is grieving. Because there are so many variations across cultures related to funeral rites and customs, we recommend focusing on developmental diversity for at least part of your lecture on death and dying. It can also be powerful to show a video that depicts widows and widowers describe their experience of the stages of grief.

Although we view a great deal of death in the movies and on TV, it is very rare for anyone in our current society to see a death occur in person. We usually start our lecture on death by asking if any students in the room have ever witnessed a death. Occasionally, a student will report being in the room when a grandparent or great-grantparent died. Additionally, you may have a student training for a health-related field with some death-relevant experience to share. For the most part, however, very few students will report seeing a death first-hand. Asking about your students' real experiences with death will begin the lecture on a serious note, but it also illustrates that we live in a society in which death is taken care of behind closed doors.

If you were to examine the experiences of your students, chances are that some variation exists in their feelings towards the deceased individual (e.g., a stranger in a hospital versus a cherished relative). Just as each individual has unique personality characteristics and talents, each death is unique as well (Nuland, 1993). Additionally, the reactions that your students report about witnessing a death are likely to be influenced by several factors including the age of the deceased individual, the student's developmental level at the time of death, and his or her previous death-related experience. Hopefully, you will be able to incorporate the experiences with death shared by your students to help explain some of the constructs related to death throughout lecture.

Speaking about death in clear and realistic terms is something that many individuals avoid. Just think of all the euphemisms that we have to describe death! You could lead your class in compiling a list of all the slang terms that exist for death in our culture (e.g., kicked the bucket, bought the farm, etc.) as well as the euphemisms that are commonly used (e.g., passed away, gone, etc.) when speaking about a dead individual. Compiling a list of slang terms for death may bring some lightness to the lecture and it can also illustrate how talking about death in clear terms is uncomfortable for some people. Kastenbaum (1985) and Kalish (1987) provide guidance on how to conduct this exercise.

Kubler-Ross (1969, 1995) was an important pioneer in the field of thanatology. Because of her seminal work, her theory is included in many articles and books about death. Her theory is a regular staple of our lecture on death and dying. However, we do try to make the point that although Kubler-Ross's theory provides an excellent framework for predicting behavior, there are some serious criticisms of her theory. We also try to mention that the stages of Kubler-Ross's theory can be used to describe responses to the loss of a marriage, relationship, job, or good health—not just death. To help explain Kubler-Ross' theory, we often incorporate the video *Death and Dying* (Magna Systems, 2001; running time 27 minutes) into our lecture as the narrator provides a good summary of the theory.

Developmental Differences in Understanding Death

As psychologists, we want to predict behavior and understand how individuals think about the world. One way to structure your lecture about death and dying is to take a developmental approach to the question "What do people of different ages understand about death?" Another perspective would be "How do people deal with death at different ages?" One aspect of teaching death and dying that we enjoy is that it is possible to consider the entire lifespan within the same lecture. Our previous lectures for specific stages of life tend to focus on one aspect of the lifespan and we relish this rare opportunity to use a true lifespan approach during a lecture.

Although research has focused on many different concepts of death, we focus on three components related to understanding death: the *permanence* of death, the *universality* of death for all living things, and the *non-functionality* of the human body after death (Speece & Brent, 1996). During our lecture on the concept of death, we walk the class through the main stages of childhood (toddlers, school-aged children, adolescence, etc.) that we covered earlier in the course and we consider the progression of the understanding of death. We provide some advice regarding how to help children deal with death. Finally, we discuss typical child and adult responses towards death as well as the most common cause of death for individuals at different ages. If you would like to include an overview of the developmental differences in understanding death, we recommend the books *Helping Bereaved Children: A Handbook for Practitioners* (Webb, 2002) or the *Handbook of Childhood Death and Bereavement* (Corr & Corr, 1996).

How children understand death

Children who are two to four years old typically do not understand any aspect (the permanence, universality, or non-functionality) of death. Most youngsters of this age have difficulty answering the question "Will you die someday?" (Speece & Brent, 1996). The main reason for a child's underdeveloped concept of death is that he or she does not yet have the cognitive resources to understand the notion of death. Additionally, many children lack death-related experience and they may be influenced by images they see in the media. We often use the example of carton characters and fairy tale heroines who may appear to die initially, but revive and return to life later in the story. Typically, these stories are misleading because the death-state may not be depicted as permanent (e.g., Sleeping Beauty) and the body may not be depicted as non-functional (e.g., Casper the Friendly Ghost, Wily Coyote).

When faced with caring for a child who has experienced the loss of a meaningful relationship, we suggest that parents designate a caretaker for the child during the funeral so the young child can take a break from the service. Some children may not be able to handle a funeral service because it will be difficult for them to maintain decorum and appropriate behavior when they do not understand completely the significance of the event. For example, we know of a small child who did not understand the significance of her great-grandfather's funeral and, instead of sitting quietly during the wake, she ran around the room and collected as many prayer cards as possible (thinking that they were like baseball cards).

By the time they are seven years old, most school-aged children understand that death is permanent and that the body is not functional after death (Speece & Brent, 1996). School-aged children may still have difficulty understanding, however, that death is universal. Children in this age range may think that death is something that happens to old people, or to other children's grandparents—not their own.

When caring for an older bereaved child, parents can be honest about the circumstances surrounding a death and explain the customs related to the funeral that the child will encounter. We suggest that parents prepare a school-aged child for a funeral service as the child may have questions about the service and the procedures related to preparation of the deceased person's remains. For example, one eight-year-old once asked during a memorial service how it was possible that his aunt was able to fit into the crematorium's urn.

We believe that it is important to cover the common reactions to grief in childhood because some children experience significant impairment in functioning following the death of a close family member (Melhem, Moritz, Walker, Shear, & Brent, 2007; Wolchik, Tein, Sandler, & Ayers, 2006). Much like our rationale for covering previous material in the course, we believe that it is important to cover the information related to children's grief responses because students may one day face the task of caring for a child who has experienced a significant loss. Many young children do not have the verbal ability—or self reflection—to indicate that they are sad, scared, or grief stricken. This lack of verbal ability can result in the child acting out behaviorally following the death of an important individual. Additionally, children need daily structure and the death of a close loved one (e.g., parent or sibling) will likely result in a marked change in family activities. As such, a child may respond to the environmental disruption caused by death in a number of ways:

- Children may act out their feelings of sadness or uneasiness in the form of temper tantrums or disruptive behavior (Van Eerdewegh, Bieri, Parrilla, & Clayton, 1982). Parents may feel that a child with acting out behaviors is taking advantage of the situation at home—or that the child is especially naughty. However, the child may need some extra attention and have no other way to gain this attention other than through acting out.
- Recalling our previous lecture on child autonomy and young children's tendency to become less autonomous and independent when they are in unfamiliar territory, some children become more dependent and clingy around caregivers following the death of a close relative. Children may become especially clingy if they have experienced the death of an important attachment figure (Baker & Sedney, 1996). The anxiety related to losing one parent may increase as the child starts to worry about the safety and well-being of the other parent. Full-fledged school refusal could

develop in a child who refuses to go to school out of fear of what might happen to the surviving parent.
- Another way that grief may express itself in the young child is through over-activity (Baker & Sedney, 1996). Occasionally, the child may present as though he or she has developed ADHD but it is the child's grief response that is responsible for the increased activity. Hyperactivity can be a sign of anxiety in children so, rather than sending the child for a Ritalin evaluation, parents and clinicians must be sensitive to the events surrounding the onset of the child's increased activity.
- There are many milestones in child development during which children outgrow immature behavior. Thumb sucking, wetting the bed, baby talk, and head banging are all behaviors that most typically developing children eventually outgrow. However, when a young child experiences grief or anxiety related to the death of a loved one, he or she may demonstrate distress by behavioral regression (e.g., he may start wetting the bed again) (Van Eerdewegh et al., 1982).

How adolescents understand death

Adolescents are able to comprehend all three aspects of death (permanence, nonfunctionality, universality). Recalling our previous lecture on adolescent cognition, we remind students that adolescents do not seriously think about how they will die one day because of the personal fable. Death is perceived as a long way in the distant future by the typical adolescent—which may help to explain why adolescents are at such high risk for accidental death. Notably, when faced with the loss of a meaningful relationship, many adolescents will mask their emotions related to loss in an effort to appear "normal" (Baker & Sedney, 1996; Lendrum & Syme, 2004).

Unlike children, some adolescents fantasize about death and what it would be like to leave the physical world (Range, 1996). Adolescents who are very depressed may contemplate what would happen if they were to solve their problems using the ultimate solution—suicide. The troubled adolescent may feel neglected in life and fantasize about how his or her funeral would be staged. Furthermore, he or she may think "just wait and see how you feel once I'm gone" and hope for emotional displays from particular individuals following his or her unexpected death. Indeed, adolescents who describe a fascination with death and who meet other risk factors related to suicide (e.g., significant depression, cognitive deficits, and recent experience with a negative life event) should be referred for a suicide-risk evaluation (Range, 1996).

How adults understand death

Most adults understand all aspects of death and they appreciate that they will one day die (Speece & Brent, 1996). Young adults typically focus on the number of years that they have lived and feel as though it is their due to have many more years of life. Most middle-aged adults report that they know death can occur at any time; however, they tend to focus on the number of years that they have left to live (Levinson, 1992). Additionally, middle-aged adults also report the greatest fears about death—perhaps because it can be disconcerting to think that the time you have left on the earth is less than the time that you have already lived. Alternatively, some middle-aged individuals report that knowing their time on earth is short provides them with a sense of vigor and purpose for their daily activities.

Adults in the older adult period are surrounded by peers who are ill or who have died. After experiencing a great deal of death in their environment, older adults know with certainty that their lives will come to an end. Notably, older adults report the fewest fears about death—perhaps because they have been able to live a full life and have adequate time to conduct a life review (Feldman, 2006).

Dealing with death

Another facet of our death and dying lecture includes a discussion of how individuals react to the news that they are terminally ill. If you have time, it can be a useful exercise to talk about some developmental differences related to facing one's own death. As part of this exercise, we describe the most common causes of death for individuals at different life stages and we cite research related to developmental reactions to impending death.

How children deal with impending death Recent survey data suggest that the most frequent cause of death for US children is accidental (National Institutes of Health, 2007). In the first year of life, preterm birth, genetic disorders, Sudden Infant Death syndrome, and low birth weight all contribute to the infant mortality rate (Centers for Disease Control, 2007). For children aged 5 to 14 years, accidents, cancer, and homicide are the leading cause of death. Data related to child mortality could provide a forum for a diversity-focused lecture in that, sadly, the causes of child death around the world vary depending on the health status and resources of the county (Seale, 2003).

In addition to describing death among children, we discuss some of the challenges faced by the child's family. Terminally ill children face a unique situation. Most children are concerned about making friends, completing homework, and the next little league game. However, the terminally ill child must face the inconvenience and pain associated with frequent hospitalizations and invasive medical procedures. These children face their own premature death and they may even find themselves in the position of comforting grief-stricken parents. Indeed, one of the most difficult parts about working with terminally ill children is helping family members—and healthcare providers—with their feelings of guilt, loss, and grief (Breyer, Sanfeliz, Cieurzo, & Meyer, 2006). Although Kubler-Ross's theory was not developed with children in mind, we like to think about how Kubler-Ross' theory might relate to a terminally-ill child or adolescent. Because terminally ill children may not comprehend the full implications of death, they may easily fall within the acceptance stage of Kubler-Ross's theory. Parental reactions, however, would likely include anticipatory grief and the entire gamut of Kubler-Ross's theory. Interestingly, research has not provided definite support for the notion that terminally ill children have a better understanding of death because of their medical condition (Speece & Brent, 1996).

To read the personal story of an individual who lived through the death of his young son, students may want to read Kushner's (1981) *When Bad Things Happen to Good People*. In a related vein, you could discuss the implications of not telling a child that he or she is terminally ill. Some parents are so concerned about protecting their terminally ill child that they request that no one tell the child that he or she is ill. Deciding not to disclose information to the child about the true nature of his or her condition is somewhat controversial and it can be interesting to engage students in a discussion on whether children should be told about their impeding death. One factor that may contribute to the discussion is that children are quite attuned to their environment and that hospital staff often talk about medical cases within earshot of the patient's hospital bed (i.e., despite parental wishes, children often learn about their condition).

How adolescents deal with impending death Motor vehicle accidents, homicide, and suicide are the three top causes of adolescent death (National Institutes of Health, 2007). Due to the sudden nature of the majority of adolescent deaths, most adolescents who die do not have time to fully grasp their impending death. In these situations, Kubler-Ross's stages of dying do not apply. However, for a small minority of adolescents it can be very clear that death is imminent. Seriously ill adolescents must face the fact that they may not have much time to live. In these chronically ill adolescents, the personal fable may not manifest itself in the same way. For example, rather than feeling invincible, the teen may feel anger related to the activities that she is not able to engage in with her friends as a result of frequent hospital visits or fatigue and pain related to their treatment regimen (Feldman, 2006). One possible reason for adolescent anger related to an anticipated death, relative to younger children, may be that they have a full understanding of death.

Summer camps that are organized around chronic illness such as cancer and cystic fibrosis may be helpful to include in your lecture on young people and death. These camps serve many useful purposes for chronically ill children and their families. For example, the camps provide much needed respite care for parents, fun activities for children and adolescents, and a way for young people to socialize with other individuals with the same diagnosis. However, one potentially negative aspect that camp-goers experience is the death of their camp friends. The news of a death spreads quickly within a community as parents, physicians, nurses, and child patients are often in close contact due to frequent hospitalizations and outpatient clinic visits. Although most of us have heard about the camps that cater for chronically ill children, the potential for bereavement as a side-effect of the camp experience is a less well considered point.

How young adults deal with impending death The most frequent causes of death in young adulthood are accidents (i.e., motor vehicle accidents, drowning, fire, falls, and poisoning) and homicide (National Institutes of Health, 2007). Thus, most young adult deaths are sudden and it is rare for young adults to have time to process an impending death. Ask your students if they know of any peers who died recently and the cause of death. Most of the deaths that students share in class will likely be accidental. Grief reactions to sudden death can be different from grief following anticipated death (Wijngaards-deMeij et al., 2005). Although both types of death can be difficult to accept, reaction to sudden death is almost always shock and disbelief, especially for parents.

Young adults with chronic illness and their families often report feeling cheated by life (Kushner, 1981). For them it is very important to maintain the meaning in life and pursue the life events that other young adults enjoy. For example, a young adult who has a poor prognosis may still want to marry his sweetheart and they may try for children with the knowledge that the ill member of the couple will likely die soon. Indeed, when a young adult dies, loved ones often experience depression and anger.

How middle-aged adults deal with impending death The most frequent causes of death in middle age are heart disease, cancer, stroke, and respiratory disease (Centers for Disease Control, 2007). Recalling the responsibilities that many middle-aged adults have at home and at work, a terminal diagnosis can be extremely disruptive—especially if young children are involved. One video that we have found helpful in describing illness in the middle age period is entitled *Tell Them You're Fine* (Aronson, 1997; running time, 17 minutes). This video offers a touching and a somewhat sad look at a group of three middle-aged individuals who have been diagnosed with cancer. Part of the video depicts the individuals in a support group—which is a nice way to tie-in the importance of providing support for individuals who are chronically ill and facing uncertainty.

How older adults deal with impending death The most frequent cause of death in old age is heart disease, cancer, stroke, respiratory disease, and accidents (Centers for Disease Control, 2007). Often the wear and tear on the human body has gradually taken its toll and the older adult has adequate time to face his or her impending death. Have you ever gone to visit an elderly relative and had him or her ask you which belongings of theirs would you like to have? These adults are getting their mental house—and physical house—in order for death. Death is not far from the thoughts of many older adults and it can be very uncomfortable for the younger adults in the family who want to say "Please don't talk like that, you are going to outlive all of us." In reality, accepting the items and the help that the older person is offering can help them to deal with their impending death.

One feature that we describe for our students regarding older adults and death is that older adults have the highest suicide rate of any age group. Firearms, hanging, and drug or gas overdose are the three most common methods of suicide for older adults (Department of Health and Human Services, 2007). It may be helpful to describe some of the risk factors for elder suicide, which include increasing age (the suicide rate is highest for individuals age 80–84 relative to those aged 70–79), depression, the loss of a spouse, and a poor support system (Department of Health and Human Services, 2007). Related to our discussion on elder suicide, we often describe the para-suicidal behavior of a former patient of ours who lost his wife of many years and would drive aimlessly along the interstate in the hopes that a semi truck would run him off the road.

Support groups and bereavement care

Students may be interested to learn about the support groups and bereavement care that are available to children and adults when they have experienced the death of a loved one (Bacon, 1996). For example, major hospitals typically offer support groups for the children of a parent diagnosed with terminal cancer. If any of your students are interested in a career as a child life specialist or pediatric psychologist, they may have the opportunity to lead a hospital-based support group for children. Another common program offered through local hospice centers is a summer camp-style program for children who have experienced the death of a loved one. These grief camps are usually offered by local hospice organizations once or twice each year. Volunteer therapists lead children through age-appropriate activities (e.g., art projects, games, role play) that allow children to process the death and to find meaning in their loss. Many of these programs attempt to bolster the resilience of bereaved children by focusing on psychological empowerment (Barnard, Morland, & Nagy, 1998).

In addition to providing end of life care for individuals who are terminally ill, hospices offer support groups for middle-aged adults and older adults as well. Much like the child-focused summer grief camps, bereavement groups offer adults an opportunity to share their experiences with other bereaved individuals. The purpose of grief groups is to help the individual process their loss and find meaning in life. Another option for bereaved individuals is support groups offered through church organizations. Such church groups may be preferable if the bereaved individual would like to incorporate strong spiritual and religious beliefs in their grief response.

Responding to death

We typically describe the difference between bereavement and grief. We also cover the stages of grief. One important point that we try to make is that individuals have different ways of dealing with the death of a loved one and that there are many feelings associated with each stage (Lendrum & Syme, 2004). Some individuals and families are comfortable showing a great outpouring of emotion following the death of a loved one. Other individuals and families will display just the hint of a sniffle during, and following, a funeral. Hopefully by the end of our lecture on the stages of grief, students recognize that individuals who do not show emotion following a death grieve in their own quiet way—and that an outward lack of emotion does not mean that the individual is unfeeling or does not care about the deceased. When it comes to emotions, we incorporate the useful metaphor of a thermostat—some people may have a *feeling* thermostat that is turned to a different (i.e., lower) setting than friends and family.

Cultural differences in the death process

There are several points at which you may decide to include a discussion of the diversity of death. The stages of grief, for example, could be one such area that you may decide to include in a discussion of the cultural differences related to death and dying. The students at our university are primarily Christian. Many of them have not been exposed to the funeral customs of other cultures so we occasionally use the first half of a video called *Death and Dying* (Magna Systems, 2001; running time, 27 minutes) to provide an introduction to Hindu, Buddhist, Amish Christian, Islamic, and Jewish traditions around death. Based on our audience, this section of lecture can be a very one-sided conversation as we often do not have much class participation from the students. However, we value diversity and still think that it is an important aspect to include in our lecture. Some cultural variations on funeral rites that you could consider, and that we often mention in class, include festive New Orleans funeral parades, Hindu funeral pyres, the tradition in the Southern US states of traffic stopping on the side of the road as funeral processions drive by, and ancient Egyptian mummification.

Final arrangements

What is it like to bury a loved one? Most students will not have experience with the steps that one must take to bury a loved one. After we spend time on the stages that an individual progresses through while he or she comes to terms with his or her illness and impending death and the grief process that loved ones progress through, we also consider what happens to the body. If you are comfortable dealing with the material related to organizing a funeral, it can be a compelling supplement to the stages of grief. After a death, something must be done with the body and few people consider what that process is like—or the number of things that could be done with a body. Although we do not go into great detail, we occasionally discuss the process of embalming and the training required to become a mortician (Williams, 2003). Sadly, one of us (EBK) had the experience of shopping for caskets at a funeral home after the death of a grandparent. The experience was eye-opening and something that we draw upon when discussing final arrangements.

Consumerism has touched even death in the US! For example, you could describe the different types of caskets that are available, how they are constructed, the average price range for a coffin, and how they are labeled with information about the life of the person whose remains are inside of the coffin. One of our favorite references to a casket is from the book *Rammer Jammer Yellow Hammer* in which football enthusiasts are described as choosing a casket emblazoned with their favorite college's school seal (St. John, 2005). In this example, the social life of the deceased individual was reflected in his choice of casket!

Death, Dying, and Saying Goodbye

Perhaps in addition to the material related to death and dying in this chapter, we should also say a few words about ending your course. We usually tell classes that we enjoyed teaching them and we urge them to keep in touch as they continue their educational and occupational pursuits. If we are saying goodbye to an especially wonderful group of students we always say so! As a teacher you will be fortunate to have students who contribute to class discussions, come prepared to class, and work hard to learn the material. Unfortunately, you will probably also teach some entitled students who would rather text message their friends during class and complain about their final grade. Whenever we are fortunate enough to have a classroom of students who fit the former description, we provide them with positive feedback at the end of the course to let them know how wonderful they were in class.

We also encourage you to end your class by soliciting feedback from your students. It can feel scary to open yourself up to criticism but it is one of the best ways that you can learn how to tweak your course for future semesters. Some students will have overly negative, nonproductive things to say and some students will be very effusive with praise for your class. Either situation is not terribly helpful in developing your skills as an educator. Students who offer concrete examples of things to try in the future will be the most beneficial to you. We always obtain feedback from students by using the university-generated class evaluation form used by our department. However, if you want more detailed information about your teaching style to supplement the official form used by your college, you may want to use an empirically based evaluation form (Keeley, Smith, & Buskist, 2006).

No matter what sort of semester we have—be it positive or merely so-so—we do our part to bring the entire human lifespan to students. In addition to learning theories, facts, and research findings, we dearly hope that our students are also better sons, daughters, spouses, parents, professionals, and citizens because of our class. With any luck, the benefits are not for our students alone. Each time we teach developmental psychology we gain a better understanding of ourselves and those around us . . . and isn't that what development is all about?

Critical Thinking Opportunities

- What are the pros and cons of using hospice care?
- What are the pros and cons of talking to elderly parents about advance directives regarding their deaths?
- Read the book *Tuesdays with Morrie* (Albom, 1997) and use Kubler-Ross's stages to describe the main protagonists.
- Listen to the Frank Sinatra song *My Way* and use Kubler-Ross's stages to describe his "life review" at the end of the song.
- A recent review of bereavement related interventions found very little support for the efficacy of grief counseling—some

interventions may even be *detrimental* for bereaved individuals (Jordan & Neimeyer, 2003). Would you recommend grief counseling for a recently widowed relative? Why or why not? How do psychologists know for sure that clinical interventions work?
- Donating your body to science is a viable alternative to burial; however, few people choose this option. Perhaps they do not like the idea of allowing medical students to practice autopsies on them. You could even donate your body to a museum exhibit. For example, Dr. Gunther Von Hagen's *Body Worlds* – the traveling museum exhibit in which 200 human specimens—sometimes entire bodies—have been preserved through the process called "plastination." This exhibit debuted in Japan in 1995 and has been on rotating display through major cities throughout the world (Museum of Science and Industry of Chicago, 2007). Would you donate your remains to science in this way? Why or why not?
- What is the best way to help an adult who is grieving? What is the best way to help a child who is grieving? For some guidance in the area of grief counseling, you could turn to a book entitled *Gift of Tears* (Lendrum & Syme, 2004).

Controversial Topics

- Should euthanasia and physician-assisted suicide be legalized? Why or why not?
- Should tax payer money be used to fund socially sanctioned death such as abortion and capital punishment if some citizens are morally opposed to these practices? Is using weapons in war and armed conflict to kill humans different from accepting abortion and capital punishment?
- The institution of capital punishment necessitates that some individuals are responsible for developing and implementing lethal devices to end human life. What are the moral implications of endorsing capital punishment from this perspective?
- What are the ethical implications of parents who refuse medical treatment for terminally ill children? Who should have the right/privilege to decide whether a child should receive life saving treatment?
- When is an individual a good candidate for organ donation (i.e., who should receive organ transplants?). Should functional death be the criteria for harvesting organs?

Developmental Diversity

Perhaps because of the ubiquity of death, there is rich variation in historical and cultural differences in dealing with death. There are several readings available to round out your discussion of cross-cultural variations in the death experience, including work on Native Americans and death (Cox, 2003), common Japanese customs (Faiola, 2005; Suzuki, 2003), common Hindu practices (Rambachan, 2003), common Muslim practices (Sultan, 2003), common Tao practices (Crowder, 2003), and Jewish customs related to death (Schindler, 2003). Some questions that you might explore with your students include:

- What are some historical and cross-cultural variations in the death experience?
- What are some religious differences in the concept of the after life?
- Is embalming used in every culture?

References

Adler, J. (2005). Children of the fallen, *Newsweek*, March 21, 2005. (27–31).
Adolph, K. E., & Berger, S. E. (2005). Physical and motor development. In M. H. Bornstein & M. E. Lamb (Eds.). *Developmental science: An advanced textbook* (5th ed.) (pp. 223–281). Mahwah, NJ: Lawrence Erlbaum Associates.
Ainsworth, M. D. S. (1979). Infant-mother attachment. *American Psychologist, 34*, 932–937.
Ainsworth, M. D. S., Blehar, M., Waters, E., & Wall, S. (1978). *Patterns of attachment: A psychological study of the strange situation*. Hillsdale, N.J.: Lawrence Erlbaum Associates.
Albom, M. (1997). *Tuesdays with Morrie*. New York: Doubleday.
Al-Qahtani, N. H. (2005). Foetal response to music and voice. *The Australian and New Zealand Journal of Obstetrics and Gynaecology, 45*, 414–417.
American Psychiatric Association. (1980). *Diagnostic and statistical manual of mental disorders* (3rd ed.). Washington, DC: Author.
American Psychiatric Association. (1994). *Diagnostic and statistical manual of mental disorders* (4th ed.). Washington, DC: Author.
American Psychiatric Association. (2000). *Diagnostic and statistical manual of mental disorders: Text Revision* (4th ed.). Washington, DC: Author.
American Psychiatric Association. (2006). *Practice guideline for the treatment of patients with eating disorders* (3rd ed.). Washington, DC: Author.

American Psychological Association Task Force on Strengthening the Teaching and Learning of Undergraduate Psychological Sciences. (2006). *Teaching, learning and assessing in a developmentally coherent curriculum.* Washington, DC: American Psychological Association.

Antonucci, T. C. (2001). Social relations: An examination of social networks, social support, and sense of control. In J. E. Birren & K. W. Schaie (Eds.), *Handbook of psychology of aging* (5th ed.) (pp. 427–453). San Diego: Academic Press.

Arabin, B. (2002). Music during pregnancy. *Ultrasound in Obstetrics and Gynecology, 20,* 425–430.

Arnold, E. H., & O'Leary, S. G. (1997). Mothers' and fathers' discipline of hard-to-manage toddlers. *Child & Family Behavior Therapy, 19,* 1–11.

Aronson, I. (Director). (1997). *Tell them you're fine.* [VHS video]. Boston, MA: Fanlight Productions.

Arquette, R. (Director and Producer). (2002). *Searching for Debra Winger* [Motion Picture]. United States: Immortal Entertainment.

Aspinwall, O. G., & Taylor, S. E. (1993). Effects of social comparison direction, threat, and self-esteem on affect, evaluation, and expected success. *Journal of Personality and Social Psychology, 64,* 708–722.

Atchley, R. C. (1985). *Social forces and aging: An introduction to social gerontology.* Belmont, CA: Wadsworth.

Atchley, R. C. (2003). Why most people cope well with retirement. In J. Ronch & J. Goldfield (Eds.), *Mental wellness in aging: Strength-based approaches* (pp. 123–138). Baltimore, MD: Health Professions Press.

Atchley, R. C., & Barusch, A. (2004). *Social forces and aging* (10th ed.). Belmont, CA: Wadsworth.

Atkinson, J., Anker, S., Braddick, O., Nokes, L., Mason, A., & Braddick, F. (2001). Visual and visuospatial development in young children with Williams syndrome. *Developmental Medicine and Child Neurology, 43,* 330–337.

Aversano, S. (Producer), & Dey, T. (Director). (2006). *Failure to launch* [Motion Picture]. United States: Paramount Pictures.

Aylward, G. P. (2003). Neonatology, prematurity, NICU, and developmental issues. In M. C. Roberts (Ed.). *Handbook of pediatric psychology* (3rd ed.) (pp. 253–268). New York: Guilford Press.

Bacon, J. B. (1996). Support groups for bereaved children. In C. A. Corr & D. M. Corr (Eds.), *Handbook of childhood death and bereavement* (pp. 285–304). New York: Springer Publishing Company.

Baillargeon, R. (1994). How do infants learn about the physical world? *Current Directions in Psychological Science, 3,* 133–140.

Baillargeon, R. (1995). A model of physical reasoning in infancy. In C. Rovee-Collier & L. P. Lipsitt (Eds.), *Advances in infancy research* (Vol. 9, pp. 305–371). Norwood, NJ: Ablex.

Baird, B. N. (2005). *The internships, practicum, and field placement handbook: A Guide for the helping professions.* Upper Saddle River, NJ: Pearson.

Baker, J. E., & Sedney, M. A. (1996). How bereaved children cope with loss: An overview. In C. A. Corr & D. M. Corr (Eds.) *Handbook of childhood death and bereavement* (pp. 109–129). New York: Springer Publishing Company.

Ball, H. L., Hooker, E., & Kelly, P. J. (2000). Parent-infant co-sleeping: Fathers' roles and perspectives. *Infant Child Development, 9,* 67–74.

Balls Organista, P., Chun, K. M., & Marin, G. (Eds.). (1998). *Readings in ethnic psychology.* New York: Routledge.

Balls Organista, P., Chun, K. M., & Marin, G. (2000). Teaching an undergraduate course on ethnic diversity. *Teaching of Psychology, 27,* 12–17.

Barkley, R. (1995). *Taking charge of ADHD: The complete, authoritative guide for parents.* New York: Guilford Press.

Barkley, R. A. (1997). *Defiant children: A clinician's manual for assessment and parent training.* New York: Guilford Press.

Barkley, R., & Murphy, K. (1998). *Attention-deficit hyperactivity disorder: A clinical workbook.* New York: Guilford Press.

Barnard, P., Morland, I., & Nagy, J. (1998). *Children, bereavement and trauma: Nurturing resilience.* London: Jessica Kingsley Publishers.

Barone, S. (2007). *Forever young living on the coast* (June issue). Destin, FL: Steve Barone.

Bartlett, N. H., Vasey, P. L., & Bukowski, W. M. (2005). Is gender identity disorder in children a mental disorder? *Sex Roles, 43,* 753–785.

Baum, C. (Producer), & Shyer, C. (Director). (1991). *Father of the bride* [Motion Picture]. United States: Sandollar Productions.

Baum, C. (Producer), & Shyer, C. (Director). (1995). *Father of the bride part 2* [Motion Picture]. United States: Sandollar Productions.

Baumrind, D. (1966). Effects of authoritative parental control on child behavior. *Child Development, 37,* 887–907.

Baumrind, D. (1996). The discipline controversy revisited. *Family Relations, 45,* 405–414.

Beck, A. T., Steer, R. A., & Brown, G. K. (1996). *Beck Depression Inventory Manual* (2nd ed.). San Antonio, TX: The Psychological Corporation.

Belsky, J. (2006). *Experiencing the lifespan.* New York: Worth Publishers.

Bergstrom, M. J., & Holmes, M. E. (2000). Lay theories of successful aging after the death of a spouse: A network text analysis of bereavement advice. *Health Communication, 12,* 377–406.

Berk, L. E. (2006). *Development through the lifespan* (4th ed.). Boston: Allyn & Bacon.

Berman, P. S. (Producer), & Minnelli, V. (Director). (1950). *Father of the bride* [Motion Picture]. United States: Metro-Goldwyn-Mayer.

Bernard, J. (1982). *The future of marriage.* New Haven, CT: Yale University Press.

Berndt, T. J. (2002). Friendship quality and social development. *Current Directions in Psychological Science, 11,* 7–10.

Bianchi, S. M., & Casper, L. M. (2000). American families. *Population Bulletin, 55,* No. 4.

Birmaher, B., Ryan, N. D., Williamson, D. E., Brent, D. A., Kaufman, J., Dahl, et al. (1996). Childhood and adolescent depression: A review of the past ten years. (part I). *Journal of the American Academy of Child and Adolescent Psychiatry, 35,* 1427–1451.

Birmaher, B., Williamson, D., Dahl, R., Axelson, D. A., Kaufman, J., Dorn, L. (2004). Clinical presentation and course of depression in youth: Does onset in childhood differ from onset in adolescence? *Journal of the American Academy of Child and Adolescent Psychiatry, 43,* 63–70.

Birney, D. P., Citron-Pousty, J. H., Lutz, D. J., & Sternberg, R. J. (2005). The development of cognitive and intellectual abilities. In M. H. Bornstein & M. E. Lamb (Eds.). *Developmental science: An advanced textbook* (5th ed.) (pp. 327–358). Mahwah, NJ: Lawrence Erlbaum Associates.

Black, M. M., & Matula, K. (1999). *Essentials of Bayley scales of infant development II assessment.* Hoboken, NJ: Wiley.

Block, P. (2002). Sexuality, parenthood, and cognitive disability in Brazil. *Sexuality and Disability, 20,* 7–28.

Bolt, M. (2001). *Instructor's resources for Psychology* (6th ed.). Myers Corp. New York: Worth Publishers.

Bornstein, M. H., & Lamb, M. E. (Eds.). (2005) *Developmental science: An advanced textbook* (5th ed.). Mahwah, NJ: Lawrence Erlbaum Associates.

Botting, N., & Conti-Ramsden, G. (2001). Non-word repetition and language development in children with specific language impairment (SLI). *International Journal of Language & Communication Disorders, 36,* 421–432.

Boyce, T. E., & Hineline, P. N. (2002). Interteaching: A strategy for enhancing the user-friendliness of behavioral arrangements in the college classroom. *The Behavior Analyst, 25,* 215–226.

Boyd-Franklin, N. (2003). *Black families in therapy* (2nd ed.). New York: The Guilford Press.

Bradburn, E. M., & Sikora, A. C. (2002). Gender and racial/ethnic differences in salary and other characteristics of postsecondary faculty: Fall 1998. [U.S. Department of Education, National Center for Education Statistics, Document NCES 2002-170]. Retrieved on July 16, 2007 from www.nces.ed.gov/pubsearch.

Brannon, L., & Feist, J. (2007). *Health psychology: An introduction to behavior and health* (6th ed.). Belmont, CA: Thomson.

Brent, D. A., Baugher, M., Bridge, J., Chen, T., & Chiappetta, L. (1999). Age-and sex-related risk factors for adolescent suicide. *Journal of the American Academy of Child and Adolescent Psychiatry, 38,* 1497–1505.

Brestan, E. V., & Eyberg, S. M. (1998). Effective psychosocial treatments of conduct-disordered children and adolescents: 29 years, 82 studies, and 5,272 kids. *Journal of Clinical Child Psychology, 27,* 179–188.
Brewaeys, A., de Bruyn, J. K., Louwe, L. A., & Helmerhorst, F. M. (2005). Anonymous or identity-registered sperm donors? A study of Dutch recipients' choices. *Human Reproduction, 20,* 820–824.
Brewer, C. L. (2006). Undergraduate education in psychology: United States. *International Journal of Psychology, 41,* 65–71.
Breyer, J., Sanfeliz, A., Cleurzo, C. E., & Meyer, E. A. (2006). Loss and grief. In R. Brown (Ed.). *Comprehensive handbook of childhood cancer and sickle cell disease: A biopsychosocial approach* (pp. 358–380). New York: Oxford University Press.
Brinkmeyer, M. Y., & Eyberg, S. M. (2003). Parent-child interaction therapy for oppositional children. In A. E. Kazdin & J. R. Weisz (Eds.). *Evidence-based psychotherapies for children and adolescents* (pp. 204–223). New York: The Guilford Press.
Bronfenbrenner, U. (1979). *The ecology of human development: Experiments by nature and design.* Cambridge, MA: Harvard University Press.
Brown, K. (2003). The medication merry go-round. *Science, 299,* 1646–1649.
Bryant, C. D. (Ed.). (2003). *Handbook of death and dying: The presence of death* Vol. 1. Thousand Oaks, CA: Sage.
Bryant, C. D. (Ed.). (2003). *Handbook of death and dying: The response to death* Vol. 2 Thousand Oaks, CA: Sage.
Buskist, W., & Davis, S. F. (Eds.). (2006). *Handbook of the teaching of psychology.* Malden, MA: Blackwell Publishing.
Buss, D. M. (2003). *The evolution of desire: Strategies of human mating* (Revised Edition). New York: Basic Books.
Buss, D. M., Abbott, M., Angleitner, A., Asherian, A., Biaggio, A., Blanco-Villasenor, A., et al. (1990). International preferences in selecting mates: A study of 37 cultures. *Journal of Cross-Cultural Psychology, 21,* 5–47.
Buxton, C. L. (1962). *A study of psychophysical methods for relief of childbirth pain.* Philadelphia: Saunders.
Cairney, T. H. (2000). Beyond the classroom walls: The rediscovery of the family and community as partners in education. *Educational Review, 52,* 163–174.
Campos, J. J., & Bertenthal, B. I. (1989). Locomotion and psychological development. In F. Morrison, K. Lord, & D. Keating (Eds.), *Applied developmental psychology* (Vol. 3, pp. 229–258). New York: Academic Press.
Carmichael, K. D. (2006). *Play therapy: An introduction.* Upper Saddle River, NJ: Pearson.
Carstensen, L. L. (1995). Evidence for a life-span theory of socioemotional selectivity. *Current Directions in Psychological Science, 4,* 151–156.

Carter, D., & Welch, D. (1981). Parenting styles and children's behavior. *Family Relations, 30,* 191–195.

Ceci, S., & Williams, W. (1999). *The nature-nurture debate: The essential readings.* London: Blackwell.

Celio, M., Karnik, N. S., & Steiner, H. (2006). Early maturation as a risk factor for aggression and delinquency in adolescent girls: A review. *International Journal of Clinical Practice, 60,* 1254–1262.

Centers for Disease Control. (2007). *Deaths: Preliminary data for 2004.* Retrieved on August 8, 2007 from the National Center for Health Statistics Web site www.cdc.gov/nchs/products/pubs/pubd/hestats

Centers for Disease Control and Prevention (CDC). Web-based Injury Statistics Query and Reporting System (WISQARS) [Online]. (2005). *Suicide.* National Center for Injury Prevention and Control, CDC (producer). Retrieved June 30, 2007 from www.cdc.gov/ncipc/dvp/Suicide/SuicideDataSheet.pdf

Chaffin, M., Silovsky, J. F., Funderburk, B., Valle, L. A., Brestan, E. V., Balachova, T. et al. (2004). Parent-child interaction therapy with physically abusive parents: Efficacy for reducing future abuse reports. *Journal of Consulting and Clinical Psychology, 72,* 500–510.

Chambless, D. L., & Ollendick, T. H. (2000). Empirically supported psychological interventions: Controversies and evidence. *Annual Review of Psychology, 52,* 685–716.

Charles, S. T., Reynolds, C. A., & Gatz, M. (2001). Age-related differences and change in positive and negative affect over 23 years. *Journal of Personality and Social Psychology, 80,* 136–151.

Christopher, A. (2006). Selecting a text and using publisher-produced courseware: Some suggestions and warnings. In W. Buskist & S. F. Davis (Eds.), *Handbook of the teaching of psychology* (pp. 36–40). Malden, MA: Blackwell Publishing.

Chugani, H. T. (1998). A critical period of brain development: Studies of cerebral glucose utlilization with PET. *Preventive Medicine, 27,* 184–188.

Chugani, H. T., Phelps, M. E., & Mazziotta, J. C. (1987). Positron emission tomography study of human brain functional development. *Annals of Neurology, 22,* 487–497.

Cobb, P., & Hodge, L. L. (2002). A relational perspective on issues of cultural diversity and equity as they play out in the mathematics classroom. *Mathematical Thinking and Learning, 4,* 249–284.

Cohen, B., Jinks, D., & Mendes, S. (1999). *American beauty.* [Motion Picture]. United States: DreamWorks SKG.

Cokley, K. O. (2002). Ethnicity, gender, and academic self-concept: A preliminary examination of academic disidentification and implications for psychologists. *Cultural Diversity and Ethnic Minority Psychology, 8,* 378–388.

Colby, A., & Kohlberg, L. (1987). *The measurement of moral adjudgment* (Vols. 1–2). New York: Cambridge University Press.

Collins, A. W. (1984). Conclusion: The status of basic research on middle childhood. In A. W. Collins (Ed.). *Development during middle childhood: The years from six to twelve.* (pp. 398–421). Washington: National Academy Press.

Collins, W. A., Maccoby, E. E., Steinberg, L., Hetherington, E. M., & Bornstein, M. H. (2000). Contemporary research on parenting: The case for nature and nurture. *American Psychologist, 55,* 218–232.

Connor-Greene, P. A. (2006). Problem-based learning. In W. Buskist & S. F. Davis (Eds.). *Handbook of the teaching of psychology* (pp. 70–77). Malden, MA: Blackwell Publishing.

Consedine, N., Magai, C., & King, A. (2004). Deconstructing positive affect in later life: A differential functionalist analysis of joy and interest. *International Journal of Aging and Human Development, 58,* 49–68.

Constantine, M. G., & Sue, D. W. (2005). *Strategies for building multicultural competence in mental health and educational settings.* Hoboken, NJ: Wiley.

Cook, R., & Golombok, S. (1995). Ethics and society: A survey of semen donation: Phase II—the view of the donors. *Human Reproduction, 10,* 951–959.

Coontz, S. (2004). The world historical transformation of marriage. *Journal of Marriage and Family, 66,* 974–979.

Coppola, B. P. (2002). Laboratory instruction: Ensuring an active learning experience. In W. J. McKeachie (Ed.). *McKeachie's teaching tips: Strategies, research, and theory for college and university teachers* (11th ed.) (pp. 235–244). Boston: Houghton Mifflin Company.

Coppola, F. F. (Producer), & Lucas, G. (Director) (1973) *American graffiti* [Motion Picture]. United States: Lucasfilm.

Corr, C. A., & Corr, D. M. (Eds.). (1996). *Handbook of childhood death and bereavement.* New York: Springer Publishing Company.

Costigan, K. A., Sipsma, H. L., & DiPietro, J. A. (2006). Pregnancy folklore revisited: The case of heartburn and hair. *Birth, 33,* 311–314.

Cox, G. R. (2003). The Native American way of death. In C. D. Bryant (Ed.). *Handbook of death and dying: The response to death Vol. 2* (pp. 631–639). Thousand Oaks, CA: Sage.

Crick, N. R., & Dodge, K. A. (1996). Social information-processing mechanisms in reactive and proactive aggression. *Child Development, 67,* 993–1002.

Crosnoe, R., & Elder, G. H. (2002). Successful adaptation in the later years: A life course approach to aging. *Social Psychology Quarterly, 65,* 309–328.

Crowder, L. S. (2003). The Taoist (Chinese) way of death. In C. D. Bryant (Ed.). *Handbook of death and dying: The response to death Vol. 2* (pp. 673–686). Thousand Oaks, CA: Sage.

Crowley, B., Hayslip, B., & Hobdy, J. (2003). Psychological hardiness and adjustment to life events in adulthood. *Journal of Adult Development*, *10*, 237–248.

Cummings, E., & Henry, W. E. (1961). *Growing old*. New York: Basic Books.

Cutler, D. M., Glaeser, E., & Norberg, K. (2000). Explaining the rise in youth suicide. *National Bureau of Economic Research (Working Paper No. 7713)*, 1–68.

Damon, W. (1977). *The social world of the child*. San Francisco: Jossey-Bass.

Damon, W., & Hart, D. (1988). *Self-understanding in childhood and adolescence*. New York: Cambridge University Press.

Damour, L. (2006). Establishing classroom etiquette: General rules of classroom conduct. In W. Buskist & S. F. Davis (eds.), *Handbook of the teaching of psychology* (pp. 228–232). Malden, MA: Blackwell Publishing.

Danforth, J. S., Barkley, R. A., & Stokes, T. F. (1991). Observations of parent-child interactions with hyperactive children: Research and clinical implications. *Clinical Psychology Review*, *11*, 703–727.

Daniels, K. R. (2000). To give or sell human gametes – the interplay between pragmatics, policy and ethics. *Journal of Medical Ethics*, *26*, 206–211.

Danner, D. D., Snowdon, D. A., & Friesen, W. V. (2001). Positive emotions in early life and longevity: Findings from the nun study. *Journal of Personality and Social Psychology*, *80*, 804–813.

Darling, N., & Steinberg, L. (1993). Parenting style as context: An integrative model. *Psychological Bulletin*, *113*, 487–496.

Davidson Films (Producer). (1999). *Adolescent cognition: Thinking in a new key* [Motion picture]. (Available from Davidson Films, Inc., 735 Tank Farm Road, Suite 210, San Luis Obispo, CA 93401).

Davidson Films. (1989). *Piaget's developmental theory: An overview*. San Luis Obispo, CA: Author.

Davidson Films. (1994). *Vygotsky's developmental theory: An introduction*. San Luis Obispo, CA: Author.

Davidson Films. (1996). *Play: A Vygotskian approach*. San Luis Obispo, CA: Author.

DeCasper, A. J., & Fifer, W. P. (1980). Of human bonding: Newborns prefer their mothers' voices. *Science*, *208*, 1174–1176.

DeCasper, A. J., & Spence, M. J. (1986). Prenatal maternal speech influences newborns' perception of speech sounds. *Infant Behavior and Development*, *9*, 133–150.

Department of Health and Human Services. (2007). *National strategy for suicide prevention*. Retrieved on August 8, 2007 from www.mentalhealth.samhsa.gov/suidideprevention/elderly.asp

Dewey, K. G., Cohen, R. J., Brown, K. H., & Rivera, L. L. (2001). Effects of exclusive breastfeeding for four versus six months on maternal nutritional status and infant motor development: Results of two randomized trials in Honduras. *Journal of Nutrition*, *131*, 262–267.

Dinehart, L. H. B., Messinger, D. S., Acosta, S. I., Cassel, T., Ambador, Z., & Cohn, J. (2005). Adult perceptions of positive and negative emotional expressions. *Infancy, 8*, 279–303.

DiNovi, D. (Producer), & Armstrong, G. (Director). (1994). *Little women* [Motion Picture]. United States: Columbia Pictures Corporation.

Dion, K. K. (1985). Socialization in adulthood. In G. Lindsey & E. Aronson (Eds.) *Handbook of social psychology* (Vol. II, pp. 123–148). New York: Random House.

Discovery Health Channel (n.d.). Retrieved September 11, 2006, from www.discovery.com

Dixon, R. A., & Lerner, R. M. (1992). History and systems in developmental psychology. In M. H. Bornstein & M. E. Lamb (Eds.), *Developmental psychology: An advanced textbook* (3rd ed.) (pp. 3–44). Mahwah, NJ: Lawrence Erlbaum Associates.

Dodge, K. A. (2006). Translational science in action: Hostile attributional style and the development of aggressive behavior problems. *Development and Psychopathology, 18*, 791–814.

Dumas, J. E., & Nilsen, W. J. (2003). *Abnormal child and adolescent psychology*. New York: Allyn and Bacon.

Duncan, C., & Loretto, W. (2004). Never the right age? Gender and age-based discrimination in employment. *Gender, Work, and Organization, 11*, 95–115.

Eisenstadt, T., Eyberg, S., McNeil, C., Newcomb, K., & Funderburk, B. (1993). Parent-child interaction therapy with behavior problem children: Relative effectiveness of two stages and overall treatment outcome. *Journal of Clinical Child Psychology, 22*, 42–51.

Engberg, M. E. (2004). Improving intergroup relations in higher education: A critical examination of the influence of educational interventions on racial bias. *Review of Educational Research, 74*, 473–524.

Erikson, E. H. (1991). *Childhood and society*. W. W. Norton & Company, Inc.

Evans, G. W. (2004). The environment of childhood poverty. *American Psychologist, 59*, 77–92.

Eyberg, S. M., & Robinson, E. A. (1982). Parent-child interaction training: Effects on family functioning. *Journal of Clinical Child Psychology, 11*, 130–137.

Faiola, A. (2005). Aging Japanese pen messages to posterity. *The Washington Post*, April 11, 2005, A13–A14.

Feldman, R. S. (2003). *Development across the lifespan* [Computer software]. Upper Saddle River, NJ: Pearson Education.

Feldman, R. S. (2006). *Development across the life span* (4th ed.) Upper Saddle River, NJ: Pearson/Prentice Hall.

Festinger, L., Schachter, S., & Back, K. (1950). *Social pressures in informal group: A study of human factors in housing*. Oxford: Harper.

Field, T., Diego, M. A., Hernandez-Reif, M., Deeds, O., & Figueiredo, B. (2006). Moderate versus light pressure massage therapy leads to greater weight gain in preterm infants. *Infant Behavior and Development, 29*, 574–578.

Field, T., Diego, M., & Hernandez-Reif, M. (2007). Massage therapy research. *Developmental Review, 27*, 75–89.

Fields, J., & Casper, L. M. (2001). *America's families and living arrangements: March 2000.* Current Population Reports (pp. 20–537). U.S. Census Bureau Washington, D.C.

Films for the Humanities & Sciences. (2005). *Prentice Hall lecture launcher: Developmental psychology.* [DVD video]. Princeton, NJ.

Forehand, R., Wells, K., & Griest, D. (1980). An examination of the social validity of a parent-training program. *Behavior Therapy, 11*, 488–502.

Freeman, E. W., Sammel, M. D., Lin, H., & Nelson, D. B. (2006). Associations of hormones and menopausal status with depressed mood in women with no history of depression. *Archives of General Psychiatry, 63*, 375–382.

Freeman, J. E. (2006). Psychology of race and ethnicity. In W. Buskist & S. F. Davis (eds.), *Handbook of the teaching of psychology* (pp. 186–190). Malden, MA: Blackwell Publishing.

Freeseman, L. J., Colombo, J., & Coldren, J. T. (1993). Individual differences in infant visual attention: Four-month-olds' discrimination and generalization of global and local stimulus properties. *Child Development, 64*, 1191–1203.

Gallagher, N. (2003). Effects of parent-child interaction therapy on young children with disruptive behavior disorders. *Bridges, 1*, 1–17.

Galler, J. R., Harrison, R. H., Ramsey, F., Forde, V., & Butler, S. C. (2000). Maternal depressive symptoms affect infant cognitive development in Barbados. *The Journal of Child Psychology and Psychiatry and Allied Disciplines, 41*, 747–757.

Gardner, H. (2004). *Frames of mind: The theory of multiple intelligences.* New York: Basic Books.

Gelman, D. (1994, April 18). The mystery of suicide. *Newsweek*, 44–49.

Genetic Science Learning Center. (2008). *Tour of the basics.* Retrieved June 19, 2008, from http://learn.genetics.utah.edu/units/basics/tour/

Gibson, E. J. (1993). Ontogenesis of the perceived self. In U. Neisser (Ed.), *The perceived self: Ecological and interpersonal sources of self-knowledge.* Cambridge MA: Cambridge University Press.

Gifford-Smith, M., & Brownell, C. (2003). Childhood peer relationships: Social acceptance, friendships, and peer networks. *Journal of School Psychology, 41*, 235–284.

Gilligan, C. (1982). *In a different voice: Psychological theory and women's development.* Cambridge, MA: Harvard University Press.

Gilligan, C. (1987). Adolescent development reconsidered. *New Directions for Child Development, 37*, 63–92.

Gilligan, C., Lyons, N. P., & Hammer, T. J. (Eds.). (1990). *Making connections.* Cambridge, MA: Harvard University Press.
Gilligan, C., Ward, J. V., & Taylor, J. M. (Eds.). (1988). *Mapping the moral domain: A contribution of women's thinking to psychological theory and education.* Cambridge, MA: Harvard University Press.
Ginzberg, E. (1972). Toward a theory of occupational choice: A restatement. *Vocational Guidance Quarterly, 12,* 10–14.
Girard, I. (Producer), & Jacquet, L. (Director). (2005). *Marche de l'empereur, La.* [Motion Picture]. France: Bonne Pioche.
Gloria, A. M., Rieckmann, T. R., & Rush, J. D. (2000). Issues and recommendations for teaching an ethnic/culture-based course. *Teaching of Psychology, 27,* 102–107.
Goldman, L. (2002). Terrorism, trauma, and children: What can we do? *Healing, 1,* 1–4.
Goldstein, S. B. (2005). Cross-cultural perspectives in the psychology curriculum: Moving beyond "add culture and stir." In B. Perlman, L. I. McCann, & W. Buskist (Eds.), *Voices of experience: Memorable talks from the National Institute on the Teaching of Psychology* (Vol. 1) (pp. 45–57). Washington, DC: American Psychological Society.
Goldstein, S., & Reynolds, C. R. (1999). *Handbook of neurodevelopmental and genetic disorders in children.* New York: Guilford Press.
Goodwin, K. A. (2002). *Instructor's resource manual* [for L. M. Barker's textbook *Psychology*]. Upper Saddle River, New Jersey: Prentice Hall.
Goodwyn, S. W., Acredolo, L. P., & Brown, C. A. (2000). Impact of symbolic gesturing on early language development. *Journal of Nonverbal Behavior, 24,* 81–103.
Gottfredson, G. D., & Holland, J. L. (1990). A longitudinal test of the influence of congruence: Job satisfaction, competency utilization, and counterproductive behavior. *Journal of Counseling Psychology, 37,* 389–398.
Gould, R. L. (1978). *Transformations: Growth and change in adult life.* New York: Simon Schuster.
Gould, R. L. (1980). Transformations during early and middle adult years. In R. Smelzer & E. Erickson (Eds.), *Themes of love and work in adulthood* (pp. 213–237). Cambridge, MA: Harvard University Press.
Grantham-McGregor, S., & Ani, C. (2001). A review of studies on the effect of iron deficiency on cognitive development in children. *Journal of Nutrition, 131,* 649S–668S.
Green, H. A. (Producer), & Hughes, J. (Director). (1984). *Sixteen candles* [Motion Picture]. United States: Universal Pictures.
Grossman, A. W., Churchill, J. D., McKinney, B. C., Kodish, I. M., Otte, S. L., & Greenough, W. T. (2003). Experience effects on brain development: Possible contributions to psychopathology. *Journal of Child Psychology and Psychiatry, 44,* 33–63.

Guest, A. M. (Ed.). (2007). *Taking sides: Clashing views in lifespan development*. Dubuque, IA: McGraw-Hill.
Gump, L. S., Baker, R. C., & Roll, S. (2000). Cultural and gender differences in moral judgment: A study of Mexican American and Anglo Americans. *Hispanic Journal of Behavioral Sciences, 22*, 78–93.
Gurney, N., & Gurney, E. (1965). *The king, the mice, and the cheese*. New York: Random House.
Gushue, G. V., Greenan, D. E., & Brazaitis, S. J. (2005). Using the multicultural guidelines in couples and family counseling. In M. G. Constantine & D. W. Sue (Eds.), *Strategies for building multicultural competence in mental health and educational settings* (pp. 56–72). Hoboken, NJ: Wiley.
Hackney, A. (2005). Teaching students about stereotypes, prejudice, and discrimination: An interview with Susan Fiske. *Teaching of Psychology, 32*, 196–199.
Hall, C. C. I. (1997). Cultural malpractice: The growing obsolescence of psychology with the changing U.S. population. *American Psychologist, 52*, 642–651.
Halpern, D. F. (1988). Assessing student outcomes for psychological majors. *Teaching of Psychology, 15*, 181–186.
Hanf, C. (1969). *A two-stage program for modifying maternal controlling during mother-child interaction*. Paper presented at the meeting of the Western Psychological Association, Vancouver, BC, Canada.
Hardee-Cleaveland, K., & Bannister, J. (1988). Fertility policy and implementation in China, 1986–88. *Population and Development Review, 14*, 245–286.
Hargraves, J. L. (2004). Trends in health insurance coverage and access among black, Latino, and white Americans. *Tracking Report, 11*, 1–6.
Harlow, H. (1959). Love in infant monkeys. *Scientific American, 200*, 68–74.
Harlow, H. (1962). Social deprivation in monkeys. *Scientific American, 207*, 136–146.
Harris, J. R. (1998). *The nurture assumption: Why children turn out the way they do*. New York: Free Press.
Hart, C. H., Ladd, G. W., & Burleson, B. R. (1990). Children's expectations of the outcomes of social strategies: Relations with sociometric status and maternal disciplinary styles. *Child Development, 61*, 127–137.
Hartmann, D. P., & Pelzel, K. E. (2005). Design, measurement, and analysis in developmental research. In M. H. Bornstein & M. E. Lamb (Eds.), *Developmental science: An advanced textbook* (5th ed.) (pp. 103–184). Mahwah, NJ: Lawrence Erlbaum Associates.
Harton, H. C., Green, L. R., Jackson, C., & Latané, B. (1998). Demonstrating dynamic social impact: Consolidation, clustering, correlation, and (sometimes) the correct answer. *Teaching of Psychology, 25*, 31–35.
Harton, H. C., Richardson, D. S., Barreras, R. E., Rockloff, M. J., & Latané, B. (2002). Focused Interactive Learning: A tool for active class discussion. *Teaching of Psychology, 29*, 10–15.

Healy, P. (2001, March 3). Data on suicides set off alarm. *Boston Globe*, B1.
Hecht, M. L., Marston, P. J., & Larkey, L. K. (1994). Love ways and relationship quality in heterosexual relationships. *Journal of Social and Personality Relationships, 11*, 25–43.
Helson, R., & Srivastava, S. (2001). Three paths of adult development: Conservers, seekers, and achievers. *Journal of Personality and Social Psychology, 80*, 995–1010.
Helson, R., & Wink, P. (1992). Personality change in women from the early 40s to the early 50s. *Psychology and Aging, 7*, 46–55.
Hembree-Kigin, T. L., & McNeil, C. B. (1995). *Parent-child interaction therapy*. New York: Plenum Press.
Hendrick, C., & Hendrick, S. (2003). Romantic love: Measuring cupid's arrow. In S. Lopez & C. Snyder (Eds.), *Positive psychological assessment: A handbook of models and measures* (pp. 235–249). Washington, D.C.: American Psychological Association.
Hewlett, S. (2004). *Creating a life*. New York: Miramax.
Hill, G. W., IV (2000). Incorporating a cross-cultural perspective in the undergraduate psychology curriculum: An interview with David Matsumoto. *Teaching of Psychology, 27*, 71–75.
Hill, N. E., Bush, K. R., & Roosa, M. W. (2003). Parenting and family socialization strategies and children's mental health: Low-income Mexican-American and Euro-American mothers and children. *Child Development, 74*, 189–204.
Hirsch, H. V., & Spinelli, D. N. (1970). Visual experience modifies distribution of horizontally and vertically oriented visual fields in cats. *Science, 168*, 869–871.
Ho, B., Friedland, J., Rappolt, S., & Noh, S. (2003). Caregiving for relatives with Alzheimer's disease: Feelings of Chinese-Canadian women. *Journal of Aging Studies, 17*, 301–321.
Hogan, J. D., & Sussner, B. D. (2000). European influences on U. S. developmental psychology: A historical perspective. In A. L. Comunian & U. P. Gielen (Eds.), *International perspectives on human development* (pp. 19–33). Lengerich, Germany: Pabst Science Publishers.
Holland, J. L. (1973). *Making vocational choices: A theory of careers*. Englewood Cliffs, NJ: Prentice Hall.
Hollingshead, A. B. (1975). *Four factor index of social status*. Unpublished manuscript, Yale University, New Haven, CT.
Hood, A. B., & Deopere, D. L. (2002). The relationship of cognitive development to age, when education and intelligence are controlled for. *Journal of Adult Development, 9*, 229–234.
Hood, K. K., & Eyberg, S. M. (2003). Outcomes of parent-child interaction therapy: Mothers' reports of maintenance three to six years after treatment. *Journal of Clinical Child and Adolescent Psychology, 32*, 419–429.

Hughes, D., & Chen, L. (1997). When and what parents tell children about race: An examination of race-related socialization among African American families. *Applied Developmental Science*, *1*, 200–214.

Isbell, L. M., & Tyler, J. M. (2005). Using students' personal ads to teach about interpersonal attraction and intimate relationships. *Teaching of Psychology*, *32*, 170–172.

James, W. (1890). *The principles of psychology*. Cambridge, MA: Harvard University Press.

Javo, C., Ronning, J. A., & Heyerdahl, S. (2004). Child-rearing in an indigenous Sami population in Norway: A cross-cultural comparison of parental attitudes and expectations. *Scandinavian Journal of Psychology*, *45*, 67–78.

Johnson, D. W., & Johnson, R. T. (1994). *Learning together and alone: Cooperative, competitive, and individualistic learning* (4th ed.). Boston: Allyn & Bacon.

Johnson, S. P. (2001). Visual development in human infants: Binding features, surfaces, and objects. *Visual Cognition*, *8*, 565–578.

Jones, E. A. (Ed.). (1995). *The national assessment of college students learning: Identifying college graduates, essential skills in writing, speech and listening, and critical thinking*. Washington, DC: National Center for Education Statistics.

Jordan, J. R., & Neimeyer, R. A. (2003). Does grief counseling work? *Death Studies*, *27*, 765–786.

Joseph, H., Reznik, I., & Mester, R. (2003). Suicidal behavior of adolescent girls: Profile and meaning. *Israel Journal of Psychiatry & Related Sciences*, *40*, 209–219.

Kagan, J. (1997). Temperament and the reactions to unfamiliarity. *Child Development*, *68*, 139–143.

Kagan, J., & Snidman, N. (1991). Temperamental factors in human development. *American Psychologist*, *46*, 856–862.

Kail, R. V., & Cavanaugh, J. C. (2007). *Human development: A life-span view* (4th ed.). Belmont, CA: Wadsworth.

Kalavar, J. (2001). Examining ageism: Do male and female college students differ? *Educational Gerontology*, *27*, 507–513.

Kalish, R. A. (1987). Death and dying. In P. Silverman (Ed.), *The elderly as modern pioneers* (pp. 389–405). Bloomington, IN: Indiana University Press.

Karrass, J., & Braungart-Rieker, J. M. (2004). Infant negative emotionality and attachment: Implications for preschool intelligence. *International Journal of Behavioral Development*, *28*, 221–229.

Kastenbaum, R. (1985). Death and dying: A life-span approach. In J. E. Birren & K. W. Schaie (Eds.), *Handbook of the psychology of aging* (2nd ed.). New York: Van Nostrand Reinhold.

Kazdin, A. E. (1995). *Conduct disorder in childhood and adolescence* (2nd ed.). Thousand Oaks, CA: Sage.

Keeley, J., Smith, D., & Buskist, W. (2006). The teacher behaviors checklist: Factor analysis of its utility for evaluating teaching. *Teaching of Psychology, 33,* 84–91.

Keller, F. S. (1968). Good-bye teacher . . . *Journal of Applied Behavior Analysis, 1,* 79–89.

Kiecolt, K. J., & Fossett, M. A. (1997). The effects of mate availability on marriage among black Americans: A contextual analysis. In R. J. Taylor, J. S. Jackson, & L. M. Chatters (Eds.), *Family life in black America* (pp. 63–78). Thousand Oaks, CA: Sage.

Kim, J. S., & Lee, E. H. (2003). Cultural and noncultural predictors of health outcomes in Korean daughter and daughter-in-law caregivers. *Public Health Nursing, 20,* 111–119.

Kipp, K., & Wilson, S. P. (2006). Teaching large classes. In W. Buskist & S. F. Davis (Eds.), *Handbook of the teaching of psychology* (pp. 115–119). Malden, MA: Blackwell Publishing.

Klusman, L. E. (1975). Reduction of pain in childbirth by the alleviation of anxiety during pregnancy. *Journal of Consulting and Clinical Psychology, 43,* 162–165.

Kohlberg, L. (1984). *The psychology of moral development: Essays on moral development* (Vol. 2). San Francisco: Harper & Row.

Kohler, H., Behrman, J. R., & Skytthe, A. (2005). Partner + children = happiness? The effects of partnerships and fertility on well-being. *Population and Development Review, 31,* 407–445.

Kornhaber, M. L., & Gardner, H. (2006). Multiple intelligences: Development in implementation and theory. In M. A. Constas & R. Sternberg (Eds.), *Translating theory and research into educational practice: Development in content domains, large-scale reform, and intellectual capacity* (pp. 255–276). Mahwah, NJ: Lawrence Erlbaum Associates.

Kreitlow, B., & Kreitlow, D. (1997). *Creative planning for the second half of life.* Duluth, MN: Whole Person Associates.

Kubler-Ross, E. (1969). *On death and dying.* New York: Macmillan.

Kubler-Ross, E. (1995). *Death is of vital importance: On life, death, and life after death.* New York: Station Hill Press.

Kuczynski, L., Kochanska, G., Radke-Yarrow, M., & Girnius-Brown, O. (1987). A developmental interpretation of young children's noncompliance. *Developmental Psychology, 23,* 799–806.

Kuhl, P. K., Stevens, E., Hayashi, A., Deguchi, T., Kiritani, S., & Iverson, P. (2006). Infants show a facilitation effect for native language phonetic perception between 6 and 12 months. *Developmental Science, 9,* F13–F21.

Kushner, H. S. (1981). *When bad things happen to good people.* New York: Schocken.

Labouvie-Vief, G. (1992). A neo-Piagetian perspective on adult cognitive development. In R. J. Sternberg & C. A. Berg (Eds.), *Intellectual development* (pp. 197–228). New York: Cambridge University Press.

Lamborn, S., Mounts, N., Steinberg, L., & Dornbusch, S. (1991). Patterns of competence and adjustment among adolescents from authoritative, authoritarian, indulgent, and neglectful families. *Child Development, 62,* 1049–1065.

Lamm, H., & Wiesman, U. (1997). Subjective attributes of attraction: How people characterize their liking, their love, and their being in love. *Personal Relationships, 4,* 271–284.

Larsen, R. W. (2001). How U.S. children and adolescents spend time: What it does (and doesn't) tell us about their development. *Current Directions in Psychological Science, 10,* 160–164.

Lasky, R. E., & Williams, A. L. (2005). The development of the auditory system from conception to term. *NeoReviews, 16,* 141–152.

Lauer, J. C., & Lauer, R. H. (1999). *How to survive and thrive in an empty nest.* Oakland, CA: New Harbinger Publications.

Leeman, Y., & Volman, M. (2001). Inclusive education: Recipe book or quest. On diversity in the classroom and educational research. *International Journal of Inclusive Education, 5,* 367–379.

Leerkes, E. M., & Crockenberg, S. C. (2003). The impact of maternal characteristics and sensitivity on the concordance between maternal reports and laboratory observations of infant negative emotionality. *Infancy, 4,* 517–539.

Lemanek, K. L., Ranalli, M. A., Green, K., Biega, C., & Lupia, C. (2003). Diseases of the blood: Sickle cell disease and hemophilia. In M. C. Roberts (Ed.), *Handbook of pediatric psychology* (3rd ed.) (pp. 321–341). New York: The Guilford Press.

Lemonick, M. D., & Mankato, A. P. (2001). The nun study: Alzheimer's. *Time,* May 14, 2001.

Lendrum, S., & Syme, G. (2004). *Gift of tears: A practical approach to loss and bereavement in counselling and psychotherapy* (2nd ed.). New York: Brunner-Routledge.

Lerman, C., Croyle, R. T., Tercyak, K. P., & Hamann, H. (2002). Genetic testing: Psychological aspects and implications. *Journal of Consulting and Clinical Psychology, 70,* 784–797.

Lerner, R. M. (1992, Winter). Diversity. *SRCD Newsletters, 2,* 12–14.

Lerner, R. M., Theokas, C., & Bobek, D. L. (2005). Concepts and theories of human development: Historical and contemporary dimensions. In M. H. Bornstein & M. E. Lamb (Eds.), *Developmental science: An advanced textbook* (5th ed.) (pp. 3–43). Mahwah, NJ: Lawrence Erlbaum Associates.

Levine, A., & Cureton, J. (1992). The quiet revolution: Eleven facts about multiculturalism and the curriculum. *Change, 24,* 25–35.

Levinson, D. J. (1986). A conception of adult development. *American Psychologist, 41,* 3–13.

Levinson, D. J. (1992). *The seasons of a woman's life.* New York: Knopf.

Lewin, T. (2003, December 22). For more people in their 20s and 30s, going home is easier because they never left. *The New York Times,* A27.

Lloyd, M. A. (2006). Psychology of gender and related courses. In W. Buskist & S. F. Davis (eds.), *Handbook of the teaching of psychology* (pp. 202–206). Malden, MA: Blackwell Publishing.

Lobell, M. (Producer), & Bergman, A. (Director). (1994). *It could happen to you* [Motion Picture]. United States: TriStar Pictures.

Lusk, A. B., & Weinberg, A. S. (1994). Discussing controversial topics in the classroom: Creating a context for learning. *Teaching Sociology, 22,* 301–308.

Luthar, S. S. (2003). The culture of affluence: Psychological costs of material wealth. *Child Development, 74,* 1581–1593.

Maassen, G. H., Goossens, F. A., & Bokhorst, J. (1998). Ratings as validation of sociometric status determined by nominations in longitudinal research. *Social Behavior and Personality: An International Journal, 26,* 259–275.

MacPhee, D., Kreutzer, J. C., & Fritz, J. J. (1994). Infusing a diversity perspective into human development courses. *Child Development, 65,* 699–715.

Magna Systems. (2001). *Death and dying.* [VHS Video]. Barrington, IL.

Magna Systems. (2002). *In their own words: Widowhood and integrity vs. despair.* [VHS Video]. Barrington, IL.

Makikallio, K., McElhinney, D. B., Levine, J. C., Marx, G. R., Colan, S. D., Marshall, A. C., Lock, J. E., Marcus, E. N., & Tworetzky, W. (2006). Fetal aortic valve stenosis and the evolution of hypoplastic left heart syndrome: Patient selection for fetal intervention. *Circulation, 113,* 1401–1405.

Manson, J. E., & Bassuk, S. S. (2006). *Hot flashes, hormones, and your health.* New York: McGraw Hill.

Marcotte, D., Fortin, L., Potvin, P., & Papillon, M. (2002). Gender differences in depressive symptoms during adolescence: Role of gender-typed characteristics, self-esteem, body image, stressful life events, and pubertal status. *Journal of Emotional and Behavioral Disorders, 10,* 29–42.

Margulis, S. (Producer), & Stuart, M. (Director). (1971). *Willy wonka and the chocolate factory* [Motion Picture]. United States: Paramount Pictures.

Marsh, H., & Ayotte, V. (2003). Do multiple dimensions of self-concept become more differentiated with age? The differential distinctiveness hypothesis. *Journal of Educational Psychology, 96,* 56–67.

Marsh, H., Ellis, L., & Craven, R. (2002). How do preschool children feel about themselves? Unraveling measurement and multidimensional self-concept structure. *Developmental Psychology, 38,* 376–393.

Martin, P., Martin, D., & Martin, M. (2001). Adolescent premarital sexual activity, cohabitation, and attitudes toward marriage. *Adolescence, 36,* 601–609.

Mash, E. J., & Wolfe, D. A. (1999). *Abnormal child psychology.* Albany, NY: Wadsworth.

McAdams, D. P., & de St. Aubin, E. (Eds.). (1998). *Generativity and adult development: How and why we care for the next generation*. Washington, DC: American Psychological Association.

McAdams, D., & Logan, R. (2004). What is generativity? In E. de St. Aubin and D. McAdams (Eds.), *Generative society: Caring for future generations* (pp. 15–31). Washington, DC: American Psychological Association.

McCaul, K. D., Ployhart, R. E., Hinsz, V. B., & McCaul, H. S. (1995). Appraisals of consistent versus similar politician: Voter preferences and intuitive judgments. *Journal of Personality and Social Psychology, 68,* 292–299.

McCrae, R. R., & Costa, P. T., Jr. (2003). *Personality in adulthood: A five-factor theory of perspective*, (2nd ed.). New York: Guilford.

McGraw Hill's annual editions on human development. (35th ed.). (2007). Dubuque, IA: McGraw Hill.

McKeachie, W. J. & Svinicki, M. (2006). *McKeachie's teaching tips: Strategies, research, and theory for college and university teachers* (12th ed.). Boston: Houghton Mifflin Company.

McKusick, V. A. (1998). *Mendelian inheritance in man: A catalog of human genes and genetic disorders* (12th ed.). Baltimore: Johns Hopkins University Press.

Medora, N. P., Wilson, S., & Larson, J. H. (2001). Attitudes toward parenting strategies, potential for child abuse, and parental satisfaction of ethnically diverse low-income U.S. mothers. *The Journal of Social Psychology, 14,* 335–348.

Melby, M. K. (2005). Factor analysis of climacteric symptoms in Japan. *Maturitas, 52,* 205–222.

Melhem, N. M., Moritz, G., Walker, M., Shear, M. K., & Brent, D. (2007). Phenomenology and correlates of complicated grief in children and adolescents. *Journal of the American Academy of Child Psychiatry, 46,* 493–499.

Mogelonsky, M. (1996, May). The rocky road to adulthood. *American Demographics, 56,* 26–35.

Montague, D. P. F., & Walker-Andrews, A. S. (2001). Peekaboo: A new look at infant's perception of emotion expressions. *Developmental Psychology, 37,* 826–838.

Mortimer, J. A., Snowdon, D. A., & Markesbery, W. R. (2003). Head circumference, education, and risk of dementia: Findings from the nun study. *Journal of Clinical and Experimental Neuropsychology, 25,* 671–679.

MTA Cooperative Group. (1999). A 14-month randomized clinical trial of treatment strategies for attention-deficit/hyperactivity disorder. *Archives of General Psychiatry, 56,* 1073–1086.

Murstein, B. I. (1987). A clarification and extension of the SVR theory of dyadic pairing. *Journal of Marriage and the Family, 49,* 929–933.

Museum of Science and Industry of Chicago. (2007). *Body worlds*. Retrieved on August 2, 2007 from www.msichicago.org/scrapbook/scrapbook_exhibits/bodyworlds

Nangle, D. W., & Erdley, C. A. (Eds.). (2001). *The role of friendship in psychological adjustment*. San Francisco: Jossey-Bass.

National Institutes of Health. (2006). Retrieved December 19, 2006, from www.nlm.nih.gov/medlineplus/ency/article/001166.htm

National Institutes of Health. (2007). *Medical encyclopedia: Death among children and adolescents*. Retrieved on August 8, 2007 from www.nlm.nih.gov/medlineplus/ency/article/001915.htm

Negro-Vilar, A. (1993). Stress and other environmental factors affecting fertility in men and women: Overview. *Environmental Health Perspectives, 101*, 59–64.

Nelson, T. D. (Ed.). (2002). *Ageism: Stereotyping and prejudice against older persons*. Cambridge, MA: MIT Press.

Nelson, T. D. (2005). Ageism: Prejudice against our feared future self. *Journal of Social Issues, 61*, 207–221.

NOVA. (1994). *Secret of the wild child*. Videotape by Boston: WGBH Boston.

NOVA (Producer). (2000, December 12). *Dying to be thin* [Television broadcast]. Boston, MA: WGBH.

Nuland, S. B. (1993). *How we die: Reflections on life's final chapter*. New York: Alfred A. Knopf.

Ocampo, C., Prieto, L. R., Whittlesey, V., Connor, J., Janco-Gidley, J., Mannix, S., & Sare, K. (2003). Diversity research in *Teaching of Psychology*: Summary and recommendations. *Teaching of Psychology, 30*, 5–18.

Osborne, J. W. (1997). Race and academic disidentification. *Journal of Educational Psychology, 89*, 728–735.

Osborne, R. E. & Renick, O. (2006). Service-learning. In W. Buskist & S. F. Davis (Eds.), *Handbook of the teaching of psychology* (pp. 137–141). Malden, MA: Blackwell Publishing.

O'Sullivan, E., & O'Sullivan, M. (2002). Precocious puberty: A parent's perspective. *Archives of Disease in Childhood, 86*, 320.

Paludi, M. A. (1986). Teaching the psychology of gender roles: Some life-stage considerations. *Teaching of Psychology, 13*, 133–138.

Park, H. C., Klinger, L. J., & Brestan, E. V. (2003, July). *Older adult interactions in cartoons: An analysis using the DPICS II*. Poster presented at the Fourth Annual Parent-Child Interaction Therapy Conference, Sacramento, California.

Patterson, C. J. (2000). *Multimedia courseware for child development* [Computer software]. Dubuque, IA: McGraw Hill.

Pekkanen, J. (2001). The mystery of fetal life: Secrets of the womb. In K. L. Freiberg (Ed.), *Human development annual editions* (35th ed.). (pp. 26–34). Dubuque, IA: McGraw-Hill.

Pelham, W., & Hoza, B. (1996). Intensive treatment: A summer treatment program for children with ADHD. In E. Hibbs & P. Jensen (Eds.), *Psychosocial treatments for child and adolescent disorders: Empirically based strategies for clinical practice* (pp. 311–340). New York: APA Press.

Pelham, W., & Waschbusch, D. (2006). Attention-Deficit Hyperactivity Disorder (ADHD). In J. E. Fisher & W. T. O'Donohue (Eds.), *Practitioner's guide to evidence-based psychotherapy* (pp. 93–100). New York: Springer Science and Business Media.

Pelham, W., Wheeler, T., & Chronis, A. (1998). Empirically supported psychosocial treatments for attention deficit hyperactivity disorder. *Journal of Clinical Child Psychology, 27*, 190–205.

Perlman, B., McCann, L. I., & Buskist, W. (Eds.). (2005). *Voices of experience: Memorable talks from the National Institute on the Teaching of Psychology* (Vol. 1). Washington, DC: American Psychological Society.

Perry, W. G. (1970). *Forms of intellectual and ethical development in the college years: A scheme.* New York: Holt, Rinehart, and Winston.

Piaget, J. (1972). Intellectual evolution from adolescence to adulthood. *Human development, 15*, 1–12.

Pinker, S. (2002). *The blank slate.* Viking Adult.

Poole, D., Warren, A., & Nunez, N. (2007). *The story of human development.* Upper Saddle River, NJ: Pearson.

Porter, L. S., & Porter, B. O. (2004). A blended infant massage-parenting enhancement program for recovering substance-abusing mothers. *Pediatric Nursing, 30*, 363–401.

Pratt, M. W., Danso, H. A., Arnold, M. L., Norris, J., & Filyer, R. (2001). Adult generativity and the socialization of adolescents: Relations to mothers' and fathers' parenting beliefs, styles, and practices. *Journal of Personality, 69*, 89–120.

Prentice Hall. (2002). *Video classics in psychology.* [Computer software]. Upper Saddle River, NJ: Author.

Public Broadcasting Service. (2001). *The aging brain: Through many lives.* [VHS Video]. New York.

Public Broadcasting Service. (2001). *The secret life of the brain.* [VHS Video Series]. New York.

Quindlen, A. (2002, May 13). Doing nothing is something. The overscheduled children of 21st-century America, deprived of the gift of boredom. *Newsweek*, 76.

Quintana, S. M. (1998). Children's developmental understanding of ethnicity and race. *Applied and Preventive Psychology, 7*, 27–45.

Quintero, R. A., Huhta, J., Suh, E., Chmait, R., Romero, R., & Angel, J. (2005). In utero cardiac fetal surgery: Laser atrial septotomy in the treatment of hypoplastic left heart syndrome with intact atrial septum. *American Journal of Obstetrics & Gynecology, 193*, 1424–1428.

Rambachan, A. (2003). The Hindu way of death. In C. D. Bryant (Ed.). *Handbook of death and dying: The response to death Vol. 2* (pp. 640–648). Thousand Oaks, CA: Sage.
Range, L. (1996). Suicide and life-threatening behavior in childhood. In C. A. Corr & D. M. Corr (Eds.). *Handbook of childhood death and bereavement* (pp. 71–88). New York: Springer Publishing Company.
Rattaz, C., Goubet, N., & Bullinger, A. (2005). The calming effect of a familiar odor on full-term newborns. *Journal of Developmental & Behavioral Pediatrics, 26*, 86–92.
Reddy, U. M., Wapner, R. J., Rebar, R. W., & Tasca, R. J. (2007). Infertility, assisted reproductive technology, and adverse pregnancy outcomes. *Obstetrics & Gynecology, 109*, 967–977.
Resnick, D. P., & Peterson, N. L. (1991). *Evaluating progress toward goal five: A report to the National Center for Education Statistics.* Washington, DC: National Center for Education Statistics. (ERIC Document ED340764).
Ridley, C. S. (2005). *Peer mediation training: Evaluating the interrater reliability of a behavior coding system for role-play practice.* Unpublished master's thesis, Auburn University, Auburn, Alabama.
Ridley, M. (2003). *Nature via nurture.* New York: Harper Collins.
Riley, K. P., Snowdon, D. A., Desrosiers, M. F. (2005). Early life linguistic ability, late life cognitive function, and neuropathology: Findings from the nun study. *Neurobiology of Aging, 26*, 341–347.
Roberts, B., Helson, R., & Klohnen, E. (2002). Personality development and growth in women across 30 years: Three perspectives. *Journal of Personality, 70*, 79–102.
Rosen, C. (2004). New technologies and our feelings: Romance on the internet. *The New Atlantis, Winter Issue,* 3–16.
Rosenbaum, P. L., Walter, S. D., Hanna, S. E., Palisano, R. J., Russell, D. J., Raina, P. et al. (2002). Prognosis for gross motor function in cerebral palsy: Creation of motor development curves. *Journal of the American Medical Association, 288*, 1357–1363.
Rovee-Collier, C. (1993). The capacity for long-term memory in infancy. *Current Directions in Psychological Science, 2*, 130–135.
Rovee-Collier, C., & Fagen, J. W. (1981). The retrieval of memory in early infancy. *Advances in Infancy Research, 1*, 225–254.
Rowe, J. W., & Kahn, R. L. (1998). *Successful aging.* New York: Pantheon.
Rudin, S. (Producer), & Wilson, H. (Director). (1996). *The first wives club* [Motion Picture]. United States: Paramount Pictures.
Rupp, D. E., Vodanovich, S. J., & Crede, M. (2005). The multidimensional nature of ageism: Construct validity and group differences. *The Journal of Social Psychology, 145*, 335–362.
Saffran, J. R., Loman, M. L., & Robertson, R. W. (2000). Infant memory for musical experiences. *Cognition, 77*, 15–23.

Saladin, K. S. (2007). *Anatomy & physiology: The unity of form and fucntion* (4th ed.). Boston: McGraw Hill.
Santos de Barona, M., & Reid, P. T. (1992). Ethnic issues in teaching the psychology of women. *Teaching of Psychology, 19,* 96–99.
Santrock, J. W. (2007). *A topical approach to life-span development* (3rd ed.). New York: McGraw Hill.
Saver, B. G., Doescher, M. P., Symons, M. P., Wright, G. E., & Andrilla, C. H. (2003). Racial and ethnic disparities in the purchase of nongroup health insurance: The roles of community and family-level factors. *Health Services Research, 38,* 211–231.
Saville, B. K., & Zinn, T. E. (2005). Interteaching versus traditional methods of instruction: A preliminary analysis. *Teaching of Psychology, 32,* 161–163.
Saville, B. K., Zinn, T. E, Neef, N. A., Van Norman, R., & Ferreri, S. J. (2006). A comparison of interteaching and lecture in the college classroom. *Journal of Applied Behavior Analysis, 39,* 49–61.
Scarborough, H. S., & Dobrich, W. (1990). Development of children with early language delay. *Journal of Speech and Hearing Research, 33,* 70–83.
Schaie, K. W. (1994). The course of adult intellectual development. *American Psychologist, 49,* 304–313.
Schindler, R. (2003). The Jewish way of death. In C. D. Bryant (Ed.). *Handbook of death and dying: The response to death Vol. 2* (pp. 687–693). Thousand Oaks, CA: Sage.
Schwartz, B. (Producer), & Apted, M. (Director). (1980). *Coal miner's daughter* [Motion picture]. United States: Universal pictures.
Scott, E. S. (1986). Sterilization of mentally retarded persons: Reproductive rights and family privacy. *Duke Law Journal, 1986,* 806–865.
Seale, C. (2003). Global mortality rates: Variations and their consequences for the experience of dying. In C. D. Bryant (Ed.). *Handbook of death and dying: The response to death Vol. 1* (pp. 198–209). Thousand Oaks, CA: Sage.
Sebastian-Galles, N. (2006). Native-language sensitivities: Evolution in the first year of life. *Trends in Cognitive Sciences, 10,* 239–241.
Segal, N. L. (1993). Twin, sibling, and adoption methods: Tests of evolutionary hypotheses. *American Psychologist, 48,* 943–956.
Segal, N. L. (2006). Fullerton virtual twin study. *Twin Research and Human Genetics, 9,* 963–964.
Segal, N. L., & Hill, E. M. (2005). Developmental behavioral genetics and evolutionary psychology: Tying the theoretical and empirical threads. In B. J. Ellis, D. F. Bjorklund (Eds.). *Origins of the social mind: Evolutionary psychology and child development* (pp. 108–136). New York: Guilford Press.
Selznick, D. O. (Producer), & Fleming, V. (Director). (1939). *Gone with the wind* [Motion Picture]. United States: Selznick International Pictures.

Settersten, R. (2002). Social sources of meaning in later life. In R. Weiss & S. Bass (Eds.), *Challenges of the third age: Meaning and purpose in later life* (pp. 55–79). London: Oxford University Press.

Sharma, S. K., Sidawi, J. E., Ramin, S. M., Lucas, M. J., Leveno, K. J., & Cunningham, F. G. (1997). Cesarean delivery: A randomized trial of epidural versus patient-controlled meperidine analgesia during labor. *Anesthesiology, 87,* 487–494.

Shelton, K. K., Frick, P. J., & Wootton, J. (1996). Assessment of parenting practices in families of elementary school-age children. *Journal of Clinical Child Psychology, 25,* 317–329.

Shi, L. (2001). The convergence of vulnerable characteristics and health insurance in the U.S. *Social Science and Medicine, 53,* 519–530.

Simoni, J. M., Sexton-Radek, K., Yescavage, K., Richard, H., & Lundquist, A. (1999). Teaching diversity: Experiences and recommendations of American Psychological Association Division 2 members. *Teaching of Psychology, 26,* 89–95.

Simpson, E., Mull, J. D., Longley, E., & East, J. (2000). Pica during pregnancy in low-income women born in Mexico. *Western Journal of Medicine, 173,* 20–24.

Smock, P. J., & Manning, W. D. (2004). Living together unmarried in the United States: Demographic perspectives and implications for family policy. *Law and Policy, 26,* 87–117.

Sorensen, M. J., Nissen, J. B., Mors, O., & Thomsen, P. H. (2005). Age and gender differences in depressive symptomatology and comorbidity: An incident sample of psychiatrically admitted children. *Journal of Affective Disorders, 84,* 85–91.

Sotiriou, A., & Zafiropoulou, M. (2003). Changes of children's self-concept during transition from kindergarten to primary school. *Psychology: The Journal of the Hellenic Psychological Society, 10,* 96–118.

Speece, M. W., & Brent, S. B. (1996). The development of children's understanding of death. In C. A. Corr & D. M. Corr (Eds.), *Handbook of childhood death and bereavement* (pp. 29–50). New York: Springer Publishing Company.

Spinrad, T. L., & Stifter, C. A. (2006). Toddlers' empathy-related responding to distress: Predictions from negative emotionality and maternal behavior in infancy. *Infancy, 10,* 97–121.

Sprecher, S., Sullivan, Q., & Hatfield, E. (1994). Mate selection preferences: Gender differences examined in a national sample. *Journal of Personality and Social Psychology, 66,* 1074–1080.

Srivastava, S., John, O., & Gosling, S. (2003). Development of personality in early and middle adulthood: Set like plaster or persistent change? *Journal of Personality and Social Psychology, 84,* 1041–1053.

St. John, W. (2005). *Rammer jammer yellow hammer: A road trip into the heart of fan mania.* New York: Crown Publishers.

Stanwood, G. D., Washington, R. A., & Levitt, P. (2001). Identification of a sensitive period of prenatal cocaine exposure that alters the development of the anterior cingulate cortex. *Cerebral Cortex, 11*, 430–440.

Sternberg, R. J. (1986). Triangular theory of love. *Psychological Review, 93*, 119–135.

Sternberg, R. J. (1987). Liking versus loving: A comparative evaluation of theories. *Psychological Bulletin, 102*, 331–345.

Stice, E., & Bearman, S. K. (2001). Body-image and eating disturbances prospectively predict increases in depressive symptoms in adolescent girls: A growth curve analysis. *Developmental Psychology, 37*, 597–607.

Stice, E., Presnell, K., & Bearman, S. K. (2001). Relation of early menarche to depression, eating disorders, substance abuse, and comorbid psychopathology among adolescent girls. *Developmental Psychology, 37*, 608–619.

Stormshak, E. A., Bierman, K. L., McMahon, R. J., Lengua, L. J., & Conduct Problems Prevention Research Group. (2000). Parenting practices and child disruptive behavior problems in early elementary school. *Journal of Clinical Child Psychology, 29*, 17–29.

Suddreth, A., & Galloway, A. T. (2006). Options for planning a course and developing a syllabus. In W. Buskist & S. F. Davis (Eds.). *Handbook of the teaching of psychology* (pp. 31–35). Malden, MA: Blackwell Publishing.

Suess, D. (1957). *The cat in the hat.* New York: Random House.

Suggett, R. (2006). *Instructor's resource manual: Development across the life span.* Upper Saddle River, NJ: Pearson.

Sultan, D. H. (2003). The Muslim way of death. In C. D. Bryant (Ed.). *Handbook of death and dying: The response to death Vol. 2* (pp. 649–655). Thousand Oaks, CA: Sage.

Suro, R. (1999, November). Mixed doubles. *American Demographics*, 57–62.

Suzuki, H. (2003). The Japanese way of death. In C. D. Bryant (Ed.). *Handbook of death and dying: The response to death Vol. 2* (pp. 656–655). Thousand Oaks, CA: Sage.

Szapocznik, J., & Kurtines, W. M. (1993). Family psychology and cultural diversity: Opportunities for theory, research, and application. *American Psychologist, 48*, 400–407.

Tanner, J. M. (1999). The growth and development of the *Annals of Human Biology*: A 25-year retrospective. *Annals of Human Biology, 26*, 3–18.

Taylor, M. G. (1996). The development of children's beliefs about social and biological aspects of gender differences. *Child Development, 67*, 1555–1571.

Taylor, S. E. (2006). *Health psychology* (6th ed.). Boston, MA: McGraw Hill.

Tercyak, K. P. (2003). Genetic disorders and genetic testing. In M. C. Roberts (Ed.). *Handbook of pediatric psychology* (3rd ed.). (pp. 719–734). New York: The Guilford Press.

Terman, L. M., & Oden, M. H. (1959). *The gifted group at mid-life: Thirty-five years follow-up of the superior child.* Stanford, CA: Stanford University Press.

The Learning Channel (Producer). (2006). *Maternity ward* [Television series]. New York: The Learning Channel.

The Learning Channel (TLC; www.tlc.discovery.com) retrieved on September 11, 2006.

Thirumurthy, V. (2004). Kaleidoscope of parenting cultures. *Childhood Education, 81,* 94–L (2).

Thomas, A., Chess, S., & Birch, H. G. (1968). *Temperament and behavior disorders in children.* New York: New York University Press.

Thompson, M. J. J., Raynor, A., Cornah, D., Stevenson, J., & Sonuga-Barke, E. J. S. (2002). Parenting behaviour described by mothers in a general population sample. *Child: Care, Health & Development, 28,* 149–155.

Tucker, M. B., & Mitchell-Kernan, C. (Eds.). (1995). *The decline in marriage among African Americans: Causes, consequences, and policy implications.* New York: Russell Sage.

Tworetzky, W., Wilkins-Haug, L., Jennings, R. W., van der Velde, M. E., Marshall, A. C., Marx, G. R., Colan, S. D., Benson C. B., Lock, J. E., & Perry, S. B. (2004). Balloon dilation of severe aortic stenosis in the fetus: Potential for prevention of hypoplastic left heart syndrome: Candidate selection, technique, and results of successful intervention. *Circulation, 110,* 2125–2131.

U.S. Department of Health & Human Services, Administration on Children, Youth and Families. (1999). *Child maltreatment 1997: Reports from the states to the National Child Abuse and Neglect Data System.* Washington, DC: US Government Printing Office.

U.S. Department of Health & Human Services, Administration on Children, Youth and Families. (2000). *Child maltreatment 1998: Reports from the states to the National Child Abuse and Neglect Data System.* Washington, DC: US Government Printing Office.

U.S. Department of Health & Human Services, Administration on Children, Youth and Families. (2001). *Child maltreatment 1999.* Washington, DC: US Government Printing Office.

U.S. Department of Health & Human Services, Administration on Children, Youth and Families. (2003). *Child maltreatment 2001.* Washington, DC: US Government Printing Office.

U.S. Department of Health & Human Services, Administration on Children, Youth and Families. (2004). *Child maltreatment 2002.* Washington, DC: US Government Printing Office.

U.S. Department of Health & Human Services, Children's Bureau. (1998). *Child maltreatment 1996: Reports from the states to the National Child Abuse and Neglect Data System.* Washington, DC: US Government Printing Office.

U.S. Department of Health & Human Services, National Center on Child Abuse and Neglect. (1996). *Child maltreatment 1994: Reports from the states to the National Center on Child Abuse and Neglect.* Washington, DC: US Government Printing Office.

U.S. Bureau of the Census. (2001). *Living arrangements of children.* Washington, DC.: US Bureau of the Census.

U.S. Census Bureau. (2005). *Current population reports (P23-209) 65+ in the United States: 2005.* Retrieved August 2, 2007, from www.census.gov/Press-Release/www/releases/archives/aging_population/006544.html

U.S. Department of Education, National Center for Education Statistics. (1999). National study of post secondary faculty (NSOPF: 99). Retrieved on July 16, 2007 from www.nces.ed.gov/pubsearch.

Uline, C. L., Tschannen-Moran, M., & Perez, L. (2003). Constructive conflict: How controversy can contribute to school improvement. *Teachers College Record, 105,* 782–816.

University of California at Davis. (2003). *Parent Child Interaction Therapy: Child Directed Interaction.* Sacramento, CA: Author.

Vaillant, G. E. (1977). *Adaptation to life.* Boston: Little, Brown.

Vaillant, G. E., & Vaillant, C. O. (1990). Natural history of male psychological health: A 45-year study of predictors of successful aging. *American Journal of Psychiatry, 147,* 31–37.

Van Eerdewegh, M. M., Bieri, M. D., Parrilla, R. H., & Clayton, P. J. (1982). The bereaved child. *British Journal of Psychiatry, 140,* 23–29.

Vygotsky, L. S. (1962). *Thought and language.* Cambridge, MA: MIT Press.

Wahler, R. G., & Afton, A. D. (1980). Attentional processes in insular and noninsular mothers: Some differences in their summary reports about child problem behaviors. *Child Behavior Therapy, 2,* 25–41.

Wahler, R. G., & Dumas, J. E. (1986). Maintenance factors in coercive mother-child interactions: The compliance and predictability hypothesis. *Journal of Applied Behavior Analysis, 19,* 13–22.

Walk, R. D., & Gibson, E. J. (1961). A comparative and analytical study of visual depth perception. *Psychological Monographs, 75,* (15, Whole No. 519).

Warren, C. S. (2006). Incorporating multiculturalism into undergraduate psychology courses: Three simple active learning activities. *Teaching of Psychology, 33,* 105–109.

Watson, J. B. (1925). *Behaviorism.* New York: Norton.

Webb, N. B. (Ed.). (2002). *Helping bereaved children: A handbook for practitioners.* New York: The Guilford Press.

Webster-Stratton, C., Kolpacoff, M., & Hollinsworth, T. (1988). Self-administered videotape therapy for families with conduct-problem children: Comparison with two cost-effective treatments and a control group. *Journal of Consulting and Clinical Psychology, 56,* 558–566.

Wechsler, D. (1958). *The measurement and appraisal of adult intelligence* (4th ed.). Baltimore: Williams & Wilkins.

Wechsler, D. (2002). *Wechsler individual achievement test* (2nd ed.). San Antonio, TX: Psychological Corporation.

Wechsler, D. (2003). *Wechsler intelligence scale for children* (4th ed.). San Antonio, TX: Psychological Corporation.

Weindruch, R. (1996, January). Caloric restriction and aging. *Scientific American, 46*, 46–52.

Welles-Nystrom, B. (2005). Co-sleeping as a window into Swedish culture: Considerations of gender and health care. *Scandinavian Journal of Caring Sciences, 19*, 354–360.

Whitbourne, S. K. (2001). *Adult development and aging: Biopsychosocial perspectives*. New York: Wiley.

White, N. (2003). Changing conceptions: Young people's views of partnering and parenting. *Journal of Sociology, 39*, 149–164.

White, S. H. (2003). Developmental psychology in a world of designed institutions. In W. Koops & M. Zuckerman (Eds.), *Beyond the century of the child: Cultural history and developmental psychology* (pp. 204–223). Baltimore, MD: University of Pennsylvania Press.

Whittlesey, V. (2001). *Diversity activities for psychology*. Boston: Allyn & Bacon.

Whyte, H., Hannah, M., Saigal, S., Hannah, W., Hewson, S., Amankwah, K., et al. (2004). Outcomes of children at 2 years after planned cesarean birth versus planned vaginal birth for breech presentation at term: The international randomized term breech trial. *American Journal of Obstetrics and Gynecology, 191*, 864–871.

Wijngaards-de Meij, L., Stroebe, M., Schut, H., Stroebe, W., van den Bout, J., van der Heijden, P., et al. (2005). Couples at risk following the death of their child: Predictors of grief versus depression. *Journal of Consulting and Clinical Psychology, 73*, 617–623.

Williams, M. J. (2003). A social history of embalming. In C. D. Bryant (Ed.), *Handbook of death and dying: The response to death Vol. 2* (pp. 534–543). Thousand Oaks, CA: Sage.

Williams, R. L., Oliver, R., & Stockdale, S. (2004). Psychological versus generic critical thinking as predictors and outcome measures in a large undergraduate human development course. *Journal of General Education, 53*, 37–58.

Willie, C., & Reddick, R. (2003). *A new look at Black families* (5th edition). Walnut Creek, CA: AltaMira Press.

Wilson, J. H., & Hackney, A. A. (2006). Problematic college students: Preparing and repairing. In W. Buskist & S. F. Davis (eds.), *Handbook of the teaching of psychology* (pp. 233–237). Malden, MA: Blackwell Publishing.

Wingert, P., & Brant, M. (2005, August 15). Reading your baby's mind. *Newsweek*, 32–39.

Winterich, J. (2003). Sex, menopause, and culture: Sexual orientation and the meaning of menopause for women's sex lives. *Gender & Society, 17,* 627–642.

Witherington, D. C., Campos, J. J., Anderson, D. I., Lejeune, L., & Seah, E. (2005). Avoidance of heights on the visual cliff in newly walking infants. *Infancy, 7,* 285–298.

Wolchik, S. A., Tein, J., Sandler, I. N., & Ayers, T. S. (2006). Stressors, quality of the child-caregiver relationship, and children's mental health problems after parental death: The mediating role of self-system beliefs. *Journal of Abnormal Child Psychology, 34,* 221–238.

Wolfe, R. H. (Producer), & Montesi, J. (Director). (2000). *Andromeda* [Television Series].United States: Fireworks Entertainment.

Woodard, S. (2006). A septuplet celebration: The septuplets at 9. *Ladies Home Journal.* Retrieved December 19, 2006, from www.lhj.com

Woodcock, R. W., & Johnson, M. B. (1989). *Woodcock-Johnson psycho-educational battery-revised.* Allen, TX: DLM Teaching Resources.

Zeanah, C. H., Boris, N. W., & Larrieu, J. A. (1997). Infant development and developmental risk: A review of the past 10 years. *Journal of the American Academy of Child and Adolescent Psychiatry, 36,* 165–178.

Zeifman, D. M. (2003). Predicting adult responses to infant distress: Adult characteristics associated with perceptions, emotional reactions, and timing of intervention. *Infant Mental Health Journal, 24,* 597–612.

Zimbardo, P. G. (1997). A passion for psychology: Teaching it charismatically, integrating teaching and research synergistically, and writing about it engagingly. In R. J. Sternberg (Ed.). *Teaching introductory psychology.* (pp. 7–34). Washington, DC: American Psychological Association.

Author Index

Acosta, S. I., 93
Acredolo, L. P., 112
Adler, J., 42
Adolph, K. E., 70, 71
Afton, A. D., 49
Ainsworth, M. D. S., 110
Albom, M., 219
Al-Qahtani, N. H., 77
Amankwah, K., 77
Ambador, Z., 93
American Psychiatric Association (APA), 18, 92, 140, 160, 162
American Psychological Association Task Force on Strengthening the Teaching and Learning of Undergraduate Psychological Sciences, 4, 9
Anderson, D. I., 98
Andrilla, C. H., 188
Ani, C., 134
Antonucci, T. C., 192
Apted, M., 93
Arabin, B., 77

Armstrong, G., 42
Arnold, E. H., 132
Arnold, M. L., 190
Aronson, I., 215
Arquette, R., 184
Aspinwall, O. G., 148
Atchley, R. C., 199, 201
Atkinson, J., 134
Aversano, S., 192
Ayers, T. S., 210
Aylward, G. P., 75, 76
Ayotte, V., 148

Back, K., 174
Bacon, J. B., 216
Baillargeon, R., 106
Baird, B. N., 15
Baker, J. E., 210, 211
Baker, R. C., 147
Ball, H. L., 93
Balls Organista, P., 16
Banister, J., 78
Barkley, R., 129–30, 142

Author Index

Barnard, P., 216
Barone, S., 181
Barreras, R. E., 13
Bartlett, N. H., 134
Barusch, A., 201
Bassuk, S. S., 186
Baugher, M., 163
Baum, C., 181
Baumrind, D., 126, 127–9, 130, 133
Bearman, S. K., 160, 161
Beck, A. T., 162
Behrman, J. R., 78
Belsky, J., 46, 51, 151, 166
Berger, S. E., 70, 71
Bergman, A., 43
Bergstrom, M. J., 199
Berk, L. E., 8
Berman, P. S., 181
Bernard, J., 176
Berndt, T. J., 149
Bertenthal, B. I., 98
Bianchi, S. M., 192
Biega, C., 70
Bieri, M. D., 210
Bierman, K. L., 129
Birch, H. G., 110–11
Birmaher, B., 162, 163
Birney, D. P., 97, 143, 151
Black, M. M., 96
Blehar, M., 110
Block, P., 78
Bobek, D. L., 40
Bokhorst, J., 150
Bolt, M., 97
Boris, N. W., 112
Bornstein, M. H., 40, 43, 87
Botting, N., 134
Boyce, T. E., 13, 14
Boyd-Franklin, N., 49
Bradburn, E. M., 173
Brannon, L., 187, 188, 198
Brant, M., 88
Braungart-Rieker, J. M., 110
Brazaitis, S. J., 49

Brent, D. A., 163–4, 210
Brent, S. B., 208, 209, 212, 213
Brestan, E. V., 133, 194
Brewaeys, A., 79
Brewer, C. L., 20
Breyer, J., 213
Bridge, J., 163
Brinkmeyer, M. Y., 38
Bronfenbrenner, U., 39, 48–50, 58, 62
Brown, C. A., 112
Brown, G. K., 162
Brown, K., 112, 142
Brownell, C., 148, 149
Bryant, C. D., 206
Bukowski, W. M., 134
Bullinger, A., 99
Burleson, B. R., 129
Bush, K. R., 128
Buskist, W., 2, 219
Buss, D. M., 177, 180
Butler, S. C., 112
Buxton, C. L., 74

Cairney, T. H., 62
Campos, J. J., 98
Carmichael, K. D., 122
Carstensen, L. L., 199
Carter, D., 128
Casper, L. M., 176, 192
Cassel, T., 93
Cavanaugh, J. C., 67, 156
Ceci, S., 43
Celio, M., 156
Centers for Disease Control and Prevention, 163, 212, 215
Chaffin, M., 132
Chambless, D. L., 133
Charles, S. T., 199
Chen, L., 134
Chen, T., 163
Chess, S., 110–11
Chiappetta, L., 163
Christopher, A., 8

Chronis, A., 142
Chugani, H. T., 89–90
Chun, K. M., 16
Cieurzo, C. E., 213
Citron-Pousty, J. H., 97, 143
Clayton, P. J., 210
Cobb, P., 62
Cohen, B., 190
Cohen, R. J., 112
Cohn, J., 93
Cokley, K. O., 171
Colby, A., 146
Coldren, J. T., 112
Collins, A. W., 148
Collins, W. A., 43
Colombo, J., 112
Conduct Problems Prevention Research Group, 129
Connor-Greene, P. A., 12
Consedine, N., 199
Constantine, M. G., 16
Conti-Ramsden, G., 134
Cook, R., 79
Coontz, S., 179
Coppola, B. P., 12
Coppola, F. F., 42
Cornah, D., 126
Corr, C. A., 209
Corr, D. M., 209
Costa, P. T., 191
Costigan, K. A., 80
Cox, G. R., 221
Craven, R., 148
Crede, M., 184
Crick, N. R., 141
Crockenberg, S. C., 110
Crosnoe, R., 199
Crowder, L. S., 221
Crowley, B., 192
Croyle, R. T., 72
Cummings, E., 199
Cunningham, F. G., 77
Cureton, J., 62
Cutler, D. M., 163

Damon, W., 149
Damour, L., 38
Danforth, J. S., 129
Daniels, K. R., 79
Danner, D. D., 197
Danso, H. A., 190
Darling, N., 127, 128
Davidson Films, 121, 122, 157–8
Davis, S. F., 2
De Bruyn, J. K., 79
de St. Aubin, E., 190
DeCasper, A. J., 71, 99, 102
Deeds, O., 76
Deguchi, T., 99
Deopere, D. L., 169
Department of Health and Human Services, 216
Desrosiers, M. F., 196
Dewey, K. G., 112
Dey, T., 192
Diego, M. A., 76, 99
Dinehart, L. H. B., 93
DiNovi, D., 42
Dion, K. K., 126
DiPietro, J. A., 80
Discovery Health Channel, 83
Dixon, R. A., 2, 3
Dobrich, W., 134
Dodge, K. A., 141
Doescher, M. P., 188
Dornbusch, S., 129
Dumas J. E., 129, 162
Duncan, C., 184

East, J., 80
Eisenstadt, T., 132
Elder, G. H., 199
Ellis, L., 148
Engberg, M. E., 62
Erdley, C. A., 149
Erikson, E. H., 189–90
Evans, G. W., 41
Eyberg, S. M., 38, 132, 133

Fagen, J. W., 112
Faiola, A., 221
Feist, J., 187, 188, 198
Feldman, R. S., 8, 40, 41, 42, 45, 46, 67, 88, 103, 156, 164, 168, 186, 190, 212, 214
Ferreri, S. J., 13
Festinger, L., 174
Field, T., 76, 99
Fields, J., 176
Fifer, W. P., 99
Figuereido, B., 76
Films for the Humanities and Sciences, 96, 98, 109
Filyer, R., 190
Fleming, V., 42
Forde, V., 112
Forehand, R., 133
Fortin, L., 162
Fossett, M. A., 176
Freeman, E. W., 185
Freeman, J. E., 16
Freeseman, L. J., 112
Frick, P. J., 127
Friedland, J., 193
Friesen, W. V., 197
Fritz, J. J., 61
Funderburk, B., 132

Gallagher, N., 133
Galler, J. R., 112
Galloway, A. T., 6, 8, 9
Gardner, H., 143
Gatz, M., 199
Gelman, D., 163
Genetic Science Learning Centre, 68
Gibson, E. J., 98
Gifford-Smith, M., 148, 149
Gilligan, C., 146, 147
Ginzberg, E., 177–8
Girard, I., 45
Girnius-Brown, O., 129
Glaeser, E., 163
Gloria, A. M., 16, 17

Goldman, L., 42
Goldstein, S. B., 16, 67
Golombok, S., 79
Goodwin, K. A., 135
Goodwyn, S. W., 112
Goossens, F. A., 150
Gosling, S., 191
Gottfredson, G. D., 178
Goubet, N., 99
Gould, R. L., 190
Grantham-McGregor, S., 134
Green, H. A., 42
Green, K., 70
Green, L. R., 13
Greenan, D. E., 49
Griest, D., 133
Grossman, A. W., 112
Guest, A. M., 44, 58, 59–60, 78
Gump, L. S., 147
Gurney, E., 71
Gurney, N., 71
Gushue, G. V., 49

Hackney, A., 16, 38
Hall, C. C. I., 15–16
Halpern, D. F., 57
Hamann, H., 72
Hammer, T. J., 147
Hannah, M., 77
Hannah, W., 77
Hardee-Cleaveland, K., 78
Hargraves, J. L., 188
Harlow, H., 109–10
Harris, J. R., 149
Harrison, R. H., 112
Hart, C., 129
Hart, D., 149
Hartmann, D. P., 50
Harton, H. C., 13
Hatfield, E., 177
Hayashi, A., 99
Hayslip, B., 192
Healy, P., 163
Hecht, M. L., 176

Helmerhorst, F. M., 79
Helson, R., 190
Hembree-Kigin, T. L., 122
Hendrick, C., 176
Hendrick, S., 176
Henry, W. E., 199
Hernandez-Reif, M., 76, 99
Hetherington, E. M., 43
Hewlett, S., 186
Hewson, S., 77
Heyerdahl, S., 93
Hill, E. M., 68
Hill, G. W., IV, 16, 22
Hill, N. E., 128
Hineline, P. N., 13, 14
Hinsz, V. B., 174
Hirsch, H. V., 90
Ho, B., 193
Hobdy, J., 192
Hodge, L. L., 62
Hogan, J. D., 3
Holland, J. L., 178
Hollingshead, A. B., 41
Hollinsworth, T., 133
Holmes, M. E., 199
Hood, A. B., 169
Hood, K. K., 132
Hooker, E., 93
Hoza, B., 143
Hughes, D., 134
Hughes, J., 42

Isbell, L. M., 174–5
Iverson, P., 99

Jackson, C., 13
Jacquet, L., 45
James, W., 88
Javo, C., 93
Jinks, D., 190
John, O., 191
Johnson, D. W., 13
Johnson, M. B., 145
Johnson, R. T., 13

Johnson, S. P., 112
Jones, E. A., 57
Jordan, J. R., 220
Joseph, H., 163

Kagan, J., 111
Kahn, R. L., 201
Kail, R. V., 67, 156
Kalavar, J., 184
Kalish, R. A., 208
Karass, J., 110
Karnik, N. S., 156
Kastenbaum, R., 208
Keeley, J., 219
Keller, F. S., 13
Kelly, P. J., 93
Kiecolt, K. J., 176
Kim, J. S., 193
King, A., 199
Kipp, K., 19
Kiritani, S., 99
Klinger, L. J., 194
Klohnen, E., 190
Klusman, L. E., 74
Kochanska, G., 129
Kohlberg, L., 18, 146–7
Kohler, H., 78
Kolpacoff, M., 133
Kornhaber, M. L., 143
Kreitlow, B., 201
Kreitlow, D., 201
Kreutzer, J. C., 61
Kubler-Ross, E., 207, 208, 219–20
Kuczynkski, L., 129
Kuhl, P. K., 99
Kurtines, W. M., 62
Kushner, H. S., 206, 213, 215

Labouvie-Vief, G., 168
Ladd, G. W., 129
Lamb, M. E., 40, 87
Lamborn, S., 129
Lamm, H., 176
Larkey, L. K., 176

Author Index

Larrieu, J. A., 112
Larson, J. H., 126
Larson, R. W., 151
Lasky, R. E., 77
Latané, B., 13
Lauer, J. C., 192
Lauer, R. H., 192
Lee, E. H., 193
Leeman, Y., 62
Leerkes, E. M., 110
Lejeune, L., 98
Lemanek, K. L., 70
Lemonick, M. D., 196
Lendrum, S., 211, 217, 220
Lengua, L. J., 129
Lerman, C., 72
Lerner, R. M., 2, 3, 40, 44, 61
Leveno, K. J., 77
Levine, J. C., 61–2
Levinson, D. J., 190, 212
Levitt, P., 112
Lewin, T., 192
Lin, H., 185
Lloyd, M. A., 16
Lobell, M., 43
Logan, R., 190
Loman, M. L., 112
Longley, E., 80
Loretto, W., 184
Louwe, L. A., 79
Lucas, G., 42
Lucas, M. J., 77
Lundquist, A., 16
Lupia, C., 70
Lusk, A. B., 60
Luthar, S. S., 41
Lutz, D. J., 97, 143
Lyons, N. P., 147

Maassen, G. H., 150
Maccoby, E. E., 43
MacPhee, D., 61–2
Magai, C., 199
Magna Systems, 191, 208, 217

Makikallio, K., 72
Mankato, A. P., 196
Manning, W. D., 176
Manson, J. E., 186
Marcotte, D., 162
Margulis, S., 93
Marin, G., 16
Markesbery, W. R., 196
Marsh, H., 148
Marston, P. J., 176
Martin, D., 176
Martin, M., 176
Martin, P., 176
Mash, E. J., 162
Matula, K., 96
Mazziotta, J. C., 89
McAdams, D. P., 190
McCann, L. I., 2
McCaul, H. S., 174
McCaul, K. D., 174
McCrae, R. R., 191
McGraw Hill's annual editions, 83
McKeachie, W. J., 2
McKusick, V. A., 67
McMahon, R. J., 129
McNeil, C., 122, 132
Medora, N. P., 126
Melby, M. K., 186
Melhem, N. M., 210
Mendes, S., 190
Messinger, D. S., 93
Mester, R., 163
Meyer, E. A., 213
Minnelli, V., 181
Mitchell-Kernan, C., 176
Mogelonsky, M., 192
Montague, D. P. F., 110
Montesi, J., 44
Moritz, G., 210
Morland, I., 216
Mors, O., 163
Mortimer, J. A., 196
Mounts, N., 129
MTA Cooperative Group, 142

Mull, J. D., 80
Murphy, K., 142
Murstein, B. I., 176
Museum of Science and Industry of Chicago, 220

Nagy, J., 216
Nangle, D. W., 149
National Institutes of Health, 69, 212, 214
Neef, N. A., 13
Negro-Vilar, A., 77
Neimeyer, R. A., 220
Nelson, B., 163
Nelson, D. B., 185
Nelson, T. D., 184
Newcomb, K., 132
Nilsen, W. J., 162
Nissen, J. B., 163
Noh, S., 193
Norberg, K., 163
Norris, J., 190
NOVA, 47, 161
Nuland, S. B., 206, 207
Nunez, N., 46, 121, 185

Ocampo, C., 16
Oden, M. H., 55
O'Leary, S. G., 132
Oliver, R., 57
Ollendick, T. H., 133
Osborne, R. E., 14, 15
Osborne, J. W., 171
O'Sullivan, E., 156
O'Sullivan, M., 156

Paludi, M. A., 179
Papillon, M., 162
Park, H. C., 194
Parrilla, R. H., 210
Patterson, C. J., 82-3, 89, 92-3, 95, 98, 102, 105, 106, 109, 111, 121, 125, 141
Pekkanen, J., 69, 72

Pelham, W., 142, 143
Pelzel, K. E., 50
Perez, L., 60
Perlman, B., 2
Perry, W. G., 44-5, 168, 169
Peterson, N. L., 57
Phelps, M. E., 89
Piaget, J., 45, 118-22, 168
Pinker, S., 43
Ployhart, R. E., 174
Poole, D., 46, 121, 185
Porter, B. O., 76
Porter, L. S., 76
Potvin, P., 162
Pratt, M. W., 190
Presnell, K., 161
Public Broadcasting Service, 197

Quindlen, A., 151
Quintana, S. M., 134
Quintero, R. A., 72

Radke-Yarrow, M., 129
Rambachan, A., 221
Ramin, S. M., 77
Ramsey, F., 112
Ranalli, M. A., 70
Range, L., 211-12
Rappolt, S., 193
Rattaz, C., 99
Raynor, A., 126
Rebar, R. W., 77
Reddick, R., 176
Reddy, U. M., 77
Reid, P. T., 17
Renick, O., 14, 15
Resnick, D. P., 57
Reynolds, C. A., 199
Reynolds, C. R., 67
Reznik, I., 163
Richard, H., 16
Richardson, D. S., 13
Ridley, C., 149, 150
Ridley, M., 43

Author Index

Rieckmann, T. R., 16
Riley, K. P., 196
Rivera, L. L., 112
Roberts, B., 190
Robertson, R. W., 112
Robinson, E. A., 133
Rockloff, M. J., 13
Roll, S., 147
Ronning, J. A., 93
Roosa, M. W., 128
Rosen, C., 179
Rosenbaum, P. L., 134
Rovee-Collier, C., 104, 105, 112
Rowe, J. W., 201
Rudin, S., 190
Rupp, D. E., 184
Rush, J. D., 16
Ryan, N. D., 163

Saffran, J. R., 112
Saigal, S., 77
Saladin, K. S., 185
Sammel, M. D., 185
Sandler, I. N., 210
Sanfeliz, A., 213
Santos de Barona, M., 17
Santrock, J. W., 67
Saver, B. G., 188
Saville, B. K., 13, 14
Scarborough, H. S., 134
Schachter, S., 174
Schaie, K. W., 168, 169, 196
Schindler, R., 221
Schwartz, B., 93
Scott, E. S., 78
Seah, E., 98
Seale, C., 213
Sebastian-Galles, N., 99
Sedney, M. A., 210, 211
Segal, N. L., 68
Selznick, D. O., 42
Settersten, R., 199
Sexton-Radek, K., 16
Sharma, S. K., 77

Shear, M. K., 210
Shelton, K. K., 127
Shi, L., 188
Shyer, C., 181
Sidawi, J. E., 77
Sikora, A. C., 173
Simoni, J. M., 16
Simpson, E., 80
Sipsma, H. L., 80
Skytthe, A., 78
Smith, D., 219
Smock, P. J., 176
Snowdon, D. A., 196–7
Sonuga-Barke, E. J. S., 126
Sorensen, M. J., 163
Sotiriou, A., 148
Speece, M. W., 208, 209, 212, 213
Spence, M. J., 71, 99, 102
Spinelli, D. N., 90
Spinrad, T. L., 110
Sprecher, S., 177
Srivastava, S., 190, 191
St. John, W., 218
Stanwood, G. D., 112
Steer, R. A., 162
Steinberg, L., 43, 127, 128, 129
Steiner, H., 156
Sternberg, R. J., 97, 143, 175, 176
Stevens, E., 99
Stevenson, J., 126
Stice, E., 160, 161
Stifter, C. A., 110
Stockdale, S., 57
Stokes, T. F., 129
Stormshak, E. A., 129
Stuart, M., 93
Suddreth, A., 6, 8, 9
Sue, D. W., 16
Suess, D., 71
Suggett, R., 61
Sullivan, Q., 177
Sultan, D. H., 221

Author Index

Suro, R., 176
Sussner, B. D., 3
Suzuki, H., 221
Svinicki, M., 2
Syme, G., 211, 217, 220
Symons, M. P., 188
Szapocznik, J., 62

Tanner, J. M., 156, 166
Tasca, R. J., 77
Taylor, J. M., 147
Taylor, M. G., 134
Taylor, S. E., 148, 187
Tein, J., 210
Tercyak, K. P., 69, 72
Terman, L. M., 55–6
The Learning Channel, 83
Theokas, C., 40
Thirumurthy, V., 136
Thomas, A., 110
Thompson, M. J. J., 126
Thomsen, P. H., 163
Tschannen-Moran, M., 60
Tucker, M. B., 176
Tworetzky, W., 72
Tyler, J. M., 174–5

Uline, C. L., 60
University of California at Davis, 133
US Census Bureau, 176, 182
US Department of Education, 173
US Department of Health and Human Services, 131

Vaillant, C. O., 177
Vaillant, G. E., 177, 190
Van Eerdewegh, M. M., 210, 211
Van Norman, R., 13
Vasey, P. L., 134
Vodanovich, S. J., 184
Volman, M., 62

Vygotsky, L. S., 118, 120, 122–5, 135

Wahler, R. G., 49, 129
Walk, R. D., 98
Walker, M., 210
Walker-Andrews, A. S., 110
Wall, S., 110
Wapner, R. J., 77
Ward, J. V., 147
Warren, A., 46, 121, 185
Warren, C. S., 16
Waschbusch, D., 142
Washington, R. A., 112
Waters, E., 110
Watson, J. B., 43
Webb, N. B., 209
Webster-Stratton, C., 133
Wechsler, D., 144
Weinberg, A. S., 60
Weindruch, R., 195
Welch, D., 128
Welles-Nystrom, B., 93
Wells, K., 133
Wheeler, T., 142
Whitbourne, S. K., 199
White, N., 176
White, S. H., 2
Whittlesey, V., 16
Whyte, H., 77
Wiesman, U., 176
Wijngaards-de Meij, L., 214
Williams, A. L., 77
Williams, M. J., 218
Williams, R. L., 57
Williams, W., 43
Willie, C., 176
Wilson, H., 190
Wilson, J. H., 38
Wilson, S. P., 19, 126
Wingert, P., 88
Wink, P., 190
Winterich, J., 186
Witherington, D. C., 98

Wolchik, S. A., 210
Wolfe, D. A., 162
Wolfe, R. H., 44
Woodard, S., 77
Woodcock, R. W., 145
Wootton, J., 127
Wright, G. E., 188

Yescavage, K., 16

Zafiropoulou, M., 148
Zeanah, C. H., 112
Zeifman, D. M., 93
Zimbardo, P. G., 123
Zinn, T. E., 13

Subject Index

AB research design, 54
academic disidentification, 171
activity theory, 199
adolescence stereotypes, 164
adolescent autonomy, 165
adolescent cognition, 157–9
   body image, 157, 158–9, 160, 161, 164, 166
   egocentrism, 157, 160
   imaginary audience, 157, 158, 160
   meta-cognition, 157, 158
   personal fable, 157, 158, 160, 211
adolescent resilience, 164
adolescents and death
   terminal illness, 214
   understanding, 211–12
adult cognitive development theories, 167–9
   Labouvie-Vief, 168–9
   Perry, 169
   Schaie, 169
adults and death
   terminal illness, 214–16
   understanding, 212

Ainsworth's strange situation, 110
ageism, 184, 194
aging
   and memory, 196–7
   successful, 198–200
aging theories, 195
alternative formats for course, 12–15
   focused interactive learning (FIL), 13
   interteaching, 13–14
   problem-based learning (PBL), 12–13
   service learning, 14–15
Alzheimer's disease, 196–7
anorexia, 50, 160–1
   male, 166
antidepressants, 162, 165
APGAR scale, 75–6
arranged marriages, 175
attachment, 109–10, 179
attention-deficit hyperactivity disorder (ADHD), 140–3, 151

Subject Index

Baumrind's parenting styles, 126, 127–9, 130, 133
Bayley Scales of Infant Development Second Edition (BSID-II), 96–7
beautiful people exercise, 158
Beck Depression Inventory (BDI), 162
beginning the course, 22–4
behavior modification, for ADHD, 142–3
   Summer Day Treatment Program, 143
behavioral coding, 94
behavioral regression, 211
bereavement, 207
   support groups, 216
big five personality traits, 191
birth complications, 76–7
body donation, 220
body image, 157, 158–9, 160, 161, 164, 166
boomerang children, 192
"bottom of the barrel" men, 176
brain imaging, 89–90
Bronfenbrenner's ecological systems theory, 39, 48–50, 58, 62
bulimia, 160–1
bullying, 149, 151

cancer, 187–8, 214, 215
career selection, 177–8
   Ginzberg's theory of career selection, 177–8
   Holland's theory of personality, 178
   Vaillant's theory of career consolidation, 177
cartoon characters, 193–4
case studies, 54
causes of death, 212–13, 214–16
Child Advocacy Centers (CACs), 15, 132
Child Development Movement, 3
child maltreatment, 15, 131, 132

Child Study Movement, 3
childhood obesity, 165
childhood resilience, 134, 151
children and death
   terminal illness, 212–13
   understanding, 209–11
Chomsky's language acquisition device, 107
choosing a textbook, 7–8
chronic illness
   children's summer camps, 214
   middle adulthood, 187–8
class discussion, 37–8
class personality, 37–8
classical conditioning, 100–1
college attendance, 170–3
college attrition, 170–1
companionate love, 176
concepts of death, 208–12
conservation *see* tasks of conservation
contexts of development, 39–50, 57–8
   age-graded influences, 40
   cultural, 40
   historical, 40
   history-graded influences, 41–2
   non-normative influences, 42–3
   sociocultural-graded influences, 41
   topical areas, 39–40
continuity theory, 199
continuous vs. discontinuous development, 39, 45–6
correlational studies, 54–5
course organization, 4–7
   summer courses, 7, 35–6
"cream of the crop" women, 176
creativity, 151
critical vs. sensitive periods, 39, 46–8
cross-sectional studies, 56
cross-sequential studies, 56
crying, 93, 102
cultural customs related to death, 217, 221

delivery options, 74
depression, 162
  adolescents, 160, 161, 162–3
  and gender, 166
  and menopause, 185
  treatment, 162
developmental psychopathology, 39–40, 162–3
Diagnostic and Statistical Manual – Fourth Edition Text Revision (DSM-IV-TR), 140–1, 145, 160, 162
Diagnostic and Statistical Manual – Third Edition (DSM-III), 140
discontinuous vs. continuous development, 39, 45–6
disengagement theory, 199
diversity, 15–18, 61–2
  and adolescent development, 165–6
  and adult development, 179–80, 202–3
  and childhood development, 135–6, 152
  and death, 217, 221
  and health, 188
  and higher education, 170, 172–3
  and infant development, 113
  and mate selection, 175, 176–7, 180
  and pregnancy and childbirth, 79–80
downward social comparison, 148
drug therapy, for ADHD, 142, 151
  amphetamines, 142
  atomoxetine, 142
  methylphenidate, 142
  pemoline, 142
dualistic thinking, 44, 169
dysthymic disorder, 162

early brain development, 88–90
eating disorders, 50, 159–61
  and gender, 166
  treatment, 160

ectoderm, 70
egg and sperm donation, 79
embalming, 218
embryonic stage, 70–1
empty nest syndrome, 192
ending the course, 218–19
endoderm, 70
EQ, 151
Erikson's stages, 189–90
estimating developmental landmarks exercise, 97
euphemisms about death exercise, 207–8
evolutionary perspective, 2
exams in pairs, 123–5
exosystems, 49
experimental design, 55

family bed exercise, 93–4
family structural change, 191–3
fertility, and menopause, 185–6
fertilization, 66–8
fetal abilities, 71
fetal stage, 71
field research video, 94
field trip to Child Advocacy Center, 132
friendship, 148–9, 152
  cyber, 165
  stages of, 149
funeral arrangements, 218

gender and undergraduate major exercise, 171–2
gender equality, 152
genetic disorders, 67, 69–70
genetic manipulation, 78–9
genetics, 68–70
  dominant traits, 68
  genotype, 68
  heterozygous genes, 69
  homozygous genes, 69
  phenotype, 68
  recessive traits, 68

Genie (feral child), 47–8
germinal stage, 70
Ginzberg's theory of career selection, 177–8
good supervisor/bad supervisor exercise, 129–31
government policy, 78
grief, 218
  childhood, 207, 209–11
  stages of, 217
grief counseling, 219–20
guest speakers
  on aging and memory, 197
  on death and dying, 206
  on eating disorders, 161
  on health, 187
  on labor and delivery, 81–2

habituation, 103
Harlow's attachment research, 109–10
health expectancy vs. life expectancy, 197–8
heart disease, 187–8, 215
Heinz dilemma, 146–7
history of developmental psychology, 2–4, 23–4
Holland's theory of personality, 178
homogamy, 176
hormone replacement therapy (HRT), 186
hospices, 207, 216

imprinting, 47
infant-directed speech, 108
infant language development, 107–8
  learning theory, 108
infant sensory development, 98–100
  auditory perception, 99
  pain and touch, 99–100
  smell and taste, 99
  visual perception, 98

infant social development, 108–11
  attachment, 109–10
  temperament, 110–11
infant states of arousal, 90–3
  awake states, 92–3
  rhythms, 91
  sleep states, 91–2
infusing diversity, 15–18
intelligence, 143–4
  adult, 195–6
  testing, 143–5, 151, 152, 196
interdisciplinary research, 3

Kubler-Ross' theory of dying, 207, 208, 213

labeled praise, 38
Labouvie-Vief's post-formal thought, 168–9
learning processes, 100–3
Levinson's seasons of life theory, 190–1
life events model, 190–1
life expectancy vs. health expectancy, 197–8
lifespan perspective, 3, 5–6
Little Albert, 101
longitudinal studies, 55–6
Lorenz, 46–7
love, 175–6

macrosystems, 49–50
major depressive disorder, 162
marriage gradient, 176
mate selection, 173–7
maternal changes, 74–5
media influence, 158
menopause, 185–6
mesoderm, 70
mesosystems, 49
meta-cognition, 157, 158
microsystems, 48–9
midlife crisis, 190–1

Subject Index

milestones of motor development, 95-7
moral development, 146-7
multiple thinking, 44-5, 169
multicultural resources, 36

naturalistic observations, 53
nature and nurture, 39, 43-5, 57-8, 60-1
neonatal appearance, 75
neonatal assessment, 75-6
neonatal psychology, 76
normative-crisis model, 189-90
nun study, 196-7

object permanence, 105-6
operant conditioning, 101-2
orienting response, 103
osteoporosis, 185
overscheduled children, 151

parent-child interaction therapy (PCIT), 38, 133
parental monitoring, 152
parenting, 126-33
　behavioral parent training, 132-3
　child maltreatment, 131
　influence of discipline on child behavior, 129
　parenting styles and discipline practices, 127-9
passionate love, 176
peer mediation programs, 150
peer nomination, 150
peer relationships, 148-50
peer status, 149-50
Perry's theory of adult cognition, 169
personal ad exercise, 174-5
personality in midlife, 189-91
phenylketonuria (KU), 69
physical appearance, middle adulthood, 183-4
　gender double standard, 184

physical changes
　middle adulthood, 183, 184-8
　older adulthood, 194-5
Piaget's theory of cognitive development, 45, 103-7
　formal operations, 157, 168
　preoperational stage, 118-22
　sensorimotor stage, 104-7
　Vygotsky compared, 125
post-formal thought, 168-9
praise, 38
prenatal development stages, 70-3
prenatal testing, 72
presbycusis, 194
proximity, 174
puberty, 156, 166
　physical milestones, 156
　precocious, 156, 165

reflexes, 95
research methods, 50-7, 59, 61
retirement, 200-1

salary and gender, 172
sandwich generation, 192-3
Schaie's theory of adult cognition, 168, 169
school violence, 149, 151
self-concept, 148
self-efficacy, 148
self-esteem, 148, 160
sensitive vs. critical periods, 39, 46-8
sickle cell anemia, 70
similarity, 174
social competence, 148
social skills programs, 150
special education, 145
stages of labor, 73-4
stimulus-value-role theory, 176
strabismus, 90
stranger anxiety, 89
student feedback, 219

suicide
  adolescents, 163–4, 211–12
  gender gap, 163–4
  older adults, 215–16
  para-suicidal behavior, 216
  suicidal ideation, 164
  suicidal intent, 164
"Swiss cheese" notes, 161
syllabus, 8–12
  class attendance, 10–11, 28–9
  exams, 9, 29
  extra credit, 11–12, 27–8
  in-class activities, 11
  lecture schedules, 8–9, 25–6, 35–6
  reading quizzes, 9, 26
  sample, 25–30
  short-project papers, 9–10, 27, 31–4

tasks of conservation demonstration, 118–22
  script, 137
teaching assistants (TAs), 18–19
teaching psychology majors vs. non-majors, 19–20
teaching today's students, 20–2
  cultural inclusivity, 22
  use of technology, 21
  variety of learning styles, 22
teen delinquency, 165
teen violence, 165

teenage sexuality, 165
television, 152
television commercial exercise, 183
temperament, 110–11
teratogens, 72–3
terminal illness, 212–16
  adolescents, 214
  adults, 214–16
  children, 212–13
  summer camps, 214
theoretical perspectives, 5
triangular theory of love, 176
twins, 67–8

university demographics, 170
US population estimates, 181–2

Vaillant's personality theory, 190
Vaillant's theory of career consolidation, 177
visual cliff, 98
Vygotsky's theory of cognitive development, 122–5
  demonstration of zone of proximal development, 122–5
  Piaget compared, 125

Watson's view of development, 43
WIAT, 145
WISC IV, 144
wisdom, 151
Woodcock-Johnson tests, 145